Praise for

In Defense of Witches

"In today's France, Chollet has emerged as a quiet revolutionary, pushing back against the clichés and the patriarchy that shapes them.... *In Defense of Witches* demonstrates that a woman's decision to go against the grain—especially by not having children—inevitably becomes a political act, even an act of resistance."
—Rachel Donadio,
The New York Times Book Review

"A smart feminist treatise reclaiming the witch and her radical way of life as a path forward for women ... Chollet's informed and passionate treatment will appeal to readers looking for more substance amid the witch trend that's otherwise been largely commodified and often scrubbed of its feminist origins."
—Jenna Jay, *Booklist*

"Allows us to understand ... [how] the witch hunts of the past influenced the representation of women today."
—*Le Monde*

"Mona Chollet demonstrates how ... those who emancipate themselves from certain social norms are, in fact, direct heirs of those that were hunted down, censored, and eliminated during the Renaissance."
—*HuffPost*

"Explores the worldview that the witch hunt has sought to promote—and its consequences on society today."
—*Vice*

In Defense

of

Witches

The Legacy of the Witch Hunts and Why
Women Are Still on Trial

Mona Chollet

Translated by Sophie R. Lewis
Foreword by Carmen Maria Machado

ST. MARTIN'S GRIFFIN
NEW YORK

Published in the United States by St. Martin's Griffin, an imprint of
St. Martin's Publishing Group

www.stmartins.com

Designed by Omar Chapa

The Library of Congress has cataloged the hardcover edition as follows:

Names: Chollet, Mona, 1973– author.
Title: In defense of witches : the legacy of the witch hunts and why
    women are still on trial / Mona Chollet ; translated by Sophie R. Lewis;
    foreword by Carmen Maria Machado.
Other titles: Sorcières. English
Description: First edition. | New York : St. Martin's Press, [2022] | Includes
    bibliographical references and index.
Identifiers: LCCN 2021046522 | ISBN 9781250271419 (hardcover) |
    ISBN 9781250272225 (ebook)
Subjects: LCSH: Feminism. | Witches—Violence against—History. |
    Sex discrimination against women—History. | Male domination (Social
    structure)
Classification: LCC HQ1122 .C54713 2022 | DDC 305.42—dc23
LC record available at https://lccn.loc.gov/2021046522

ISBN 978-1-250-89487-8 (trade paperback)

Originally published in France in 2018 under the title *Sorcières*
by Editions La Découverte

First St. Martin's Griffin Edition: 2023

10 9 8 7 6 5 4 3 2

There is no "joining" WITCH.
If you are a woman
and dare to look
within yourself,
you are a Witch.

WITCH Manifesto
(Women's International Terrorist Conspiracy from Hell),
New York, 1968[1]

Contents

FOREWORD

For me, it was Strega Nona: the wily, no-nonsense witch from the eponymous picture book, who owns a magic pasta pot, commands the respect of her community (even the local priests and nuns!) and holds her dopey helper, Big Anthony, to account for his disobedience and mischief. For my spouse, it was Angela Lansbury's character, Eglantine Price, in *Bedknobs and Broomsticks,* who wears knitted cardigans and fights Nazis via witchcraft she has learned through a correspondence course. For Mona Chollet, it was Flutter Mildweather—a character in a Swedish children's book, *The Glassblower's Children*—who makes carpets, consorts with a one-eyed crow and wears an indigo cloak and a tall violet hat festooned with flowers and butterflies. Imagine, for a moment, your witch. Not your earliest witch, necessarily, but the one who first captured your attention. Are you holding her in your mind?

I imagine I can tell you some things about her. She is a woman, single and childless. She has her own little house, which she may or may not share with an animal.[1] She is an artist, or a craftswoman, or a scientist, if you imagine magic as a kind of science. She has an undeniable air of poise and a wonderful sense of style. Whether or not she is evil (after all, we have *The Wizard of Oz*, Grimms' fairy tales, and decades of Disney movies to contend with), it cannot be denied that she is wily, self-satisfied, and in charge of her own affairs. She commands respect. She is, to interesting people, someone worth learning from, if not emulating entirely. She is what happens when women get to direct the warp and weft of their own lives.

In Defense of Witches is a spirited account of the way the perpetrators of witch-hunts have endured, albeit in modern form and with altered tactics; so much so that the people responsible can plausibly say they have no connection to their forebears. Here, Chollet ties a litany of modern gendered indignities—from the minor, aggravating, day-to-day nego-tiations to large-scale injustices and human-rights abuses—back to historic witch-hunts, which historian Anne Llewellyn Barstow calls a "burst of misogyny without parallel in West-ern history."

The phrase "witch-hunt" is a curiously loaded one; de-ployed nowadays, the speaker is almost certainly using it incorrectly and acting in bad faith (and would unquestion-ably minimize witch-hunts as historic fact). One cannot help but think of Woody Allen's defense of Harvey Weinstein, in which he blamed "a witch-hunt atmosphere" for Wein-stein being held accountable for decades of wide-scale sexual abuses and predations.[2]

But, here, Chollet is far more interested in returning to the roots of the metaphor—how our cultural and societal response to women cannot be unthreaded from our historic treatment of women perceived to be witches. We do not burn, hang, or drown as many women now as we did in the past, but there is no shortage of ways women's lives continue to be destroyed. Women are abused, assaulted, economically disempowered, raped, shoved into the margins, pressured, silenced, ignored, treated as guinea pigs, co-opted, stolen from, misrepresented, forced into pregnancy or servitude, imprisoned, and, yes, sometimes murdered. Every possible decision modern women make or role they occupy, outside of the most rigorous and regressive, can be tied back to the very symptoms of witchcraft: refusal of motherhood, rejection of marriage, ignoring traditional beauty standards, bodily and sexual autonomy, homosexuality, aging, anger, even a general sense of self-determination.

You'd be hard-pressed to find a more enduring and potent archetype than the witch; she has served as a shorthand for women's power and potential—and, for some, the threat of those things—for much of human history. And yet, nowadays, witches have become a neo-liberal girlboss-style icon. That is to say, capitalism has gotten ahold of her; and, like so many things capitalism touches, she is in danger of dissociating from her radical roots. What could have once gotten a woman killed is now available for purchase at Urban Outfitters. (Within limits, of course. You can sell her crystals but refuse to pay her fair wages.)

I have long been fascinated—and horrified!—by the contemporary commodification of feminism, the way capitalism's interest has clouded its necessity. Many people seem to fall for this line of thinking, however unconsciously: If feminism is something that can be commodified, then it follows that it's ultimately frivolous, maybe even unnecessary. But, instead of thinking of feminism as archaic, capitalism's cheapening co-option proves that it's more necessary than ever: Women's liberation remains at odds with the patriarchal structures that govern our society.

If we forget—even now, in an age of the consequences of hard-won political battles—that women occupy the literal margins, we will continue to lose all ground. It is not an accident that I write this foreword at a moment in US history where abortion rights are in jeopardy, and the COVID pandemic—aided by decades of misogynist policies and a nonexistent social safety net—has gutted all of the economic advances American women have made in the last half-century. The fact is, no matter how many advances societies make, they cannot help but treat women in the same predictable ways. The past, as they say, is hardly past at all.

Are you still thinking about her? Your witch? Here's the thing: she's fictional. But you are surrounded by witches; you might even be one yourself. Grab your broomstick, your cloak, your familiar. In these pages, you will find the witch-hunters' playbook; may their unbroken chain of successes become your own.

Carmen Maria Machado
June 7, 2021
Philadelphia, PA

In Defense

of

Witches

Introduction

Their Descendants

Of course, there was the one in Walt Disney's *Snow White*, all stringy gray hair under her black hood, a wart on her crooked nose, her inane rictus revealing a single tooth left in her lower gum, and the heavy brows over her crazy eyes further exaggerating her wicked expression. But she is not the witch who made the biggest impression on my childhood: that honor goes to Flutter Mildweather.

Flutter appears in *The Glassblower's Children,* a children's novel by the Swedish writer Maria Gripe, which is set in an imaginary Nordic country. She lives in a house perched on a hilltop and nestled beneath a very old apple tree, the shape of which is visible from far away, outlined against the sky. The region is peaceful and lovely, but the inhabitants of the nearby village avoid wandering that way, for a gallows once stood there. At night, you may catch a faint glimmer at the window while the old woman weaves and chats to her crow, Wise Wit, who has been one-eyed ever since he lost the other by looking too deeply into the Well of Wisdom. More than the witch's magical powers, I was impressed by the aura she had, a blend of deep serenity, mystery and insight.

I was fascinated by the way Flutter was depicted: "she always walked about wearing a big indigo cloak with a shoulder cape. The deep, scalloped edge flapped like huge wings on her shoulders"—hence her first name, "Flutter."[1] "And on her head she wore a very remarkable hat. Its flower-strewn brim belled out beneath a high violet peak decorated with butterflies." All who crossed her path were struck by the vitality of her blue eyes, which "were changing all the time and had great power over people." Perhaps, much later, with my adult interest in fashion, it was this image of Flutter Mildweather that allowed me to appreciate the imposing creations of Yohji Yamamoto—his capacious garments, his vast hats, like shelters of fabric—the polar opposite to the dominant aesthetic diktat that women should show as much of their skin and shape as possible.[2] A benevolent shadow, Flutter remained stored away in me like a talisman, a memory of what a woman of *stature* could be.

I also used to like the somewhat withdrawn life Flutter led and her relationship with the nearby community, at once distant and connected. The hill where her house stands, Gripe writes, seems to keep the village safe, as if it is "resting comfortably in its protection." The witch weaves extraordinary carpets: "She sat at her loom day in and day out, brooding somewhat anxiously about the people and the life down in the village. And then one day she discovered that she knew what was going to happen to them. She could see it in the carpet design that grew under her hands."[3] Her appearances in the village streets, infrequent and fleeting as they are, become a sign of hope for those who see her go by: she owes the second part of her nickname—no one seems to know her true name—to the fact that she is never seen in winter and that her reappearance is a sure sign of spring's imminence, even if that day the thermometer is still at "thirty degrees below freezing."

Even the scary witches—the one in "Hansel and Gretel"; Baba Yaga of the Russian fairy tales, lurking in her *izba* perched on chicken feet—all inspired in me more excitement than repugnance. They stirred my imagination, sparked delicious shivers of terror, gave me a sense of adventure and opened doors onto other worlds. At primary school, faced with the inexplicable composure of the teaching staff and left to our own devices, my schoolmates and I would spend our breaks tracking down the witch who had set up home behind the playground hedge. Danger danced hand in hand with intrigue. Suddenly we felt that anything might happen, and perhaps, too, that unthreatening prettiness and cooing sweetness were not the only fate imaginable for women. Without this excitement, childhood would have lacked depth of flavor. But, in Flutter Mildweather, the figure of the witch ultimately became a positive one for me. It was the witch who had the last word, who made the baddies bite the dust. She offered the promise of revenge over any adversary who underestimated you; like Fantômette, in a way, only with the power of her wit rather than her talents as a Lycra-clad gymnast—which suited me, as I hated sport.[4] Through Flutter, I arrived at the idea that being a woman could mean having additional power, whereas up to that point my vague impressions suggested quite the opposite. Since then, wherever it appears, the word "witch" has had a magnetic hold on me, as if still promising some power that could one day be mine. Something about it fizzes with energy. The word speaks of a knowledge that lies close to the ground, a vital power, an accumulated force of experience that official sources disdain or repress. I also like the idea of an art that we can go on perfecting throughout our lives, to which we dedicate ourselves and which protects us against everything, or almost everything, if only due to the passion we invest in it. The witch embodies woman free of all domination, all limitation; she is an ideal to aim for; she shows us the way.

A Victim of the Moderns

It has taken me a surprisingly long time to appreciate the degree of misunderstanding within this magnet for fantasy, this image of a heroine with superpowers—as witches are portrayed in all dominant cultural productions going. Half a lifetime to understand that, before becoming a spark to the imagination or a badge of honor, the word "witch" had been the very worst seal of shame, the false charge which caused the torture and death of tens of thousands of women. The witch-hunts that took place in Europe, principally during the sixteenth and seventeenth centuries, occupy a strange place in the collective consciousness. Witch trials were based on wild accusations—of night-time flights to reach sabbath meetings, of pacts and copulation with the Devil—which seem to have dragged witches with them into the sphere of the unreal, tearing them away from their genuine historical roots. To our eyes, when we come across her these days, the first known representation of a woman flying on a broomstick, in the margin of Martin Le Franc's manuscript *Le Champion des dames* (*The Champion of Women*, 1441–2), appears unserious, facetious even, as though she might have swooped straight out of a Tim Burton film or from the credits to *Bewitched,* or even been intended as a Halloween decoration. And yet, at the time the drawing was made—around 1440—she heralded centuries of suffering. On the invention of the witches' sabbath, historian Guy Bechtel says: "This great ideological poem has been responsible for many murders."[5] As for the sexual dimension of the torture the accused suffered, the truth of this seems to have been dissolved into Sadean imagery and the troubling emotions that provokes.

In 2016, Bruges' Sint-Janshospitaal museum devoted an exhibition to "Bruegel's Witches," the Flemish master being among the first painters to take up this theme. On one panel, he listed the names of dozens of the city's women who were burned as witches in the public square. "Many of Bruges' inhabitants still bear these surnames and, before visiting the exhibition, they had no idea they could have an ancestor accused of witchcraft," the museum's director commented in the documentary *Dans le sillage des sorcières de Bruegel.* This was said with a smile, as if the fact of finding in your family tree an innocent woman murdered on grounds of delusional allegations were a cute little anecdote for dinner-party gossip. And it begs the question: which other mass crime, even one long-past, is it possible to speak of like this—with a smile?

By wiping out entire families, by inducing a reign of terror and by pitilessly repressing certain behaviors and practices that had come to be seen as unacceptable, the witch-hunts contributed to shaping the world we live in now. Had they not occurred, we would probably be living in very different societies. They tell us much about choices that were made, about paths that were preferred and those that were condemned. Yet we refuse to confront them directly. Even when we do accept the truth about this period of history, we go on finding ways to keep our distance from it. For example, we often make the mistake of considering the witch-hunts part of the Middle Ages, which is generally considered a regressive and obscurantist period, nothing to do with us now—yet the most extensive witch-hunts occurred during the Renaissance: they began around 1400 and had become a major phenomenon by 1560. Executions were still taking place at the end of the eighteenth century—for example, that of Anna Göldi, who was beheaded at Glarus, in Switzerland, in 1782. As Guy Bechtel writes, the witch "was a victim of the Moderns, not the Ancients."[6]

Likewise, we tend to explain the persecutions as a religious fanaticism led by perverted inquisitors. Yet, the Inquisition, which was above all concerned with heretics, made very little attempt to discover witches; the vast majority of condemnations for witchcraft took place in the civil courts. The secular court judges revealed themselves to be "more cruel and more fanatical than Rome"[7] when it came to witchcraft. Besides, this distinction is only moderately useful in a world where there *was* no belief system beyond the religious. Even among the few who spoke out against the persecutions—such as the Dutch physician Johann Weyer, who, in 1563, condemned the "bloodbath of innocents"—none doubted the existence of the Devil. As for the Protestants, despite their reputation as the greater rationalists, they hunted down witches with the same ardour as the Catholics. The return to literalist readings of the Bible, championed by the Reformation, did not favor clemency—quite the contrary. In Geneva, under Calvin, thirty-five "witches" were executed in accordance with one line from the Book of Exodus: "Thou shalt not suffer a witch to live" (Exodus 22:18). The intolerant climate of the time, the bloody orgies of the religious wars—3,000 Protestants were killed in Paris on St. Bartholomew's Day, 1572—only boosted the cruelty of both camps toward witches.

Truth be told, it is precisely because the witch-hunts speak to us of our own time that we have excellent reasons not to face up to them. Venturing down this path means confronting the most wretched aspects of humanity. The witch-hunts demonstrate, first, the stubborn tendency of all societies to find a scapegoat for their misfortunes and to lock themselves into a spiral of irrationality, cut off from all reasonable challenge, until the accumulation of hate-filled discourse and obsessional hostility justify a turn to physical violence, perceived as the legitimate defense of a beleaguered society. In Françoise d'Eaubonne's words, the witch-hunts demonstrate our capacity to "trigger a massacre by following the logic of a lunatic."[8] The demonization of women as witches had much in common with anti-Semitism. Terms such as witches' "sabbath" and their "synagogue" were used; like Jews, witches were suspected of conspiring to destroy Christianity and both groups were depicted with hooked noses. In 1618, a court clerk, whiling away the longueurs of a witch trial in the Colmar region, drew the accused in the margin of his report: he showed her with a traditional Jewish hairstyle, "with pendants, trimmed with stars of David."[9]

Often, far from being the work of an uncouth, poorly educated community, the choice of scapegoat came from on high, from the educated classes. The origin of the witch myth coincides closely with that—in 1454—of the printing press, which plays a crucial role in it. Bechtel describes a "media campaign" which "utilized all the period's information vectors": "books for those who could read, sermons for the rest; for all, great quantities of visual representations."[11] The work of two inquisitors, Heinrich Kramer (or Henricus Institor) from Alsace and Jakob Sprenger from Basel, the *Malleus Maleficarum* was published in 1487 and has been compared to Hitler's *Mein Kampf*. Reprinted upward of fifteen times, it sold around 30,000 copies throughout Europe during the great witch-hunts. "Throughout this age of fire, in all the trials, the judges relied on it. They would ask the questions in the *Malleus* and the replies they heard came equally from the *Malleus*."[12] Enough to put paid to our idealized visions of the first uses of the printing press! By giving credence to the notion of an imminent threat that demanded the application of exceptional measures, the *Malleus Maleficarum* sustained a collective delusion. Its success inspired other demonologists, who became a veritable gold mine for publishers. The authors of these contemporary books—such as the French philosopher Jean Bodin—whose writings read like the ravings of madmen, were in fact scholars and men of great reputation, Bechtel emphasizes: "What a contrast with the credulity and the brutality demonstrated by every one of them in their demonological reports."[13]

All the Tall Poppies

One emerges from these accounts chilled to the bone, and especially as a woman. Of course, many men were executed for witchcraft, but misogyny was at the heart of the persecutions. "Male witches are of small concern," as one author of the *Malleus* confirmed.[14] Its authors feel that "if the evil of women did not in fact exist—not to mention their acts of sorcery—the world would remain unburdened of countless dangers."[15] Weak in body and mind, spurred on by insatiable licentious drives, women were thought to make easy prey for the Devil. In the trials in most areas, women represented on average 80 percent of those accused and 85 percent of those condemned.[16] Women were also at a disadvantage when it came to the judicial machine: in France, men made up 20 percent of those accused, but they originated 50 percent of the appeal cases brought to the French parliament. Whereas previously the courts disallowed their testimony, European women only achieved the status of subjects in their own right, in the eyes of the law, for the purpose of being accused, en masse, of witchcraft.[17] The campaign led between 1587 and 1593 in twenty-two villages in the region of Trier, in Germany—the starting point and also the epicenter, along with Switzerland, of the witch-hunts—was so relentless that, in two of the villages, only one woman was left alive; in total, 368 women were burned. Entire family lines were wiped out: the charges were not very clear against Magdelaine Denas, who at seventy-seven was burned as a witch in the Cambrésis region of Northern France in 1670, but her aunt, mother and daughter had already been executed and it was thought that witchcraft was hereditary.[18]

For some time, the accusations tended to spare the upper classes, and when they in turn came under scrutiny from accusers, the trials rapidly fizzled out. The political enemies of certain high-born figures would occasionally denounce the latter's daughters or wives as witches; this was easier than attacking their enemies directly. However, the great majority of victims belonged to the lower classes. They were at the mercy of entirely male institutions: interrogators, priests or pastors, torturers, guards, judges and executioners—all were men. We can imagine the panic and distress of these women, exacerbated for most by having to face their ordeal entirely alone. The men of their families rarely attempted to support them— sometimes even adding their voices to those of the accusers. For some, this reticence can be explained by fear: men accused of witchcraft were for the most part accused due to their intimacy with "witches." Others took advantage of the climate of general suspicion "to free themselves from unwanted wives and lovers, or to blunt the revenge of women they had raped or seduced," as Silvia Federici explains; in her analysis, the "years of propaganda and terror sowed among men the seeds of a deep psychological alienation from women."[19]

Some of the women accused were both sorceresses and healers, a combination that reads strangely to us now, but was seen as natural and obvious at the time. They cast or lifted spells, they brewed philtres and potions, but they also cared for the sick and injured, and helped women to give birth. They were the only option available to most people suffering from ill health and had always been respected members of their communities, until their activities became associated with the workings of the Devil. More generally, however, any woman who stepped out of line risked arousing the interest of a witch-hunter. Talking back to a neighbor, speaking loudly, having a strong character or showing a bit too much aware-ness of your own sexual appeal: being a nuisance of any kind would put you in danger. According to a paradoxical dynamic familiar to women in all eras, every behavior and its oppo-site could be used against you: it was suspicious to miss Sun-day Mass too frequently, but it was also suspicious never to miss it; it was suspicious to gather regularly with friends, but also to have too solitary a lifestyle . . . [20] The trial by ducking sums up these contradictions. The suspect was thrown into deep water: if she drowned, she was innocent; if she floated, she was a witch and must then be executed. There are also many contemporary references to a "rejection of alms" rou-tine: wealthy people who disdained the outstretched hand of a beggar and then fell ill or suffered some misfortune would rush to accuse her of putting a spell on them, thus displacing their guilty obligation back on the beggar. In other cases, we find the logic of the scapegoat in its purest form: "Ships are in trouble out at sea? Digna Robert, in Belgium, is arrested, burned, displayed upon a wheel (1565). A windmill outside Bordeaux has broken down? It is claimed that Jeanne Nichols, known as Gache, has 'blocked' it (1619)."[21] No matter that these were perfectly inoffensive women, their fellow citizens were convinced they held unlimited powers of destruction. In Shakespeare's *The Tempest* (1611), it is said of the enslaved Caliban that "His mother was a witch, and one so strong /

That could control the moon," and, in the introduction to his 1864 French translation, François Guizot expanded on this point, asserting: "In all the ancient accusations of witchcraft in England, we find constantly the epithet *strong* connected to the word *witch*, a kind of special, expansive qualification. The courts were obliged to rule, in contrast with popular opinion, that the word *strong* added nothing to the prosecuting case."[22]

Having a woman's body could be enough to make you suspect. After their arrest, accused women were stripped naked, shaved and handed to a witch pricker, who would carry out a meticulous search for the Devil's mark, on the surface or within their body, by pricking them with needles. Any birthmark, scar or irregularity could serve as proof— which explains why older women were condemned in such great numbers. This mark was understood to be unaffected by pain; many of the suspected women were so shocked by the pricker's violation of their modesty—by the violation the entire business represented—that they were, by then, in a state of semi-consciousness and so did not react to the pricking. In Scotland, witch prickers even traveled through towns and villages offering to unmask the witches hidden among their inhabitants. In 1649, the city of Newcastle hired one with the incentive of twenty shillings' payment per condemned witch. Thirty women were taken to the town hall and undressed. And—what a surprise—most were pronounced guilty.[23]

"My response to studying this material has often been the same as reading the daily newspaper, namely, that I learn more about human cruelty than I want to," admits Anne L. Barstow in the introduction to her study of the European witch-hunts.[24] Indeed, her cataloguing of the tortures is unbearable: joints dislocated by strappado, bodies burned on white-hot metal chairs, leg bones broken by brodequins. Demonologists would urge that we not be moved by the victims' tears, which were attributed to diabolical cunning and were of course faked. Witch-hunters are revealed as both obsessed with and terrified by female sexuality. Their interrogations included asking, tirelessly, what the Devil's penis looked like. The *Malleus Malleficarum* confirms that witches have the power to make men's genitals disappear and that they keep whole collections of them in chests or in birds' nests, where they go on desperately wiggling (although no such collection has ever been found). In addition to being a household symbol turned upside down, the phallic form of the broom that witches sit astride bears witness to their sexual freedom. The sabbath is understood as an occasion of wild, untrammeled sexual exhibition. Torturers enjoyed the absolute control they exercised over their prisoners; they could give free rein to voyeuristic and sexually sadistic inclinations. To all this was added rape by the women's guards: when a prisoner was discovered strangled in her cell, it was said that the Devil had come to collect his servant. By the time of their execution, many of the condemned women were no longer able to stand upright. But, although they might have been relieved to put an end to their torture, an appalling death still lay ahead. The demonologist Henry Boguet described the last hours of Clauda Jam-Guillaume, who found the strength to escape her funeral pyre three times. The executioner had not kept his promise to strangle her before the flames reached her, so she effectively forced him to honor his word: the third time, he knocked her out, so that she died unconscious.[25]

Either Denied or Glamorized

It is difficult not to conclude that the witch-hunts amounted to a war against women. And yet . . . Carol F. Karlsen, a specialist on the New England witch trials, deplores how her "gender analysis has been ignored, trivialized or obliquely challenged" in the numerous publications, scholarly and generalist, that were written to mark the 300th anniversary of the Salem witch trials, in 1992.[26] Anne L. Barstow considers it "as extraordinary as the historical facts themselves"[27] that historians seem determined to deny that witch-hunts constituted "a burst of misogyny without parallel in Western history."[28] She cites the astounding contortions that her colleagues—male and female—will engage in to contradict conclusions arising from their own research. Guy Bechtel offers one illustration of this when, after describing the "demonization of women" that preceded the witch-hunts, he asks, "Does this mean that anti-female sentiment explains the pyres?" and then replies, decidedly, "Of course not."[29] In support of this conclusion, he calls on some rather weak arguments: first, "men too were burned," and then, "anti-female attitudes—which developed from the end of the thirteenth century—substantially predated the period of the pyres." Now, although some men were indeed victims of denunciation by "possessed" women, as in the famous cases of Loudun and Louviers, the majority were only, as we have seen, accused of witchcraft by association with women, or otherwise as a secondary charge, this crime being added to other primary charges. As for the fact that anti-woman sentiment originated much earlier, we can instead read this as confirmation of the decisive role it came to play in these events. Centuries of hatred and obscurantism seem to have culminated in this wave of violence, born of fear in the face of the increasing space taken up by women in the social realm.

Jean Delumeau sees Alvarus Pelagius's *De Planctu Ecclesiae*, which was written in about 1330 at the request of Pope John XXII, as the major document of clerical hostility toward women, a "call to take up holy war against the Devil's female allies" and the precursor of the *Malleus Maleficarum*. In this text, the Spanish Franciscan states, notably, that women, "beneath a humble exterior, hide a proud and wayward temperament, in which they resemble the Jews," as Delumeau summarizes it.[30] From the end of the medieval era, Bechtel states, "even the most unreligious texts are imbued with misogyny."[31] On this point, the Church fathers and their successors were, in any case, building on Greek and Roman traditions. Before Eve ate the forbidden fruit, Greek mythology's Pandora had already opened the urn that held all the ills of humanity. Fledgling Christianity borrowed much from Stoicism, which was already opposed to pleasure and therefore to women. "No other group in the world has been so deeply and continually insulted," says Bechtel. Reading these texts, it can feel as though such rhetoric must inevitably, one day, lead to some kind of action on a grand scale. In 1593, a German pastor who was somewhat more peaceable than most became alarmed about the "little leaflets that peddle in all regions insults against women," the reading of which "serves as a pastime for the idle." He felt that "by dint of hearing and reading these things, our menfolk have become exasperated with women, and when they learn that one of them has been condemned to perish on the pyre, they cry: 'A good thing too!'"[32]

"Hysterics" and "unfortunate women:" Barstow also highlights the condescension of many historians toward the victims of the witch-hunts. Colette Arnould finds the same attitude in Voltaire, who wrote of witchcraft, "Philosophy alone has at length cured men of this abominable delusion, and has taught judges that they should not burn the insane."[33] Whereas, she protests, the first victims of "the madness" were the judges, and they did their work so well that their particular insanity became contagious.[34] We also find instances of a victim-blaming reflex: studying the witch-hunts in southern Germany, eminent American scholar Erik Midelfort observes that the women seemed "to provoke somehow an intense misogyny at times" and calls for further study as to "why that group *attracted to itself* the scapegoating mechanism."[35] Karlsen rejects the portraits often drawn of New England's accused women, which, by dwelling on their "bad character" or "deviant personality," adopted the accusers' point of view. She discerns here a manifestation of the "deeply embedded tendency in our society to hold women ultimately responsible for the violence committed against them."[36] Perhaps this contempt and these prejudices simply indicate that, although they would not condone them and although they do comprehend the horror of them, like Voltaire, those who make the witch-hunts the object of their study are nonetheless still products of the world that hunted those witches. Perhaps we should infer that the work required to expose how this episode transformed European societies is still only in its infancy.

The witch-hunts' toll of human lives remains deeply disputed and will probably never be established with certainty. In the 1970s, there was talk of a million victims, or possibly many more. These days, we talk instead of between 50,000 and 100,000.[37] These figures exclude those who were lynched, who committed suicide or who died in prison—whether from the effects of torture or due to the poor conditions of their imprisonment. Others who did not lose their lives were banished instead or saw their reputation and that of their family ruined. Yet all women, even those who were never accused, felt the effects of the witch-hunts. The public staging of the tortures, a powerful source of terror and collective discipline, induced all women to be discreet, docile and submissive—not to make any waves. What's more, one way or another, they were compelled to assume the conviction that they were the incarnation of evil; they were forcibly persuaded of their own guilt and fundamental wickedness.

Thus the previously lively and supportive subculture among women in the Middle Ages came to an end, according to Barstow. For her, the rise of individualism—in the sense of an inward turn and focus on personal interests—over the period that followed should largely, in the case of women, be attributed to fear. There was plenty of encouragement for women to keep a low profile, as certain incidents show. In 1679, in Marchiennes, in France, Péronne Goguillon managed to escape a rape attempt by four drunk soldiers, who then made her promise to pay them to leave her in peace.

When he reported the soldiers' actions, Goguillon's husband drew attention to his wife's previously poor reputation; as a result, she was burned as a witch.[38] Something similar happened in the case of Anna Göldi; her biographer, the Swiss journalist Walter Hauser, picked up the trail of a complaint about sexual harassment that she had made against the doctor who employed her as a servant. The latter had then accused her of witchcraft by way of counterattack.[39]

From *The Wizard of Oz* to *Starhawk*

By reclaiming the story of the women accused of witchcraft, Western feminists have—whether deliberately or not—both perpetuated their subversive effect and defiantly reasserted the terrifying powers accorded them by their judges. "We are the granddaughters of the witches you weren't able to burn," as the famous slogan goes; or, in 1970s Italy: "Tremble, tremble, the witches are back!" ("*Tremate, tremate, le streghe son tornate!*") Feminists have also called for justice by fighting back against shallow and sugar-coated treatments of the witches' story. In 1985, the German town of Gelnhausen turned its "witches' tower" into a tourist attraction—a building in which women accused of witchcraft had once been walled-up alive. The morning of the public opening, demonstrators dressed in white paraded around the edifice holding signs with the victims' names.[40] Whatever their origin, these awareness-raising efforts have sometimes paid off: in 2008, the Swiss canton of Glarus officially exonerated Anna Göldi, thanks to her biographer's persistence, and dedicated a museum to her.[41] Freiburg and Cologne, in Germany, and Nieuport, in Belgium, all followed suit. In 2013, Norway unveiled the

Steilneset Memorial, a collaboration between architect Peter Zumthor and artist Louise Bourgeois that pays homage to ninety-one people on the very site where they were burned in the northern county of Finnmark.

The first feminist to disinter the witches' story and to claim this title for herself was the American Matilda Joslyn Gage, who fought for women's right to vote and also for the rights of Native Americans and the abolition of slavery—she was given a prison sentence for helping slaves to escape. In *Woman, Church and State* (1893), she offered a feminist reading of the witch-hunts: "When for 'witches' we read 'women,' we gain fuller comprehension of the cruelties inflicted by the church upon this portion of humanity."[42] Gage inspired the character of Glinda, the good witch in *The Wonderful Wizard of Oz*, which was written by her son-in-law, L. Frank Baum. When he adapted the novel for cinema in 1939, Victor Fleming created the first "good witch" in popular culture.[43]

Then, on All Hallows' Eve 1968, in New York, the Women's International Terrorist Conspiracy from Hell ("WITCH") movement took to the streets, its members parading down Wall Street and dancing, hand in hand, dressed in black cloaks, outside the Stock Exchange. "With closed eyes and lowered heads, the women incanted the Berber Yell (sacred to Algerian witches) and proclaimed the coming demise of various stocks. A few hours later, the market closed 1.5 points down, and the following day it dropped 5 points," according to the account published a few years later by Robin Morgan, one of the witches.[44] Yet she also highlights their striking ignorance, at the time, of the history of witches:

We demanded an audience with Satan, our superior,
at the Stock Exchange—an ignorant faux pas which
now makes me cringe: the members of the Old Religion never worshipped Satan. They were followers of
a tripartite Goddess: it was the Christian church who
invented Satan and then claimed that witches were
Satanists. We had bitten the patriarchal bait on that
one, and on so many others . . . We were plain dumb.
But we were dumb with style.[45]

It's true: photos from the occasion provide ample evidence. In France, among the highlights of our second wave
of feminism was the launch of *Sorcières* ("Witches") magazine, published in Paris from 1976 to 1982 under the edi-
torship of Xavière Gauthier, and including contributions
from Hélène Cixous, Marguerite Duras, Luce Irigaray, Julia
Kristeva, Nancy Huston and Annie Leclerc, among other
stars of French feminist thought.[46] And we must not forget
the very lovely songs of Anne Sylvestre who, in addition to
her children's nursery rhymes, created a substantial repertoire
of feminist work, particularly encapsulated in her 1975 album
Une sorcière comme les autres ("A witch like any other").[47]

In 1979, *The Spiral Dance*, Starhawk's first book, was published in the US. This was to become a key reference work on
the neopagan cult of the Goddess. The name of this Califor-
nian witch—who was born Miriam Simos in 1951—would
reach European ears only in 1999, on the occasion of Starhawk and her friends' much discussed participation in the
demonstrations against the World Trade Organization
ministerial conference in Seattle, which itself marked a key

date in the early days of the anti-globalization movement. In 2003, publisher Philippe Pignarre and philosopher Isabelle Stengers published *Femmes, magie et politique*, the first French translation of one of Starhawk's books, originally published in English as *Dreaming the Dark: Magic, Sex and Politics* (first published in 1982). When, in an online group, I happened to mention an article I'd written about this book, I unleashed enraged sarcasm from another subscriber, a thriller writer who couldn't find words sufficiently damning to describe the pit of despair into which the notion of "neopagan witchcraft" plunged him. Fifteen years later, his opinion may not have changed, but my reference has lost much of its perceived absurdity. These days, witches are everywhere. In the US, they take part in the Black Lives Matter movement, put spells on Donald Trump, protest against white supremacists and against those who question a woman's right to abortion. In Portland, Oregon, and elsewhere, groups are reviving WITCH. In France, in 2015, Isabelle Cambourakis created a new feminist list within her brother's eponymous publishing house, calling it *Sorcières*—"Witches." And she opened the list with a republication of the French edition of *Dreaming the Dark* (she chose to keep the original title, *Rêver l'obscur*), which was much better received on this occasion than it had been the first time round—especially as the French translation of Federici's *Caliban and the Witch* had also just been published. What's more, at the September 2017 demonstrations against labor law reforms in France, a feminist and anarchist "Witch Bloc" paraded in pointed hats under the banner "*Macron au chaudron*"—"Macron for the cauldron."

Misogynists too, as ever, appear to be obsessed with the

figure of the witch. "Feminism encourages women to leave their husbands, kill their children, practice witchcraft, destroy capitalism and become lesbians," the American televangelist Pat Robertson railed as recently as 1992, in a speech that remains famous (and prompted many to respond, "Where do we sign up?"). During the 2016 US presidential campaign, the hatred shown toward Hillary Clinton far outstripped even the most virulent criticisms that could legitimately be pinned on her. She was linked with "evil" and widely compared to a witch, which is to say that she was attacked as a woman, not as a political leader. After her defeat, some of those critics dug out the song "Ding Dong, the Witch is Dead," sung in *The Wizard of Oz* to celebrate the Witch of the East's death—a jingle already revived in the UK at the time of Margaret Thatcher's death in 2013. This reference was brandished not only by Donald Trump's electors, but also by supporters of Bernie Sanders, Clinton's main rival in the primaries. On Sanders' official site, a fundraising initiative was announced under the punning title "Bern the Witch"—an announcement that the Vermont senator's campaign team took down as soon as it was brought to his attention. Continuing this series of limp quips, the conservative commentator Rush Limbaugh quipped, "She's a witch with a capital B"—he can't have known that, at the Salem witch trials in the seventeenth century, a key figure had already exploited this consonance by calling his servant, Sarah Churchill, who was one of his accusers, "bitch witch." In reaction, female Democrat voters started sporting badges calling themselves "Witches for Hillary" or "Hags for Hillary."[48]

Over the last few years, there has been a substantive

change in the way French feminists approach the figure of the witch. The publisher's initial description of Starhawk's *Dreaming the Dark* read:

> In France, those who engage in politics have grown used to distrusting everything to do with spirituality, which was rapidly written off as part of far-right discourse. Magic and politics do not sit naturally together, so when women choose to call themselves witches, they shed all that they consider mere superstition and old-fashioned ideas and retain only the persecution that once beset them at the hands of patriarchal authorities.[49]

Today, this observation is no longer true. In France, as in the US, young feminists—a group that includes gay and trans people—comfortably proclaim their use of magic. Between the summer of 2017 and spring of 2018, French journalist and writer Jack Parker published *Witch, Please*, "the modern witch's newsletter," with thousands of subscribers. In it she shared photos of her altar and her personal spell books, interviews with other witches and recommendations for rituals linked to the positions of the stars and the moon's phases.

These new witches maintain no shared liturgy: "As witchcraft is a practice, it has no need of organized religious worship, although it can easily be combined with one," explains Mæl, a French witch. "There is no fundamental incompatibility, here. Indeed, we find witches coming from the big monotheistic religions (Judaism, Christianity, Islam) as well as atheist and agnostic witches, but also witches adhering to pagan and neopagan religions (polytheists, Wiccans, Helle-nists, etc.)."[50] Starhawk—who operates within the very broad church of the neopagan religion, Wicca—also advocates the invention of new rituals as the need arises. She describes, for instance, how the ritual with which she and her friends now celebrate the winter solstice began when they decided to light a great fire on the beach and then plunged together into the ocean, hands in the air, chanting and making jubilant cries:

> On one of the first Solstices I celebrated with my early women's coven, we went to the beach to watch the sunset before our evening ritual. One woman said, "Let's take off our clothes and jump in. Come on, I dare you!" "You're out of your mind," I remember saying, but we did it anyway. After a few years, it occurred to us to light a fire, staving off hypothermia, and so a tradition was born. (Do something once, it's an experiment. Do it twice, and it's a tradition.)[51]

Visitors at Nightfall

How to explain this new trend? Those who are practicing witchcraft today grew up with the Harry Potter books, but also with the *Charmed* series—whose heroines are three witch sisters—and *Buffy the Vampire Slayer*—in which shy schoolgirl Willow becomes a powerful witch—which may have played a part in this turnaround. Paradoxically, magic now seems a very pragmatic solution, a life-affirming jump-start, a way of anchoring ourselves in the world and in our own lives at a time when everything seems to be conspiring to destabilize us and exploit our vulnerabilities. In her 16 July 2017 newsletter,

Jack Parker refused to decide one way or the other on the question of "placebo effect versus genuine ancestral magic:"

> What's important is that it works and that it does us good, right? [. . .] We are always looking for life's meaning, for meaning in our own lives, and why and how and where-am-I-going and who-am-I and what-will-I-become, so if we can hang on to two or three things that reassure us and that we can get the knack of along the way, why reject them out of hand?

Without having a magical practice in the literal sense myself, I feel that there is something in this that I have tried to advocate elsewhere: time to oneself, regular withdrawals from the world, confidence in letting the forces of imagination and reverie take over.[52] With its insistence on positive thinking and its invitation to "discover your inner goddess," the witchcraft trend forms a completely distinct sub-genre within the vast realm of self-improvement. There is a fine line between the self-help aspect—which leans heavily on spirituality—and feminism and political empowerment, both of which entail the critique of systems of oppression; however, precisely on that fine line, things are happening that are unquestionably worthy of our attention.

Perhaps the ever more visible ecological catastrophe has also diminished the prestige and the bullying power of our technocratic society, thus removing previously inhibiting factors for would-be witches. When a system for apprehending the world which presents itself as supremely rational ends up destroying humanity's fundamental, life-supporting substrate, we may be (over)due a reboot of our standard classifications of what is rational and what irrational. Indeed, the mechanistic view of the world reveals an understanding of science that no longer applies. Far from relegating them to the realm of fantasy or writing them off as charlatans, the most recent scientific discoveries actually converge with the witches' intuitions. Starhawk writes that, "Modern physics no longer speaks of separate, discrete atoms of dead matter, but of waves of energy, probabilities, patterns that change as they are observed; it recognizes what Shamans and Witches have always known: that matter and energy are not separate forces, but different forms of the same thing."[53] Just as Starhawk saw then, so we are now seeing the reinforcement of all kinds of domination, symbolized by the election to lead the world's most powerful country of a billionaire who unashamedly professes misogyny and racism—such that, once again, magic can be a weapon for the oppressed. The witch appears at nightfall, just when everything seems to be lost. It is she who can uncover reserves of fresh hope amid the depths of despair. "When we set a new course, all the powers of life and growth and regeneration will be flowing with us. And when we ally with those powers, miracles can happen," Starhawk wrote in 2005, in an account of her time spent in New Orleans helping the survivors of Hurricane Katrina.[54]

The confrontation between those who defend the rights of women and sexual minorities and those who adhere to reactionary ideologies is increasingly fraught. On 6 September 2017, in Louisville, Kentucky, the local WITCH group demonstrated in support of the state's last abortion clinic, which was threatened with closure, claiming that "American religious fanatics [have been] crucifying women's rights since the 1600s."[55] The effect is a strange cultural climate combining technological sophistication with oppressive traditionalism, and it is nicely depicted in the series *The Handmaid's Tale,* adapted from Margaret Atwood's novel of the same name. It was in this context that, in February 2017, a group of witches—among them, the singer Lana Del Rey—agreed to meet at the foot of Trump Tower in New York to try to bring about the President's impeachment. The organizers asked members to bring a black thread, sulfur, feathers, salt, an orange candle and a white one, and an "unflattering" photo of Donald Trump.[56] In reaction, Christian nationalists invited their adherents to counteract this spiritual offensive by reciting a psalm from the Book of David. They spread the word on Twitter with the hashtag #PrayerResistance. A strange moment indeed . . .

In a (rather left-field) report published in August 2015, the New York design agency K-Hole announced that it had identified a new cultural trend: "chaos magic." And they weren't wrong. Alex Mar, who wrote an account, published that same year, of the million American followers of pagan traditions,[57] described how, "When I started working on [the book], I would talk to people about the project and be met with blank looks . . . Then by the time the book came out, I was being accused of riding a trend."[58] Whether a spiritual and/or a political practice, witchcraft is also an aesthetic, a fashion . . . and a lucrative money-spinner. It has its hashtags on Instagram and its virtual aisles on Etsy, its influencers and its indie entrepreneurs, selling their spells, candles, grimoires, superfoods, essential oils and crystals online. Witchcraft is a fashion inspiration; the big brands are adopting and adapting it. And there's nothing surprising in this: after all, capitalism is always engaged in selling back to us in product form all that it has first destroyed. But there may also be a natural affinity at work here. In 1970, Jean Baudrillard highlighted the degree to which the ideology of consumption was impregnated with magical thinking, writing of a "mentality based on miraculous thinking."[59] In its report, K-Hole sets up a parallel between the logic of magic and that of brand strategy: "Like branding, Chaos Magic is mostly concerned with inception. But where branding is about implanting ideas in the brains of an audience, Chaos Magic is about implanting ideas into your own." Magic has its symbols and mantras; brands have their logos and slogans.[60]

Even before witchcraft turned into a profitable concept, we may consider that the cosmetics industry, in particular, had succeeded in exploiting an obscure nostalgia for magic found among many women, by selling them its pots and vials, its miraculous ingredients, its promises of transformation and its immersion in a world of enchantment. This mode is flagrantly pursued by the French brand Garancia, whose products are called "Bewitching Oil with Super Powers," "Magic Spritz," "Eau de Sourcellerie" (a pun on *eau de source,* meaning "spring water," and *sorcellerie,* meaning "witchcraft"), "Diabolic Tomato," "The Sorcerers' Masked Ball" and "Redness Begone!" But we also find this tendency with the luxury natural cosmetics brand Susanne Kaufmann: its founder is an Austrian who grew up in the "idyllic" Bregenzerwald. As a little girl, she was "immersed in an understanding of the local traditions and the beauty and wellness benefits that could be found in the plants that grew in abundance in the area."[61] Similarly, the word "glamor" (like the

French word *charme*) has lost its former meaning of "spell," to retain only the meanings "beauty" or "glow;" it is now associated with showbiz and the women's magazine whose title it provides. "Patriarchy has stolen our cosmos and returned it in the form of *Cosmopolitan* magazine and cosmetics," American philosopher Mary Daly says, in a nutshell.[62]

The daily beauty routine, a perennial feature of women's magazines, in which a woman in the public eye describes the ways she takes care of her skin and, more broadly, her figure and her health, generates a fascination that is very widely shared (by me too). YouTube channels and websites (the best known being the American site, Into the Gloss) are dedicated to the subject, and it even pops up on the feminist media platforms. Cosmetics are a jungle, demanding a lot of time, energy and money if you're to come through it alive, and these beauty-routine pieces play their part in keeping female consumers in there, maintaining their obsessions with brands and products. Implying the cultivation of special expertise, secrets passed down from woman to woman (reference is often made to what the interviewee has learned from her mother), knowledge of active ingredients and protocols, and discipline—yet also lending a feeling of order, control and pleasure within a sometimes chaotic everyday grind—the "daily routine" could well be seen as a watered-down form of the witches' initiation. We talk elsewhere of beauty "rituals," and of those who master them as "high priestesses."

How This Story Has Shaped Our World

The pages that follow will not, however, spend much time on contemporary witchcraft, at least not in its literal sense.

What I'm interested in, given the story that I have roughly sketched out here, is rather to explore the afterlife of the witch-hunts in Europe and the US. The hunts both translated and amped up prejudices about women, especially the stigma that attaches to some women. The hunts effectively repressed certain behaviors and lifestyles. We have inherited these representations as they have been forged and perpetuated over centuries. The negative associations continue to produce, at best, censorship and self-censorship, and barriers wherever we turn; at worst, hostility and even violence. And even if there were a genuine and widely shared desire for a critical analysis, we have no alternative with which to replace these historical associations. As Françoise d'Eaubonne writes: "Our contemporaries are shaped by events they may know nothing about and which may not even be remembered by others; yet this does not mean they could not have been different and would not have thought quite differently, had those events not happened."[63]

The field is vast, and I shall focus on only four aspects of the story. First, there is the blow dealt to all forms of women's independence (chapter 1). Among those accused of witchcraft, we will note the over-representation of single women and widows—that is, of women not formally bound and subordinate to a man.[64] In this period, women were driven out of roles they had been used to occupying in the world of work. They were expelled from businesses; professional apprenticeship was formalized and women were thereby denied access. Women living alone, in particular, were subjected to "unbearable economic pressure."[65] In Germany, the widows of master craftsmen were no longer permitted to continue their

husbands' work. As for married women, the reintroduction
of Roman law in Europe from the eleventh century formalized their juridical ineligibility; a small margin of autonomy
remained to them, but this was finally formally closed off in
the sixteenth century. Jean Bodin, whose delightful sideline
in demonology we conveniently forget, remains famous for
his political treatise, the *Six Books of the Republic* (1576). Yet,
as Armelle Le Bras-Chopard remarks, his analysis is distin-
guished by its view that the well-governed family and well-
governed state, both guaranteed by masculine authority, will
create a cycle of mutual reinforcement—which may not be
unrelated to his obsession with witches. The married woman's social debarment would be formalized in France with the
civil law of 1804. The witch-hunts had by then fulfilled their
function: there was no further need to burn women alleged
to be witches; now, the law "enabled the curtailment of *all*
women's independence."[66] Nowadays, despite being legally
and practically sanctioned, women's independence continues
to elicit general skepticism. Women's bond with men and
with children, carried out in the mode of selflessness, is still
considered the core of their identity. The way girls are brought
up and socialized teaches them to avoid isolation and leaves
their faculty for independence largely undeveloped. Behind
the famous figure of the "spinster with a cat," left behind by
her peers and the object of pity and derision, we can detect
the shadow of the fearsome witch of the bad old days, flanked
by her diabolical familiar.

Over the same period as the witch-hunts, we also see the
criminalization of contraception and abortion. In France, a
law issued in 1556 obliged all pregnant women to declare their

pregnancy and to ensure a witness at the birth. Infanticide in France became a *crimen exceptum*—"an exceptional crime that was not subject to regular judicial procedures or standards of proof"[67]—a status even witchcraft was not accorded there.[68] Among the accusations made against "witches," murder of infants came up frequently; it was often said that witches consumed children's cadavers at their sabbaths. The witch becomes the "antimother." Many of the accused were healers who played the role of midwife—but who also used to help women wishing to prevent or terminate a pregnancy. For Federici, the witch-hunts paved the way for the gendered labor division required by capitalism, reserving remunerated work for men and assigning to women the birthing and education of the future labor-force.[69] This division has endured into the present day: women are free to have children or not . . . on condition they choose to have them. Those who choose not to are often likened to heartless creatures, obscurely evil and malevolent toward the children of others (chapter 2).

The witch-hunts also branded a very negative image of old women deep into the collective consciousness (chapter 3). Of course, very young "witches" were burned, and even children of seven or eight, girls and boys, but older women, considered both repugnant to look at and especially dangerous due to their experience, became the "favored victims of the witch-hunts."[70] Gage wrote: "Instead of the tenderness and care due to aged women, they were so frequently accused of witchcraft that for years it was an unusual thing for an old woman in the north of Europe to die in her bed."[71] The hate-filled obsession with old women shown by painters (Quentin

Metsys, Hans Baldung, Niklaus Manuel Deutsch) and poets (Ronsard, Du Bellay) can be explained by the cult of youth that flourished at this time and by the simple fact that women were now beginning to live longer. Moreover, the privatization of land that had been common space—known in the UK as "enclosure," part of the early amassing of property that prepared the ground for capitalism—was especially damaging for women. Men were more easily able to access remunerated work, which became the sole means of subsistence. Women depended disproportionately on common land, on areas where it was possible to graze cows, to gather firewood or herbs.[72] The enclosure process both dissolved their independence and, for all who could not count on their children's support, reduced the oldest among them to begging. Although occasionally freer in her behavior and her speech, as soon as she turned into a mouth not worth feeding, the post-menopausal woman became a millstone round the neck of her community. These women were believed to be subject to even stronger sexual urges than in their youth, hence they were driven to seek copulation with the Devil; in them, desire was considered grotesque and repulsive. Nowadays, given that women are considered to wither with time, whereas men age attractively, and given that age exacts penalties on women's sexual and married lives, and that, for women, the competition for youthfulness has taken on an ever more desperate tone, we may assume that the representations of old women during the witch-hunts continue to haunt us, from Goya's witches to those of Walt Disney. One way or another, old age in women remains ugly, shameful, threatening and satanic.

According to Federici's analysis, the subjugation of women required by capitalist systems occurred in parallel with that of peoples branded "inferior," who, enslaved and colonized, became providers of free resources and free labor.[73] But capitalism also entailed the systematic plundering of natural resources and the establishment of a new conception of knowledge. The emerging new science was arrogant and imbued with contempt for femininity, which was associated with irrationality, sentimentality and hysteria, as well as with a natural world requiring domination (chapter 4). Modern medicine, in particular, was built on this model, and the witch-hunts enabled the official doctors of the period to eliminate competition from female healers—despite their being broadly more competent than the doctors. The legacy for healthcare today includes a systematically aggressive stance toward patients, and especially toward female patients, as shown by the mistreatment and violence exposed over recent years, particularly through social media. Our enshrinement of a single "correct view," often less rational than it appears, and our aggressive stance on nature, now so ordinary we hardly notice it, have always been dubious—a serious critique is needed more urgently now than ever, as we face global warming and the increasing destruction of nature. Such challenges to the status quo sometimes arise without any reference to gender, but sometimes they are formulated from a feminist angle. Indeed, some female thinkers consider it essential that the two tyrannies that were imposed together be toppled together. In addition to challenging the inequities they encounter within the system, they are daring to oppose the system itself: their aim is to overturn a symbolic order and a system of knowledge that were explicitly built to work against them.

Eating the Sailor of Hydra's Heart

It would be impossible to provide a comprehensive coverage of any of these subjects in a single volume. I shall provide only, for each of them, a route through, with my thoughts and readings offered as stages along the way. In doing so, I will be drawing on the work of the women writers who, to my mind, best represent a challenge to the barriers described above—for, leading an independent life, growing old and retaining control of one's body remain, in many ways, off-limits for women. In short, I'll be relying on the work of those who are, for me, modern witches, whose strength and perspicacity spur me on, just as Flutter Mildweather did when I was a child, helping to ward off the heavy artillery of the patriarchy and to navigate between its strictures. Whether or not they define themselves as feminists, these women refuse to give up the full exercise of their abilities and their liberty, the exploration of their desires and potential; they will not sacrifice the full enjoyment of their own lives. They thereby lay themselves open to social punishment, which may happen simply through the unthinking reactions and condemnations of those around them, so deep-rooted is the narrow definition of what a woman should be. Reassessing the prohibitions that they subvert will allow us to measure both the everyday oppression we experience and the audacity of those who dare to live differently.

I have written elsewhere—and only half-jokingly—that I was stepping up to found the "scaredy-cat" branch of feminism.[74]

I am a nice, well-brought-up, middle-class woman and I hate to make myself stand out in a crowd. I stick my head above the parapet solely when I can do nothing else, when my convictions and aspirations force me to. I write books like this one to boost my courage. Hence, I do appreciate the galvanizing power of role models. A few years ago, a magazine interviewed a selection of women of all ages, none of whom dyed their white hair—an apparently banal decision, but one that instantly revives shades of witchery. One of the women, the designer Annabelle Adie, recalled the shock she'd had on discovering Marie Seznec, a young model for Christian Lacroix in the 1980s, whose hair was completely white: "When I saw her at a fashion show, I was floored. I was in my twenties and already going gray. She confirmed my determination: no dye, ever!"[75] More recently, the fashion journalist Sophie Fontanel wrote a book about her own decision to stop dyeing her hair; she called it *Une apparition* ("an appearance" or "an apparition"). Her "apparitions" are of both the dazzling person who had been hidden by the dye, and the impressive white-haired woman on a café terrace, the sight of whom prompted Fontanel to take the plunge.[76] In the 1970s, in the US, *The Mary Tyler Moore Show* put the real-life figure of Moore—a happily single journalist—center stage, and proved a revelation for many female viewers. In 2009, Katie Couric, who in 2006 became the first solo female presenter on one of America's major evening news programs, remembered: "I saw this woman out on her own, making a life for herself, and I always thought: I want into that."[77] Retracing the path that led to her not having a child, the writer Pam Houston describes the influence of Nan Nowik, her tutor in feminist studies at the University of Denison, Ohio, in 1980: tall and elegant, she wore IUDs as earrings . . . [78]

Back from a trip to Hydra, a Greek girlfriend tells me that, on display in the local museum, she saw the embalmed heart of the Hydriot sailor who most fiercely fought off the Turks. "Do you think, if we were to eat it, we could become as brave as he was?" she asks me, thoughtfully. But there's no need for such extreme steps: when you want to channel someone else's potency, an encounter with an image or a thought of theirs can be enough to produce spectacular effects. In the way women have of helping each other out, offering each other a leg-up—whether deliberately or unwittingly—we can see the exact opposite of the logic of ostentation that rules the gossip columns and endless Instagram feeds: not keeping up the illusion of a perfect life—good for nothing but exciting envy and frustration, and even self-hatred and despair—but instead extending a generous invitation to constructive and stimulating self-fashioning, without wishing away our flaws and weaknesses. The former attitude dominates the vast and lucrative competition for the title of best representative of traditional femininity—the fashion plate, the mother and/or mistress of the perfect home. The latter attitude, on the other hand, fosters divergence from these models. It shows that it's possible to live and flourish outside them, and that, contrary to what the subtly intimidating discourse would have us believe, perdition does not await as soon as we stray from the straight and narrow. There is doubtless always an element of idealization or delusion in the belief that others "know," that they are party to a secret that eludes us, but, at least in this case, rather than depressing or paralyzing us, this is an idealization that can lend us wings.

Some of the photos of the American intellectual Susan Sontag (1933–2004) show her with a thick streak of white in the midst of her dark hair. That streak was the sign of a partial albinism. Fontanel, who is affected by the same phenomenon, describes how, in Burgundy, in 1460, a woman called Yolande was burned as a witch: upon having her head shaved, she was found to have an area of depigmentation related to this albinism, which appeared to her accusers as the Devil's mark. I recently came across one of those Sontag photos again. I realized that I find her beautiful, despite, twenty-five-odd years ago, having seen something hard, something disturbing about her. At the time, although I hadn't articulated it, she reminded me of the hideous and terrifying Cruella de Vil, in Disney's *One Hundred and One Dalmatians*. Simply identifying this connection conjured away the shadow of the evil witch that had been skewing my perception of this woman and all who look like her.

In her book, Fontanel lists the reasons she finds her white hair beautiful: "White like so many beautiful white things: the whitewashed walls of Greece, Carrara marble, white sand beaches, mother-of-pearl in their shells, chalk on a blackboard, a bath of milk, the glow of a kiss, a snow-covered slope, Cary Grant's head as he accepts his honorary Oscar, my mother taking me out to see the snow, the winter."[79] So many references that gently dissipate associations with ideas arising from a deeply misogynist past. I find a kind of magic in this.

In a documentary about his life and work, Alan Moore, who created the graphic book *V for Vendetta*, said:

> I believe that magic is art, and that art . . . is literally magic. Art is, like magic, the science of manipulating symbols, words or images, to achieve changes in consciousness . . . Indeed, to cast a spell is simply to spell, to manipulate words, to change people's consciousness, and this is why I believe that an artist or writer is the closest thing in the contemporary world to a shaman.[80]

To try to dig out, from among the strata of accumulated images and discourses, what we take to be immutable truths, to shine a light on the arbitrary and contingent nature of the views to which we are unwittingly in thrall, and to replace them with others that allow us to live fully realized lives, that surround us in positive feedback: this is a kind of witchcraft I would be happy to practice for the rest of my life.

1

A Life of One's Own

THE SCOURGE OF WOMEN'S INDEPENDENCE

"Hi, Gloria. I'm so excited to finally get to talk to you . . ."

One day, in March 1990, on CNN, Larry King is hosting Gloria Steinem, the American feminist superstar. A member of the TV audience calls from Cleveland, Ohio. Her tone is warm; we assume this is a fan. But we soon realize this is not the case. "I really believe that your movement was a total failure . . ." the silky voice goes on. "You are one of the primary causes of the downfall of our beautiful American family and society today. A couple of questions. I'd like to know if you're married . . . If you have children." Twice, an unruffled Steinem gallantly replies, "No." Interrupted by the presenter, who diplomatically attempts to sum up her case, the anonymous avenger looses her final bombshell: "I have said for the last fifteen years that Gloria Steinem should rot in hell."[1]

A journalist who, in the early 1970s, became an ardent defender of women's rights, Gloria Steinem has always offered her critics a good run for their money. First, her beauty and her many lovers give the lie to the old chestnut that feminist protest only masks the bitterness and frustration of plain

Janes whom no man has done the honor of rescuing from the shelf. What's more, the full and dynamic life Steinem has led and leads today, a whirlwind of travels and new vistas, of activism and writing, of love and friendship, seriously complicates the picture for those who believe a woman's life means nothing without partnership and motherhood. To a journalist who asked why she wasn't married, Steinem gave the justly celebrated reply: "I can't mate in captivity."

She departed from this rule at the age of sixty-six, so that her companion at the time—David Bale, a South African—could obtain his green card and remain in the US. She married Bale in Oklahoma, at the house of her friend Wilma Mankiller, a Native American leader and activist, in a Cherokee ceremony, followed by a "wonderful breakfast." She wore her "best jeans" for the occasion.[2] Her husband died of cancer three years later. "Some people still assume that, because we got legally married, he was the love of my life—and I was his," Steinem confided, years later, to the journalist Rebecca Traister, who was investigating the history of single women in the US. "That's such a misunderstanding of human uniqueness. He had been married twice before and he had wonderful grown children. I had been happily in love with men who are still my friends and chosen family. Some people have one partner for life, but most don't—and each of our loves is crucial and unique."[3]

Up to the end of the 1960s, as Traister reminds us, American feminism was dominated by Betty Friedan's approach. The author of *The Feminine Mystique* (1963) and an outspoken critic of the ideal of the housewife, Friedan spoke up for "women who wanted equality, but who also wanted to keep on loving their husbands and children."[4] Critiques of marriage itself only surfaced in the feminist movement later on, with the birth of the fight for gay rights and with lesbians' increased visibility. But, even then, it seemed unthinkable for many activists that a woman could be heterosexual and not wish to marry; "at least until Gloria came along."[5] Thanks to Steinem and a few others, in 1973, *Newsweek* observed that it was "finally becoming possible to be both single and whole."[7] By the end of the decade, the divorce rate had exploded, reaching almost 50 percent.

On Welfare, Fraudsters and Free Spirits

We must be clear that, once again, white American feminists seem to have been reinventing the wheel. On the one hand, descended from slaves, black American women had never been subject to the domestic ideal denounced by Friedan. They proudly owned their status as workers, as the lawyer Sadie Alexander (in 1921, the first African-American woman to achieve a PhD in economics) theorized in the 1930s.[8] And this pride in independence was part of a long tradition of political and community engagement. The formidable Annette Richter, for example, has also lived essentially single and without children, and unquestionably deserves to become just as well known as Steinem, who is the same age as her. After a brilliant university career, Richter spent her whole professional life within the government at Washington, while also leading the semi-secret black women's mutual aid organization that her great-great-grandmother founded in 1867, while the latter was still a slave.[9] Further, because of the deterioration in their economic position after the Second World

War, African-American women became much less likely to marry, and began to have children, outside marriage, much earlier than white women. In 1965, this won them a reproof from the then assistant secretary of state for labor, Daniel Patrick Moynihan, who accused them of endangering "the patriarchal structure" of American society.[10]

With the advent of Ronald Reagan's presidency in the 1980s, conservative discourse created the reviled figure of the "welfare queen," who could be black or white, although the racist connotations were clear when this term was used of black women. For ten years, the President himself peddled the unfounded story of one of these "queens," who, he shamelessly insisted, used "80 names, 30 addresses and 12 Social Security cards," thanks to which, he claimed, "Her tax-free cash income alone is over $150,000."[11] In short, the normalized denunciation of social spongers and fraudsters—a political tack also familiar in France—was now specifically applicable to women too. During his 1994 gubernatorial campaign for Florida, Jeb Bush opined that women receiving welfare assistance would do better to "get their life together and find a husband."[12] In Ariel Gore's novel *We Were Witches* (2017), set in early 1990s California, the heroine (also called Ariel), a young (white) single mother, makes the mistake of confiding to her new neighbor, in the suburb she's just moved to, that she's living on food stamps. On learning this, the neighbor's husband shows up to insult her from the street—and steals her welfare check from her letterbox. Ariel moves house in a panic the day that, arriving home with her daughter, she finds a doll pinned to the front door, daubed in red with the words: "Die, welfare slut."[13] In 2017, a Michigan court carried out a paternity test for an eight-year-old child born of a rape; without consulting any of those involved, it awarded joint parental authority and rights to visit to the rapist, whose name it also added to the child's birth certificate and to whom it gave the victim's address. The young mother commented: "I was receiving about $260 a month in food stamps for me and my son, and health insurance for him. I guess they were trying to see how to get some of the money back."[14] A woman must have a master, even if he's the man who kidnapped and assaulted her when she was twelve.

Robert Rector, one of the architects of the disastrous 1996 US social care reform, led by Bill Clinton, which tore apart a safety net already riddled with large holes, was still talking in 2012 about marriage as the "strongest anti-poverty weapon."[15] This, Traister argues, amounts to topsy-turvy thinking: "If politicians are concerned about dropping marriage rates, they should increase welfare benefits. It's that simple"—for we're more inclined to get married when we have a minimum of economic security. And, "if they're concerned about poverty rates? They should increase welfare benefits."[16] Moreover, she comments, even if unmarried women truly wanted a "hubby state," what would be so scandalous about that, when white men "and especially married wealthy white men" have long benefited from the support of a "wifey state" to ensure their independence by means of grants, loans and tax reductions?[17] But the idea that women are sovereign individuals, not mere appendages, still has a long way to go before it becomes the accepted norm—and not only among conservative politicians.

In 1971, Gloria Steinem co-founded the feminist monthly *Ms. Magazine*. Not "Miss" or "Mrs," but "Ms," an exact female equivalent of Mr—a title that reveals nothing of the holder's matrimonial status. The word was invented in 1961 by Sheila Michaels, a civil-rights activist. She had the idea upon spotting a typo on a letter addressed to her housemate. She herself had never been a "father's property," for her parents had not married, and she didn't intend to find a husband, and she was looking for a term to express this. At the time, many girls were marrying at eighteen and Michaels was twenty-two: being a "Miss" meant being "left on the shelf." For ten years, she introduced herself as "Ms," putting up with the laughter and the jibes. Then, a friend of Steinem who'd heard of her idea passed it on to the magazine's founders, who were yet to settle on its name. By adopting "Ms," they at last brought the new word into common parlance—and it became a great success. That year, Bella Abzug, a Congressional Representative for the state of New York, passed a law authorizing the use of "Ms" on federal forms. Unexpectedly questioned about this in a 1972 television interview, Richard Nixon answered with a brief irritable laugh that he was "a little old-fashioned," preferring to stick with Miss or Mrs.[18] In a secret recording from the White House after the show, Nixon can be heard muttering to his adviser Henry Kissinger: "For shit's sake, how many people really have read Gloria Steinem and give one shit about that?" In 2007, tracing the history of the word, *Guardian* journalist Eve Kay recalled her own pride the day she opened her first bank account as a "Ms": "I was my own person with my own identity and Ms. summed that up better than any other title. It was a small symbolic step—I knew it didn't mean that women were equal, but it was important to at least announce to the world my intent to be free." And Kay encouraged her readers to follow suit: "Choose Miss and you are condemned to childish immaturity. Choose Mrs. and be condemned as some guy's chattel. Choose Ms. and you become an adult woman in charge of your whole life."[19]

When, in France, forty long years after Nixon's comment, the feminist organizations *Osez le féminisme!* ("Dare to be a feminist!") and the *Chiennes de garde* ("Bitches on guard") eventually put this question on the table with their campaign "'*Mademoiselle,' la case en trop*" ("Miss: a tick-box too far"), which called for the elimination of the "Miss" option on administrative forms, the move was seen as the nth nutty fad from feminists with too much time on their hands. The reactions ranged from sighs of nostalgia to eulogies on the murder of gallantry *à la française* by these harpies, and dyspeptic exhortations to campaign on "more serious subjects." "At first, we thought it was a joke," Alix Girod de l'Ain mocked in a column in *Elle* magazine.[20] She recalled the honorary and rare usage of "Mademoiselle" for famous actresses who've had no long connection to a single man: "We must defend mademoiselle because of Mademoiselle Jeanne Moreau, Mademoiselle Catherine Deneuve and Mademoiselle Isabelle Adjani." From this stance, she insisted, somewhat disingenuously, that making "Madame" the only option—French doesn't yet have any third term equivalent to Ms—amounted to addressing all women as if they were married: "Would this mean, for these feminists, that it's better—more respectable—to be officially married off?"—which of course was not the intention of the organizations behind the campaign. That said, it rapidly emerged that her real concern was for Mademoiselle's youthful connotations: "We must save mademoiselle because, when the greengrocer on Rue Cadet uses it for me, I'm not taken in, but I get a notion that my basil may be mine for free." (Girod de l'Ain was forgetting that, as it happens, the big guns of the feminist dictatorship were trained only on bureaucratic forms, and so did not necessarily pose a threat to her free basil.) She concluded by calling instead for the addition of a new box to tick: "Pcsse"—in defense of "our inalienable right to be princesses."

Dispiriting as this is, Girod de l'Ain's piece at least reveals the degree to which women are conditioned to value their infantilization and to derive their sense of self-worth from their objectification—or at least French women do, for, that year too, Canadian *Marie Claire* was assuring us that, in Quebec, "the term reveals such archaic thinking that calling a woman 'mademoiselle' will guarantee you a slap in response."[21]

Adventuress: No Role Model for a Lady

While this realm is not exclusively hers, the single woman embodies female independence in its most obvious and visible form. This makes her a magnet for reactionary hate, but it also makes her an intimidating figure for a substantial number of other women. The gender-divided labor model that still constrains us has significant psychological consequences. Nothing in the way most girls are educated encourages them to believe in their own strength and abilities, nor to cultivate and value their independence. They are taught not only to consider partnership and family the foundations of their personal achievements, but also to look on themselves as delicate and helpless, and to seek emotional security at all costs, such that their admiration for intrepid female adventurers remains purely notional and without impact on their own lives. In 2017, one reader of the *Cut,* an American online magazine for modern women, posted a cry for help: "Tell me not to get married!" Aged twenty, she had lost her mother two and a half years earlier. Her father was preparing to remarry and to sell the family home, and her two sisters were already married—one with children, the other hoping for them. On her forthcoming trip back home, she faced having to share a bedroom with her father's new nine-year-old stepdaughter—and found the prospect depressing. She had no boyfriend, but, although aware that this state of mind might lead to bad decisions, she was obsessed by the feeling that she too should get married. In the *Cut*'s response to the piece, journalist Heather Havrilesky emphasized the disadvantage girls can suffer on facing the turmoil of adult life, due to the way they are socialized:

> Boys are encouraged to map out their adult trajectory in the most adventurous manner possible. Conquering the world all alone is the most romantic path possible for a guy, and he can only pray that some lady doesn't slow him down along the way, thereby ruining everything. But for women, the romance of forging out into the world is painted as pathetic and dreary if there's no dude there. [. . .] And Jesus, does it take hard work to reinvent the world outside those narrow conventions![22]

This doesn't mean a man can't suffer from emotional insecurity or loneliness, but at least men are not surrounded by a culture of exemplars that exacerbates—or even *creates*— these miserable situations. On the contrary: our culture looks after its men. Even the introverted, awkward geek has had his revenge, becoming the Prometheus of the contemporary world, garlanded with money and success. As one interviewee in Charlotte Debest's book, *Le choix d'une vie sans enfant*, explained, "in male culture there is no Princess Charming, no fabulous wedding with glorious suits."[23] Whereas women learn to dream of "romance" rather than "love," in line with a distinction established by Steinem. She writes: "The more patriarchal and gender-polarized a culture is, the more addicted to romance." Instead of developing a full palette of human qualities, we make do with the restricted range of those considered either masculine or feminine, and then seek fulfillment by means of a partner, in superficial relationships pursued in the manner of an addiction. And this substantially disadvantages women: "Since most human qualities are labeled 'masculine,' and only a few are 'feminine'—and even those are marginalized [. . .]—*women have an even greater need to project life-giving parts of themselves onto another human being*" (emphasis in the original).[24]

In this context, independent women arouse skepticism in all fields. Sociologist Érika Flahault shows how this skepticism has been expressed in France since the appearance, in the early twentieth century, of single women living alone—where they would once have been "taken in by relations, by their extended family or local community in almost every case."[25] She disinters journalist Maurice de Waleffe's observation from 1927:

A man is never alone, short of being shipwrecked like Robinson Crusoe on a desert island: when he turns lighthouse-keeper, shepherd or anchorite, it's because he feels like it; the mood is upon him. And we should admire him, for a soul's greatness is measured by the wealth of its inner life, and a man must be fiendishly rich in that to sustain himself solo. But you will never see a woman choose such greatness. Gentler because they are weaker, they have a greater need than we do for society.[26]

And, in a widely read book from 1967, André Soubiran, a doctor, reflected: "One wonders whether feminine psychology can accommodate freedom and the absence of men's domination as well as we imagine."[27]

We must not underestimate our need for examples— whether shared by the majority or drawn from a counterculture—that support us, even if only subconsciously, that provide meaning, impetus, resonance and depth to our life choices. We need to discern a pattern beneath the trajectory of women's lives, in order to motivate, support and legitimize our choices, to weave others' lives into our own and make their presence, their approbation felt. Having come to prominence with the second feminist wave, a few films of the 1970s have played this role for independent women. In Gillian Armstrong's *My Brilliant Career* (1979), for example, Judy Davis plays Sybylla Melvyn, a young woman in nineteenth-century Australia who is pulled to and fro between her mother's rich family and the poverty of her father's farm. Imaginative, joyous and wild about art, Sybylla rebels against the idea of marrying. She finds love in the figure of a rich childhood friend. When, after various peripeteia, he asks her to marry him, she refuses, painfully: "I can't lose myself in somebody else's life when I haven't lived my own, yet." She confides that she wants to be a writer: "I've got to do it now. And I've got to do it alone." In the last scene, she completes a manuscript. On the point of sending it to her publisher, she savors her happiness, leaning on a gatepost, facing into the golden sunlight.

A happy ending involving neither man nor love: this is so exceptional that even I, who chose the film looking for precisely this, was a little horrified. Watching the scene in which Sybylla rejects her suitor, a part of me understood (she tells him: "The last thing I want is to be a wife, out in the bush, having a baby every year"), but another part could not help wanting to shout, "Come on, girl, are you sure?" At the time the film is set, refusing marriage implies the entire renunciation of a partnership, yet this would cease to be the case as time went on: "Fuck marriage, not men," urged a tract handed out at the 1969 Congress to Unite Women, in New York.[29] This lends a tragic dimension to Sybylla's decision, but also allows her to take a radical stance: yes, a woman too may choose above all to pursue her vocation.

"Damned clever, I thought, how men had made life so intolerable for single women that most would gladly embrace even bad marriages instead," sighs Isadora Wing, heroine of Erica Jong's 1973 novel *Fear of Flying*, which explores this female damnation through all its ramifications. A young poet, Wing flees her second husband in order to follow another man she has fallen hard for. She describes the uncontainable yearning that fills her after five years of marriage: "Those longings to hit the open road from time to time, to discover whether you could still live alone inside your own head, to discover whether you could manage to survive in a cabin in the woods without going mad"; but she also feels waves of nostalgia and tenderness for her husband: "If I lost him, I wouldn't be able to remember my own name."[30] This tension between our need for security in love and our need for freedom is largely common to men and women; this is what makes exclusive relationships both so desirable and so problematic. But Wing realizes that, as a woman, she is poorly equipped for independence, even when she really needs it. She fears her courage may not be equal to her ambitions. She would like to care less about love, to be able to concentrate on her work and her books, to fashion herself through them just as a man would, but she sees that her writing is still fundamentally about seeking love. She's afraid she might never enjoy her freedom without a taint of guilt. Her clinically unstable first husband had tried to throw himself out of a window and to take her with him, yet, even after this, she can't entirely accept having left him: "I chose me. My guilt about this haunts me still."[31] She realizes she "simply couldn't imagine [her]self without a man": "without one, I felt lost as a dog without a master; rootless, faceless, undefined."[32] And yet, the marriages that play out around her are mostly appalling: the question isn't, "When did it all go wrong? But: when was it ever right?"[33] It seems that single people dream only of marriage, while the married dream of nothing but escape.

"The dictionary defines 'adventurer' as 'a person who has, enjoys or seeks adventures,' but 'adventuress' is 'a woman who uses unscrupulous means in order to gain wealth or social position,'" Gloria Steinem points out.[34] Thanks to her very unconventional upbringing, she escaped the conditioning which compels most girls to seek security: her father always refused formal employment and earned a living in a multitude of jobs, such as itinerant secondhand dealing, and he brought the whole family on the road with him, so that Steinem was more often to be found reading on the back seat of their car than attending school. Indeed, she only attended school regularly from the age of twelve. Her father had such a "fear of the siren song of home," she recalls, that if they found they'd left something behind, even having only just set out, he preferred to buy the missing things than turn back.[35] From the age of six, when she needed clothes, he would give her money and wait for her in the car while she chose what she fancied; there resulted "such satisfying purchases as a grown-up ladies' red hat, Easter shoes that came with a live rabbit and a cowgirl jacket with fringe."[36] In other words, Steinem's father left her free to define who she wanted to be. Later, always looking ahead to the next plane flight, she reproduced her beloved father's way of life. The day that the company, which she'd been working for remotely, asked her to come into the office two days a week, she "quit, bought an ice cream cone and walked the sunny streets of Manhattan."[37] Her apartment had long been a jumble of cardboard boxes and suitcases, and it was only in her fifties that she developed some sense of homemaking: after months of "nesting—shopping for such things as sheets and candles with a pleasure that bordered on orgasmic,"[38] she discovered that feeling happy at home actually sharpened her taste for travel, and vice versa. But, whatever the reasons, sheets and candles have never been high on her agenda. She did not start out by learning how to be "like a girl" (she tells how, as a child, when a man went to kiss her on the cheek, she bit him[39]), and this has likely served her very well.

In *Une vie à soi* ("A life of one's own"), a sociological inquiry into French women living alone, Érika Flahault distinguishes between women "*en manque*"—who feel something is missing but put up with their situation, despite some suffering; women "*en marche*"—who are learning to appreciate their situation; and the "*apostates du conjugal*"—women who have left marriage behind, who are deliberately organizing their lives, loves and friendships outside the framework of the couple. Of the first set, Flahault observes that, no matter their personal trajectory or social class (her interviewees include a one-time farmer as well as one very wealthy woman), these women are quite at a loss once deprived of the option to play the good wife or good mother: they share "the same socialization experience, one strongly marked by the gendered division of their roles and a deep attachment to these traditional roles, whether or not they have the opportunity to realize them." In contrast, the conjugal apostates have always cultivated a critical distance, sometimes even wholesale defiance in relation to these roles. And they are creative women, who tend to read a lot and lead a rich life of the mind: "They live beyond the range of the male gaze, beyond that of most others, for their solitude is populated with works of art and with people, living and dead, dear as well as unknown, encounters with whom—whether in flesh and blood or in thought, through their oeuvres—form the foundations to the women's sense of identity."[40] These women consider themselves individuals, not representatives of female types. Far from the miserable isolation that prejudice associates with women living alone, the ongoing shaping of their own identities creates a dual effect: it allows women to overcome, even to enjoy, a solitude which most people, married or unmarried, must confront, at least at times in their lives; and it allows them to nurture particularly intense relationships, connections built from the core of their personalities rather than on conventional social roles. In this light, self-knowledge is not an egoism, not navel-gazing, but a fast track to meaningful engagement with others. Contrary to the line peddled by unending propaganda, traditional femininity is not our best hope for survival: far from ensuring our immunity, seeking to embody traditional roles, to adhere to their values, only weakens and impoverishes us.

The pity reserved for single women may well conceal a bid to ward off the threat they represent. Witness the cliché of the "cat lady," where the pet is considered to fulfill unmet emotional needs.[41] Journalist Nadia Daam develops this idea further in her book *Comment ne pas devenir une fille à chat: l'art d'être célibataire sans sentir la croquette* ("How not to become a cat lady: the art of being single without a whiff of Sheba").[42] In her show *Je parle toute seule* ("Talking to myself"), comedian Blanche Gardin describes how her friends advised her to get a cat—a sign, as she read it, that her situation was really desperate: "No one says, 'Get a hamster, they live two or three years, by then you'll have found someone.' No, what they propose is a twenty-year-long solution. I ask you!" Cats are, in fact, witches' favorite choice of "familiar spirit"—usually simply called their "familiar"—a supernatural creature who assists in their magical practice and allows them sometimes to change their appearance. In the original animated opening credits for the series *Bewitched*, Samantha turns into a cat and rubs against her husband's legs, before jumping into his arms and becoming her human self again. In Richard Quine's film *Bell, Book and Candle* (1958), the witch played by Kim Novak, who keeps a shop selling African art in New York, asks her Siamese cat Pyewacket—a classic name for a familiar—to bring her a man for Christmas. In 1233, a bull issued by Pope Gregory IX declared cats to be "the Devil's servants." Then, in 1484, Pope Innocent VIII ordered that all cats seen in the company of women be considered their familiars; these witches were to be burned along with their animals. The cats' extermination contributed to the growth of the rat population, so aggravating subsequent outbreaks of disease—which were blamed on witches . . . [43] In 1893, Matilda Joslyn Gage remarked on the persistence of mistrust toward black cats, inherited from these earlier times, which translated into a substantially lower market value for their fur.[44]

Death to Rebels

When women have the audacity to strike out for independence, they are met by a war machine that's unafraid to use blackmail, intimidation and threats in order to make them give up. According to journalist Susan Faludi, throughout history, each step forward in women's emancipation, however small, has brought its counteroffensive. After the Second World War, American sociologist Willard Waller proposed that "independent-minded women had gotten 'out of hand,'"[45] thanks to the transformations wrought by the conflict—as if echoing the *Malleus Maleficarum:* "When a woman thinks alone, she thinks evil." Men, it seems, experience the merest breeze of equality as something like a catastrophic hurricane—there's a similar exaggeration involved when majority groups feel under attack and consider themselves practically overwhelmed as soon as victims of racism show the least sign of standing up for themselves. Apart from resistance to renouncing their privilege (whether as men or as white people), this reaction displays the inability of the dominant to comprehend the experience of the dominated, but perhaps also, despite their indignant protestations of innocence, an appalling guilty conscience, acknowledging something along the lines of: "We are hurting them so badly that, if we give them the tiniest room for maneuver, they will destroy us."

In her 1991 book *Backlash*, Faludi sets out in minute detail the many manifestations of what she calls the "revenge" or "backlash": a veritable propaganda campaign which gathered momentum in the US throughout the 1980s—in the press and through television, cinema and psychology books—to counteract the feminist advances of the preceding decade. With the quarter-century of hindsight gained since Faludi identified this backlash, the crudeness of the means utilized is even more striking. This demonstrates that, as ever, the various media thrive on ideology rather than information: biased studies are quoted without any critical distance, there's a complete absence of scruples or rigor, and rampant intellectual laziness, opportunism, sensationalism and herd mentality shape a hermetic echo chamber, untroubled by contact with any genuine reality. "Trend journalism attains authority not through actual reporting but through the power of repetition," Faludi observes.[46] The thesis insisted on and repeated across all platforms over this period can be summed up in the following two lies: 1) the feminists have won, they have achieved equality; 2) they are now unhappy and lonely.

The second assertion makes no attempt to describe a situation, but rather aims to create fear, to send out a warning: women who dare to desert their posts and, instead of remaining in the service of their husband and children, try to live their own lives, are the architects of their own misery. Key to this campaign of dissuasion is that women are attacked on what is, thanks to their conditioning, their most vulnerable point: their absolute terror of being left to their own devices. "She dreads nightfall, when darkness hugs the city and lights go on in warm kitchens," the *New York Times* snidely opined in a piece about single women.[47] A popular scholarly book entitled *The Cost of Loving* warned of the "myth of independence."[48] *Newsweek* shrieked that single women over forty are "more likely to be killed by a terrorist" than marry.[49] From all sides, women are warned to beware the rapid decline in their fertility, to abandon their absurd castles in the air and to have children as early as possible. Wives who have not been able to make their husbands "the focus of their life" are singled out for opprobrium.[50] "Experts" point to a supposed increase in the number of heart attacks and suicides among working women. The press published endless doom-laden articles about nursery schools, with sober headlines such as: "MOMMY, DON'T LEAVE ME HERE!" At the San Francisco Zoo, a local daily paper cooed: "Koko the Gorilla Tells Keeper She Would Like to Have a Baby."[51] Films and magazines were filled with glowing housewives and mothers, and also with pallid single women whose problem was they expected "too much from life."

The French press took up the same refrain, as demonstrated by this selection of headlines from *Le Monde* between 1979 and 1987: "When solitude equals freedom," "Women, free but lonely," "A France of single women," "When I come home, no one is waiting for me . . ."[52] Yet Flahault observes that, even in other periods, the discourse about independent women has *never* been positive. It has always been tainted with pessimism or condescension. Again, it has tended to be more about provoking an emotional reaction than describing a situation: "Planted in the mouth of a woman who claims to be fulfilled in her solitude, lines such as 'a woman is not made to live without a man' have a much more pernicious impact than in any other context."[53] You have to trawl through the feminist press of the time to find a few articles on the subject that are not striving to save the flock's stray (black) sheep. This branch of the press stands alone in addressing the "prolonged cultural onslaught" to which we subject women living alone, and in envisaging how this might explain the unhappiness of many among them.[54] There is something quite intriguing in the way that society forces independent women into miserable lives, the better to confound them thereafter: "Ah! See how unhappy you are!" In the feminist press, according to Flahault's analysis, "instead of being rejected, the choice of a life alone is restored to its true status: that of a victory over multiple pressures that act upon the individual from the moment of her birth and condition a large number of her actions, 'a pitched battle against the archetypes we carry within us, the conventions, the constant and ever-renewed social pressure.'"[55] Only in this space do we suddenly discover other stories and other points of view, such as this one, from the *Revue d'en face* of June 1979: "Slow blossoming of desires, repossession of one's body, of one's bed, of space and time. An apprenticeship in pleasures for oneself, in reverie, in availability to others and to the world."[56]

Today, these calls for a return to the norm have not gone away: in 2011, author and screenwriter Tracy McMillan (one of the writers on the *Mad Men* series, among other projects) hit a nerve with her post—the most read in the history of *HuffPost*—titled "Why You're Not Married." Claiming to describe a real situation, the piece turned out mainly to reveal the remarkably contemptuous and hate-filled image McMillan had of her single female readers. She begins by making a show of digging into the psychology of single women, suggesting that, despite their attempts to put on a brave face and pretend to be happy with their lot, they are in fact riddled with envy toward friends who are already married. Full of the authority gained via her three experiences of matrimony, McMillan sets out her theories: if you're not married, it's because "you're a slut," because "you're shallow" and/or because "you're a liar . . ." She pre-empts her readers' anger, saying:

> You're pissed. At your mom. At the military-industrial complex. At Sarah Palin. And it's scaring men off. [. . .] Most men just want to marry someone who is nice to them. [. . .] Have you ever seen Kim Kardashian angry? I didn't think so. You've seen Kim Kardashian smile, wiggle, and make a sex tape. Female anger terrifies men. I know it seems unfair that you have to work around a man's fear and insecurity in order to get married—but actually, it's perfect,

since working around a man's fear and insecurity is a big part of what you'll be doing as a wife.

McMillan invites us not to appear too picky as we try to select a partner, for "This is the thinking of a teenaged girl. And men of character do not want to marry teenaged girls. Because teenage girls are never happy. And they never feel like cooking, either." Finally, of course, she admonishes the "selfish": "If you're not married, chances are you think a lot about you. You think about your thighs, your outfits, your naso-labial folds.[57] You think about your career, or if you don't have one, you think about doing yoga teacher training."[58] To read these lines and think of the long history of women's sacrifices, and of the dose of misogyny that McMillan must have absorbed for her not to see that a desire for personal fulfillment could take other forms than this, makes me feel slightly queasy. I don't know of any equivalently crude call for submission and self-denial in the French media, where promotion of the traditional family is more often carried out under cover of what's "chic and in good taste," through images of idyllic interiors and interviews in which trendy parents describe their daily lives, their leisure pursuits and holidays, and name their favorite shops and restaurants.[59]

The Long Shadow of the Pyres

In the cinema, the demonic single female character most representative of the 1980s is Alex Forrest—played by Glenn Close—in Adrian Lyne's *Fatal Attraction* (1987). In the film, Michael Douglas plays Dan Gallagher, a lawyer who, in a moment of weakness, while his wife and daughter are away for a couple of days, gives in to the advances of a sexy editor whom he meets over drinks. They spend a torrid weekend together, but, when he wants to go, leaving her alone once more in her sad and empty loft, she clings to him and slashes her wrists to try to keep him there. Subsequently, scenes showing Dan's happy family life with his sweet and well-balanced wife (she doesn't work) alternate with scenes showing Alex, in tears, left to her miserable solitude, listening to *Madame Butterfly* while turning a lamp on and off, over and over. Both pathetic and scary, Alex begins to harass Dan, then to attack his family—in a famous scene, she kills his daughter's rabbit and boils it in a pan. She discovers she's fallen pregnant by Dan and refuses to have an abortion: "I'm thirty-six years old; it may be my last chance to have a child." The confident, emancipated professional woman's mask falls off, to reveal a miserable creature, languishing as she awaits a savior to unlock the coveted status of companion and mother.

The film ends with Forrest's murder by Gallagher's wife in the bathroom of the family villa, which she has broken into. In an earlier version, Alex was to commit suicide. However, after showing that ending to a test audience, the producers demanded a different final sequence, an ending more in tune with its audience's wishes—to Close's great dissatisfaction, for she opposed the change in vain. "The audience viscerally wanted to kill Alex, not allow her to kill herself," Douglas explained placidly.[60] In cinemas at the time, men showed their enthusiasm during this scene by shouting, "Beat that bitch! Kill her off now!"[61] After the tragedy's conclusion, with the police making their exit, the couple head back into their house, holding each other close, and the camera pans over to a family photo displayed on a chest of drawers. Already, at intervals throughout the film, we have been made to linger over shots of Gallagher's family photos, using canny crops to emphasize now the remorse of the unfaithful husband, now his lover's helpless rage. In 2017, on *Fatal Attraction*'s thirtieth anniversary, Adrian Lyne complained, "The idea that I was trying to condemn career women and say they're all psychotic is just nuts. I'm a feminist."[62] It's true that these days feminism is back in fashion. In any case, his protests feel rather paltry, given the way in which, according to Faludi, the screenplay was relentlessly revised in a more reactionary direction. At first, Dan's wife was a teacher, then she became a housewife; the producers insisted the character of the husband be made more sympathetic, laying an extra burden of guilt at the door of his lover. Lyne had the idea of dressing Alex in black leather and locating her home in New York's meatpacking district. Beneath her apartment, fires burn in metal drums, like "witches' cauldrons."[63]

But the revenge that Faludi charts is not limited to the symbolic realm—despite its very real effects there. Just as, at the time of the witch-hunts, women who wished to work as men did were often prevented on multiple fronts—finding their access to education blocked or themselves expelled from the family business—so, in recent decades, women have met with merciless hostility. Witness the story of Betty Riggs and her colleagues, employees of American Cyanamid (it has since become Cytec Industries), in West Virginia. In 1974, the management were obliged by the state to hire women on their production lines. Spotting a rare opportunity to escape the round of dollar-an-hour jobs in which she'd been stuck—to support her parents and son, and, eventually, to leave her violent husband—Betty Riggs waged a determined campaign to be hired, despite the company rejecting her applications on a number of different pretexts. After a year, she was eventually hired, along with thirty-five other women. She was placed in the pigments workshop, where, during her first year, the production showed considerable improvement. But the women were harassed by their male colleagues. On one occasion, they found a sign handwritten over their section: "SHOOT A WOMAN, SAVE A JOB." As if that weren't enough, Riggs's husband broke in, first setting fire to her car in the parking lot, then coming to attack her inside the factory, where he punched her in the face. And then, toward the decade's end, the company suddenly showed an interest in the effects of the substances they were handling on the reproductive health of their female employees. While refusing to put additional protective measures in place, and knowing the same substances posed a similar risk to their male employees, the company decided that fertile women under fifty years old could no longer work in that department . . . unless they were sterilized. The seven affected employees were devastated. Because they absolutely depended on these jobs, five of them decided to have the operation, among them Betty Riggs, who was only twenty-six at the time. Less than two years later, at the end of 1979, at daggers drawn with the Occupation Safety and Health Administration authority, Cyanamid's management reacted by closing the pigments department altogether: "The jobs the five women had sacrificed their wombs to keep were gone."[64] The women went on to lose the legal action they pursued against the company: a federal judge ultimately ruled that they had had "the option" of sterilization.[65] Riggs was obliged to go back to "women's work" and earn her living cleaning houses. No burning at the stake here, but nonetheless a patriarchal authority that excluded, that ground down goodwill and energy, and readily adopted mutilation in order to keep all rebels in their place: eternally subaltern.

Who is the Devil?

Who is this Devil who, from the fourteenth century onward, in the eyes of powerful European men, began to loom behind the figure of every female healer, every sorceress, every woman who was slightly too forward or too much of a stirrer, to the point that they became a mortal threat to society? What if this Devil were in fact independence?

As essayist Pacôme Thiellement observes:

> The whole power question comes down to separating people from what they can do. There is no power issue if people are self-sufficient. For me, the history of witchcraft could equally be called the history of independence. Anyway, a married witch, like in *Bewitched*, is peculiar [. . .] Those in power must constantly be making examples out of people, demonstrating that we couldn't go on without them. On the international political level, the most troubled territories are always those that want to be independent.[66]

Even today, in Ghana, among the women reduced to living in "witch camps," 70 percent were accused of witchcraft following their husband's death.[67] In Rungano Nyoni's fictional film

I Am Not a Witch (2017), set in a camp like this in Zambia, every witch has a long white ribbon attached to their back, tying them to their own giant wooden reel and restricting their range of movement to hardly more than a meter. This system is designed to stop them flying away to commit murders—without the reels, it's said they would be capable of flying "as far as the UK." If they cut the ribbons, they will turn into goats. Showing us the reel that once restricted her, the local government representative's wife explains to Shula, a nine-year-old girl sent to the camp, that she too was once branded a witch. Only the respectability acquired with marriage, combined with absolute deference and obedience, she insists, has enabled her to cut the ribbon without being turned into a goat.

In Europe, in the fifteenth century, before the major wave of witchcraft trials, the dismantling of the special dispensation given to the beguines can be seen as a harbinger of what was to follow. These communities of women were principally to be found in France, Germany and Belgium. Neither wives nor nuns, though often widows, free of all male authority, they lived communally in rows of small individual houses, with medicinal and kitchen gardens, free to come and go as they pleased. In her vivid novel of 2017, Aline Kliner brings to life the great royal beguinage in Paris, vestiges of which can still be seen today in the Marais quarter. Her heroine, the aged Ysabel, a herbalist at the beguinage, whose home is fragrant with "charred wood and bitter herbs," has "strange eyes, neither green nor blue, that reflect the changing hues of the sky, of the plants in her garden, of the droplets shot through with light when it rains"—clearly, she is a cousin of Flutter Mildweather. Some of the beguines even lived and worked outside the beguinage—for example, Jeanne du Faut, who kept a flourishing silk business. They were used to a physical, intellectual and spiritual prosperity that was quite the opposite of the withering to which so many thousands of women locked up in convents were condemned. (In the nineteenth century, the poet Théophile Gautier, who entrusted his daughter to the nuns of Notre-Dame de la Miséricorde, observed one day that she stank; when he requested a weekly bath for her, the scandalized nuns replied that "a nun's toilette consists simply of airing her blouse."[68]) The execution of Marguerite Porete—a beguine from Hainaut who, in 1310, was burned for heresy in the Place de Grève, in front of Paris's town hall—rang the death knell of the tolerance these women had enjoyed, for they were increasingly ill appreciated due to their "double rejection of obedience, to both Church and husband."[69]

The state no longer organizes public executions for alleged witches, but the death penalty for women who wish to be free has, in a sense, been privatized: when a woman is killed by her partner or ex-partner (which, in France, occurs every three days, on average), it is often because she has left the partner or announced her intention to do so—as was the case with Émilie Hallouin, whose husband tied her to the rails of the high-speed Paris–Nantes line on 12 June 2017, on her thirty-fourth birthday.[70] And the media treats these murders with the same flattening triviality used to describe the witches' pyres.[71] When, in September 2017, a man burned his wife to death in Le Plessis-Robinson, outside Paris, the tabloid daily *Le Parisien* opened with the headline: "*Il met le feu à sa femme et incendie l'appartement*" ("He sets fire to his wife and his apartment is gutted"), as if the victim were a piece of furniture and the key news item were the burned-out apartment; the journalist almost seems to find the husband's clumsiness cause for humor. The only occasions—in France, at least—on which the murder of women is treated appropriately, and the gravity of the crime is recognized, are when the murderer is black or of Arab origin, but then it's a case of fanning the flames of racism, not defending the cause of women.

Looking beyond its dimension as a light Hollywood comedy, René Clair's 1942 film *I Married a Witch* can be seen as an uninhibited celebration of the crushing of independent women. Executed for witchcraft along with her father in seventeenth-century New England, Jennifer (Veronica Lake) is reincarnated in the twentieth century with a plan to take revenge on her accuser's descendant. But she accidentally drinks the philtre herself, and so it's she who falls in love with him. From here on in, her powers serve only to ensure her man's victory in the elections—a proper patriarch's dream come true—after which, when he comes home, she rushes to bring him his slippers and announces her intention to give up magic and become "just a simple, helpful wife." In truth, right from the start, this childish, whimsical and charming witch, her father's charge before becoming that of her husband, has nothing in common with the uncontrollable creature supposed to have terrified her persecutors. It is literally the masculine authorities around her who bring her to life. When she and her father are resurrected in spirit, she begs him, "Father—give me a body," for she dreams of having lips once more: "lips to whisper lies; lips to kiss a man and make him suffer"—and here, this portrait of a witch links back to the well-trodden tropes of everyday misogyny. He grants her wish and turns her into a "little bit of a thing," as an older lady who lends her a dress says indulgently—a pretty little ethereal thing, as elegant as Hollywood could make then and still churns out now: women who don't take up too much space and dress in lacy nighties and fur coats, the better to seduce their future husbands. Then, when Jennifer's father decides to deprive her of her fleshly appearance, to punish her for falling in love with a mortal, it's the kiss from her candidate of choice that brings her back to life, just like Sleeping Beauty. Jennifer ends up knitting by the fire, surrounded by her family, in what is apparently meant to be a happy ending. Naturally, her little girl begins rushing around the house astride a broom— "I'm afraid we're going to have trouble with her someday," Jennifer sighs. But don't panic: the daughter will be brought to heel, like her mother. Thanks to "love," of course, which is "stronger than witchcraft." This theme of the witch who happily gives up her powers in order to get married also drives *Bell, Book and Candle*.[72]

In contrast, in George Miller's film *The Witches of East-wick* (1987), which is set in the 1980s, in a small Rhode Island town, Daryl Van Horne, aka the Devil, played by Jack Nicholson, declares he doesn't believe in marriage: "Good for the man, lousy for the woman. She dies, she suffocates!" When, at their first encounter, Alexandra (played by Cher) tells him she's a widow, he replies, "Well, sorry, but you're one of the lucky ones. When a woman unloads a husband, or a husband unloads a woman, however it happens—death, desertion, divorce—the three *d*s—when that happens, a woman blooms! She blossoms. Like flowers. Like fruit. She is ripe. That's the woman for me." There were once witch-killings in the castle where he's now living, which leads him to offer his interpretation of the phenomenon: "[Men's] dicks get limp when confronted by a woman of obvious power, and what do they do about it? Call them witches, burn them, torture them, until every woman is afraid. Afraid of herself . . . Afraid of men . . ." Before Van Horne's arrival in the town, the three witches, who are played by Cher, Michelle Pfeiffer and Susan Sarandon, hardly believe in their magical powers. Yet it's they who summon him, unintentionally, one rainy night while discussing their ideal man, and they manage, over cocktails, to wish him into their lives—before concluding sadly that men are not "the answer to everything" and wondering why they always end up talking about them. Until Van Horne's shattering entrance into their world, the women have been constantly holding back, restraining themselves, pretending to be "half of what they are" and conforming to the rules of a patriarchal and puritanical society. He, on the other hand, encourages them to reach their full potential, to give free rein to their energy, their creativity and their sexuality. Van Horne presents himself as a man operating above ordinary men, whom they should not be afraid of frightening: "Use me . . . I can take it," he says to them, again and again. Here, not only are we well outside the usual conjugal scenario, but love and desire are enhancing the witches' powers instead of wiping them out. What's more, the three heroines ultimately rid themselves of their dear Daryl Van Horne. It's an opportunity to ponder the paradox that the Devil represents: he is the master of unmastered women. The Renaissance demonologists couldn't even imagine women's absolute autonomy; for them, the freedom of those they accused of witchcraft had to be understood as part of a further subordination: they were necessarily under the Devil's sway and therefore still subject to a masculine authority.

The Amazing Dissolving Woman

But independence is not the sole preserve of widows and singles. It can also occur in the home itself, right under a husband's nose. This is indeed the symbolism of the witch's nocturnal flights, which lead her to desert the marital bed, escaping the sleeping man's vigilance, to straddle her broomstick and take off for the sabbath. In the demonologists' tirades, which betray the masculine obsessions of their times, the witch's flight, as Armelle Le Bras-Chopard describes it, represents:

> a freedom to come and go, not only without the husband's permission but generally without his knowledge (unless he is a witch himself) and even to his disadvantage. By picking up a broomstick or chair leg and placing it between her legs, the witch awards herself a simulacrum of the virile member that she lacks. And by artificially stepping outside her sex and giving herself that of a man, she is also stepping outside her female gender: the witch is able to accord herself the ease of movement that, within the standard social order, is the unique privilege of men. [. . .] Granting herself this autonomy, and thereby escaping the man whose principal freedom is manifest

through his dominance over her, the witch spirits a portion of the man's power away from him: her liberation is also a larceny.[73]

Contrary to what today's "backlash" would have us believe, women's autonomy does not entail a severing of connections, but rather the opportunity to form bonds that do not infringe on our integrity or our freedom of choice, bonds that promote our personal development instead of blocking it—whatever lifestyle we choose, whether solo or in a partnership, with or without children. As Pam Grossman writes, "the Witch is arguably the only female archetype that has power on its own terms. She is not defined by anyone else. Wife, sister, mother, virgin, whore—these archetypes draw meaning based on relationships with others. The Witch, however, is a woman who stands entirely on her own."[74] Whereas the example promulgated over the period of the witch-hunts, imposed first by violence and then, later, with the nineteenth-century invention of the housewife ideal, by a clever mix of flattery, seduction and menace, locks women into their role as reproducers and disenfranchises them from participation in the world of work. Thus, women are positioned in such a way that their own identity is constantly at risk of being muddled with others,' of atrophying, of being swallowed up altogether. They are prevented from living and fashioning their own lives, for the sake of representing an imagined quintessence of femininity. In New York, in 1969, the WITCH group caused havoc at a weddings trade fair by releasing mice into the main hall. One of their slogans railed, "Always a Bride, Never a Person."[75]

These days, any woman who shares her life with a man and children must keep fighting tooth and nail if she doesn't want to be a "dissolving woman"—a "*femme fondue.*" The expression was coined by Colette Cosnier in her study of the forty volumes of *Brigitte,* a series of sentimental novels written by Berthe Bernage that began appearing in the 1930s. Through the eponymous heroine, who is eighteen in the first book and a great-grandmother in the last volumes, the author attempted "to put together a kind of manual for modern life intended at first for young women, then for young wives and mothers," Cosnier explains.[76] So, when Brigitte looks tenderly at her children, Bernage writes: "Some day Roseline would melt seamlessly into another family, while he, the little man who clenches his tiny and already willful fists, why, he would become simply 'himself.'"[77] We may imagine ourselves as light years ahead of this reactionary world (during the Second World War, Brigitte was, of course, although never explicitly, pro-Vichy and, occasionally, anti-Semitic too). And yet . . . At the heart of the heteroparental family, the woman's needs must always give way to those of her partner and of their children. "Women are often told that blurring into the lives of the others *is the right way to mother,*" writes sociologist Orna Donath.[78] While this archaic logic is no longer expressed among more progressive couples—it would be unacceptable—it nonetheless takes place, almost magically, when the burden of housework lands on the mother's shoulders like a massive avalanche. Thirty-something journalist and author Titiou Lecoq describes how she had never felt personally affected by sexual discrimination, "And then, bam . . . I had children. It was then that I—who had been operating as an absolute first-person singular

'I'—I suddenly clicked, this was what it meant to be a woman, and, no way out, I was one of them." Not only does a vast portion of women's identities become folded into their domestic and maternal roles, but they are lumbered with the least rewarding aspects of parenting. Lecoq notes that, according to studies, "only the activities of games and children's socialization are fairly shared." And she comments, "I understand the guys' attitude. I would also much rather go for a walk in the woods with the kids than go through the clothes they've outgrown."[79]

Moreover, the dissolution of women's identity into their maternal roles goes beyond the issues of who takes charge of educational and domestic tasks. American poet and essayist Adrienne Rich remembered that, during her first pregnancy (in 1955), she stopped writing poetry and even reading, and made do instead with taking sewing lessons: "I had made curtains for the baby's room, collected baby clothes, blotted out as much as possible the woman I had been a few months earlier. [. . .] I felt myself perceived by the world simply as a pregnant woman, and it seemed easier, less disturbing, to perceive myself so."[80] Those around Rich did indeed seem determined not to let her be both a writer and a future mother. When she was due to give a reading of her poetry at a prestigious New England boys' school, the teacher canceled her invitation upon learning that Rich was seven months pregnant, assuming that her condition "would make it impossible for the boys to listen to [her] poetry."[81] As recently as 2005, in her autobiographical novel *Un heureux événement* ("A happy event"—adapted for film under the same name by Rémi Bezançon, in 2011), Éliette Abécassis demonstrated the pervasiveness of this prejudice around the thinking mother. One morning, at a late stage in her pregnancy, the protagonist has a meeting to attend with her thesis supervisor, and she wonders, shattered: "If by some miracle I managed to get up, how was I going to show myself to him in this state? I'd had enough trouble establishing our relationship as one of equals. What lie could I possibly spin for him to justify my transformation?"[82] As if the hormones of pregnancy inhibit the brain's functioning, or as if it were scandalous to wish both to think and to bear children.

This reflex recalls the "conservation of energy" theory, developed by doctors in the nineteenth century, in which the human body's organs and functions were thought to be in competition for the limited amount of energy circulating among them. From that point on, knowing their lives' ultimate goal to be reproduction, women were obliged to "concentrate their physical energy internally, toward the womb," as Barbara Ehrenreich and Deirdre English explain.[83] When pregnant, they were expected to remain horizontal for most of the day and avoid all other activity, especially anything intellectual: "Doctors and educators were quick to draw the obvious conclusion that, for women, higher education could be physically dangerous. Too much development of the brain, they counseled, would atrophy the uterus. Reproductive development was totally antagonistic to mental development."[84] Are we not still unwittingly in thrall to the mental world resulting from these fanciful theories and their use in justifying women's social relegation? These long-outdated fantasies about women's bodies still feed the social exclusion—whether open or discreet—that affects mothers: we celebrate them as icons of a rather sentimental ideal, but we deny them as people.

You will remember Tracy McMillan's recommendation that women suppress their anger in order to increase the chances that a man will deign to marry them.[85] (Self-)censoring of anger plays a significant role in the erasure of identity. "Female anger threatens the institution of motherhood," writes Adrienne Rich, and she quotes Marmee's reply to her daughter Jo in *Little Women:* "I am angry nearly every day of my life, Jo; but I have learned not to show it; and I still hope to learn not to feel it, though it may take me another forty years to do so."[86] Since the mother's "job" is to guarantee the peace and serenity of her home, to look after the well-being, both mental and material, of all the other members of her household, "her own anger becomes illegitimate."[87] These days, we prefer to prioritize non-violent education: the need to respect children, not to traumatize them. "You have to put on a good show and push yourself, whatever the circumstances, to talk appropriately and pleasantly with them; a *public-spirited* approach. No harshness. Neutral. Compassionate" (emphasis in the original), as Corinne Maier expresses the mother's duty in her satirical pamphlet *No Kid.*[88] In Titiou Lecoq's analysis, "We must break out of this modern paradox through which this notion of children as individuals whom we help to grow into themselves relegates women to the status not of individuals living their own lives but to that of their maternal function, thereby denying women's own individuality."[89]

At work, too, we run the risk of "dissolving" away. The same subjection, the same reduction to stereotype also occurs here. The oppression of female medical workers—whether lay

healers or officially recognized practitioners—and the establishment of a male monopoly in medicine, which happened
in Europe during the Renaissance and in the United States
toward the end of the nineteenth century, provides a perfect
illustration of this. When women were allowed to return to
the medical profession, it was as nurses; that is, in the subordinate position of assistants to the Great Men of Science, a
position that was assigned them in recognition of their "natural" qualities.[90] In France, these days, not only are a substantial proportion of women employed part-time (a third of
women work part-time, compared with 8 percent of men[91])
and therefore not financially independent—which is to say
they aren't independent at all—but women are also siloed
off into professions focused on education, on caring for children and older people, or into assistant roles: "Almost half of
women (47 percent) are concentrated in a dozen professions,
such as nursing (87.7 percent of nurses are women), care work
and nursery assistant roles (97.7 percent are women), cleaning,
secretarial and school teaching."[92] Whereas, in the Middle
Ages, like their male counterparts, European women could
access a great range of professions, as Silvia Federici points
out: "In the medieval towns, women worked as smiths, butch-
ers, bakers, candlestick makers, hat-makers, ale-brewers,
wool-carders and retailers."[93] In England, "seventy-two out
of eighty-five guilds counted women among their members"
and some were "dominated" by them. It was, then, not a con-
quest but a re-conquest that women began to attempt in the
twentieth century. And their coup remains far from complete:
women are still intruders in the world of work. Psychologist
Marie Pezé sees a direct connection between the subordinate

positions they occupy and the harassment and sexual aggressions they experience. She asserts that, "As long as we aren't tackling the derogation of women's contribution, we will not be able to fix anything."[94]

The Service Reflex

Even when they are in a position to envisage a prestigious and/or creative profession, a psychological block or lack of encouragement from those around them can hold women back. They often elect to pursue their vocation through a proxy occupation instead: by taking advisory roles, as amanuenses or foils to some admired man, whether friend, employer or life partner, always following the doctor–nurse model. This is the inhibition that the classic feminist T-shirt slogan—"Be the doctor your parents always wanted you to marry"—means to blow out of the water. Of course, the history of science and art is filled with men who have appropriated the work of a female partner—F. Scott Fitzgerald, for example, who studded his books with his wife Zelda's writing, and who, when she was preparing a collection of texts for publication, suggested *Authors Wife* [sic] for the title.[95] But to these external factors we must also add women's own internalization of their status as second or assistant to a principal actor.

Isadora Wing, Erica Jong's heroine, is put on her guard against artists and aspiring artists by her mother, who herself paid a high price for this lesson, as her daughter recalls: "My grandfather . . . used to paint over my mother's canvases instead of going out to buy new canvas. She switched to poetry for a while, to escape him, but then met my father who was a song writer and stole her images to use in lyrics."[96] As for Isadora, however sincere and profoundly felt her desire to write ("I wanted to make myself anew, to make a new life for myself by writing"[97]), she constantly doubts herself. The first two novels she writes have male narrators: "I just assumed that nobody would be interested in a woman's point of view."[98] All the subjects she knows well seem "trivial" and too "feminine" to her. And she can hardly count on any enthusiasm from her peers for encouragement. Her sister, a mother of nine, calls her poetry "masturbatory and exhibitionistic" and reproaches her for her "sterility," screaming, "You act as if writing is the most important thing in the world!"[99] In the afterword written for the fortieth anniversary edition of *Fear of Flying*, in 2013, Erica Jong admitted that, even having sold 27 million copies, in dozens of languages, and with a film adaptation in the works, she still felt "like a poet who fell into the bad habit of writing novels." And yet, there's her book with its female narrator and "feminine" subjects—and millions of female readers have recognized themselves in its pages, while millions of male readers have appreciated it too. It's an emblem of both Isadora's triumph and that of Jong herself, a triumph over their doubts and complexes, over their fears of never managing to find their voices and make themselves heard.

For my part, I recall the alarm bell that rang in my head just at the point of no return, when, about fifteen years ago, a philosopher I admired proposed that we put together a book of interviews with him—a good deal for him, in the sense that I would be the one who'd be doing all the writing. He had feminist ideas; surely I needn't have any concerns? I hadn't quite clocked that his approach was actually an excellent way of guaranteeing I'd be onside and, therefore, at his beck and call. But when he said, "You know, your name will be on the cover too, not just mine," the shabby way he persisted in dangling this superb honor before me suddenly set me thinking. I began to sense a sign that read "sucker" flashing on my forehead. A few days later, he called again: he'd just hooked up with an old friend, a famous journalist, and they had recorded their conversation with an idea to make a book out of it. He wondered if it might "interest" me to transcribe the recording. When I replied, probably rather brusquely, "Er . . . *no*," he hastened to add, "No matter, no matter! It was only if you were interested!" He had taken a chance on the likelihood that my enthusiasm for his work, combined with my feminine servility and sense of inferiority, would turn me into a voluntary secretary, to be exploited at will—and I almost proved him right. Decisively turned off, I stepped away from our joint project. Instead, I wrote a book on the cover of which my name eventually appeared solo.

But to refuse to sacrifice yourself or to want to pursue your own goals can still attract instant condemnation. If your rebellion occurs in a professional setting, you will be accused of being pretentious, individualist, careerist or simply of being big-headed. A phalanx of men are forever ready to praise the glory of devotion to any cause greater than a little bit of a thing such as yourself, and the infinitely superior gratifications this would bring you—they themselves do such things rather rarely, it's true, but anyway, they've heard about it. By some incredible luck, furthering this or that cause will tend, generally, to align with furthering their own career. And their blackmail does work, for it is that difficult to challenge men over the intangible but effective aura of legitimacy and prestige that surrounds them when they choose to write, create or film, or launch any ambitious project whatsoever.

If you're rebelling at home, amid family—for example, by refusing to organize your entire life around your offspring—you will be called a virago and a bad mother. Here too you will be invited to look beyond the concerns of your own little interests. The sovereign effects of maternity upon the deplorable tendency toward navel-gazing that seems to be typical of women will be extolled, as in one young American woman's revelation: "having a baby is the only way a woman will ever stop being all about herself."[100] You will inevitably be reminded that "no one has forced you to have children," so effectively have the rights to contraception and abortion been co-opted to reinforce the norms of "good" mothering.[101] Curiously, "good" fathering has been much less of a target, despite men theoretically being equally involved in the decision to procreate. It is almost always mothers on the receiving end of those little quips apparently born of simple common sense, such as: "You don't have children just for someone else to bring them up." Sure; but we also don't have children with the intention of remaining glued permanently to their sides, nor with the intention of giving up our cultivation of all other aspects of our lives. And part of bringing them up can include presenting them with a model of a well-balanced adult, rather than one who is unstable or frustrated.[102] Some women, too, will be accused of acting like spoiled children, like little snowflakes incapable of working with the elementary constraints of human life. Whereas, Adrienne Rich insists, "The institution of motherhood is not identical with bearing and caring for children, any more than the institution of heterosexuality is identical with intimacy and sexual love."[103]

At the publication of Simone de Beauvoir's book *The Second Sex* (1949), writer and critic André Rousseau sighed, "How can we make [women] understand that it is through the giving of oneself that one attains the infinite glories?"[104] In the 1960s, in the Éditions Nathan *Encyclopédie de la femme* ("Encyclopedia of Woman"), Monsarrat, a female doctor, was still describing girls' education in these terms:

> It must be done in the most altruistic way. A woman's role in life is to give everything to those around her—comfort, joy, beauty—while keeping a smile on her face, without making herself out to be a martyr, without ill humor, without visible fatigue. It's a major task; we must lead every daughter toward this happy, lifelong renunciation. From her very first year, a girl must know how to share her toys and sweets spontaneously and to give what she has to those around her, especially whatever she most treasures.[105]

A contemporary American author admitted to puzzlement on realizing that, since becoming a mother, when she eats crackers, she takes the broken ones and leaves the whole biscuits for her husband and daughter.[106] In 1975, when the French collective Les Chimères took a stand against "motherhood as servitude," it found that even a feminist like Évelyne Sullerot would talk of the time when her children were young as years of "expiation."[107] Women internalize the conviction that their purpose in life is to be found in serving others, which then augments their suffering if they are unable to have children. In the early 1990s, a Mexican-American called Martina described how, upon learning that she needed a hysterectomy for medical reasons, she called her mother in tears: "So I said to her, 'I guess you could say now I'm totally useless, because it's not like I have the sparkly shiny house for [my husband]. It's not like I do any of the traditionally womanly things. I mean, he does the cooking, and now I can't even do this.'"[108]

Self-sacrifice remains the only fate imaginable for women. More precisely, it is a self-sacrifice that operates by way of abandoning one's own creative potential rather than by its realization. Fortunately, we can also nurture those around us, whether they are from our innermost or wider circle, by developing our own particular strengths and giving free rein to our personal aspirations. This may even be the only form of self-sacrifice that we should seek to achieve, sharing out as best we can the portion of irreducible sacrifice that is inevitable, if there is some. Meanwhile, women's potential continues to be largely wasted. "A 'real woman' is a graveyard of desires, of dreams unfulfilled, of delusions," the Chimères collective wrote.[109] It is time that women—so often lacking in confidence, so uncertain of their capabilities, of the pertinence of what they can bring, of their right to a life of their own— learn to defend themselves against accusations inducing guilt and against intimidation, that they take their own aspirations seriously and preserve them without bending when faced by male authority figures who may try to deflect their energy for their own benefit. "Always choose yourself first," advises

Aminatou Sow, a writer who spoke to Rebecca Traister. "If you put yourself first, it's this incredible path you can forge for yourself [. . .] If you choose yourself, people will say you're selfish. But *no*. You have agency. You have dreams."[110]

Many middle- and upper-class mothers give up on making full use of their own education in order to devote themselves to that of their children, for whom they want the very best education, and this self-abnegation reveals a fundamental contradiction. The time, money and energy spent on ensuring the success and fulfillment of their children conveys, at least implicitly, the hope that the latter will accomplish great things. Many psychologists, authors and educators who claim to guide and help gifted or "high potential" children confirm the ubiquity of this concern. We may infer from this the existence of a broad consensus on the importance of self-realization and the legitimacy of the need for recognition. And, of course, our efforts focus as much on girls as on boys. No one would expect any difference in their treatment: we are no longer in the nineteenth century. And yet, if later on these girls themselves have children, it is likely that a proportion of our resources will have been spent in vain. When they reach adulthood, suddenly, by some weird hocus-pocus, everyone decides that women should no longer be trying to succeed in their own lives, but rather, more than anything, should be aiming to succeed in their family lives—as if the whole carry-on of their own education was actually just meant to keep their mother busy. And it is these girls who generally shoulder the responsibility of ensuring their own children's future success. If they wish simultaneously to pursue family, personal and professional lives, there is a high chance that motherhood will exact penalties along the way, whereas fatherhood has no deleterious effects on careers or vocation—the opposite, in fact. In short, if we want to be consistent, we should either be easing off on girls' education or building into it some serious guerrilla-style training in opposing the patriarchy, all the while ourselves working actively to change the situation.

The Millstone of Motherhood as Institution

Of course, nothing should prevent a woman from having children and a satisfying personal life in other fields. On the contrary, you are actively encouraged to attempt this: by setting the cherry of personal accomplishment atop the cake of motherhood, you flatter our collective conscience and our narcissism. We don't like to admit to ourselves that we primarily see women as reproducers. (As one Québécoise academic said to a pregnant colleague: "Good luck with your *real* project!"[111]) But then, you really ought to have plenty of energy, good organizational skills and great capacity to resist fatigue; you should also not be overfond of sleep or chilling out, nor be allergic to timetables, and you also need to be a dab hand at multitasking. Besides, women writers are falling over themselves to help you pursue your mission, offering titles such as *Choose Everything* and *Having a Child Without Losing Yourself.*[112] The art of finding your "work–life balance" is fertile ground for publishing; it has its female experts, who are interviewed in dedicated columns across the press, on blogs and in women's magazines—I once saw a single father invited to describe the shape of his day, and, another time, a gay mother, but in the vast majority of cases only heterosexual women are asked to contribute. This is understandable, in the sense that they are the majority of those struggling to balance the demands of their lives with children, but it also contributes to normalizing this situation—and skirts around the profound social injustice of it.[113] We are given the impression that there is no external element to the equation, that everything depends on these women and their sense of organization, and it loads guilt on the shoulders of those who cope less well, making them feel that they are in fact the source of the problem.

A few years ago, for a radio program, Nathacha Appanah interviewed five Paris-based fellow writers—three women and two men—about their work. Of the men, she recalls, one arranged to meet her in front of the Sacré-Coeur basilica and the other in a Belleville cafe. All three of the women invited her to do the interviews in their homes:

> While we talked about their books, the genesis of each one, and about their working rituals and discipline, one of them finished washing her dishes and made me a cup of tea, and another put away toys that were scattered around the living room while keeping an eye on the time for the end of the school day. The latter confided that she was getting up at five a.m. every day so she could write.

At that point, Appanah had no children and was free of responsibilities to others. When she became a mother, it was her turn to try this "parceling-out of time," the "mental acrobatics required to handle a last-minute cancelation by the babysitter and the block that is stalling your novel at page twenty-two." "I spent months looking for the old me, the one that could concentrate, the efficient person I used to be," she admits. When, chatting to a writer who had three children and traveled a lot, she asked him how he managed, he replied that he was "very lucky." She comments: ""Very lucky" is, I suspect, a modern way to say, "I have a fantastic wife."" And Appanah tots them up: "Flannery O'Connor, Virginia Woolf, Katherine Mansfield, Simone de Beauvoir: no children. Toni Morrison: two children, published her first novel at thirty-nine. Penelope Fitzgerald: three children, published her first novel at sixty. Saul Bellow: four children, many books. John Updike: four children, many books."[114]

Appanah does not say whether her interviewees were among the tiny minority of writers who make their living from writing. Self-fulfillment is obviously even harder to attain when it's accomplished through another activity that runs in parallel to paid work, rather than their being one and the same thing. Of course, the experience of motherhood can stimulate creativity, but you still have to achieve the necessary practical conditions for your work to see the light of day, and these don't fall into place for everyone: there are great disparities between professional industries, family set-ups, finances, health and energy. In her autobiographical writing, Erica Jong, who had a daughter at thirty-six and loved being a mother, made fun of what she called "the blue-stocking either-or (the baby *or* the book)," a choice she had previously believed in—but it is probably easier to make fun of such things when one is a bestselling author than when one is fighting to exercise one's talent in the slim interstices left by the job that puts food on the table.[115]

"I'm not under any illusions that I could have been where I am now in literary terms if I had been heterosexual," explained British novelist Jeanette Winterson, in 1997. "Because—and this has gotten me into huge trouble before, but I suppose I may as well get into trouble again—I can't find a model, a female literary model who did the work she wanted to do and led an ordinary heterosexual life and had children. Where is she?" She explains that she did have a few affairs with men, but they were something she had always "instinctively" avoided, in order to protect her vocation. "The issue of how women are going to live with men and bring up children and perhaps do the work they want to do has in no way been honestly addressed."[116]

Whether they live with men or not, and whether or not they have a vocation, some women do find another way to escape being sucked into the role of devoted servant: by not having children to bring up; by focusing on their own self-realization, rather than on giving life to others; and by fashioning a feminine identity that has no need of motherhood.

2

Wanting Sterility

THE NO-CHILD OPTION

"As soon as we have truly understood what our society has done with motherhood, the only coherent attitude is to reject it," wrote the Chimères collective, forty-five years ago. "But the question is not nearly as simple as that, for in doing so we are rejecting a significant human experience."[1] For Adrienne Rich, it was clear that "motherhood as institution has ghettoised and degraded female potentialities."[2] Being among the first women to write with such honesty about the ambivalence mothers can feel—she had three sons—she states: "The depths of this conflict, between self-preservation and maternal feelings, can be experienced—I have experienced it—as a primal agony. And this is not the least of the pains of childbirth."[3] As for Corinne Maier, such qualms are not her style: "You want equality between men and women? Start by not having children."[4] Wombs on strike: this great fear was at the heart of the debates (among men) that preceded the legalization of contraception, which amounts to a peculiar admission—for, really, if motherhood is such a universally wonderful experience in our society, why would women choose anything else?

It follows that those women who don't feel the desire to procreate enjoy a certain advantage. They are spared the heartache described by Rich and see one of their greatest obstacles—perhaps *the* greatest one—to equality (although not all obstacles; fear not) melt away, as if by magic: one reason for genuine euphoria. Sure that she did not want children, one young woman who had a tubal ligation delightedly recalls her first post-operative sexual intercourse as an "enormous feeling of freedom": "I remember while we were having sex, saying 'This is how men feel!' There was just not the remotest possibility that I was going to get pregnant."[5]

In Europe, governing politicians became obsessed with contraception, abortion and infanticide from the time of the witch-hunts onward.[6] Although I would never put the third item on a par with the first two, it's safe to say that all three have often been weaponized in protests against women's situation in particular and against the social order more broadly. In Toni Morrison's 1987 novel *Beloved*, the heroine, Sethe, kills her baby girl in order to spare her a life of slavery. In Maryse Condé's novel, *I, Tituba, Black Witch of Salem*, dedicated to the real historical slave Tituba, who was among those accused of witchcraft at the Salem trials in 1692, the heroine decides to abort upon realizing that she is pregnant by her lover John Indian.[7] At the time, both belong to the sinister pastor Samuel Parris, and they feel lost in freezing Massachusetts, surrounded by villagers who are hostile and obsessed with Evil. Tituba explains her situation thus:

There is no happiness in motherhood for a slave. It is little more than the expulsion of an innocent baby, who will have no chance to change its fate, into a world of slavery and abjection. Throughout my childhood I had seen slaves kill their babies by sticking a long thorn into the still viscous-like egg of their heads, by cutting the umbilical cord with a poison blade, or else by abandoning them at night in a place frequented by angry spirits. Throughout my childhood I had heard slaves exchange formulas for potions, baths and injections that sterilize the womb forever and turn it into a tomb lined with a scarlet shroud.[8]

When Tituba is subsequently accused of witchcraft, John Indian begs her to name everyone she is asked to denounce, to do everything she can to stay alive, for the sake of their future children. But she shoots back, "I shall never bring children into this dark and gloomy world."[9] Upon her release from prison, when the smith smashes the chains at her wrists and ankles with a blow to each, she screams, "Few people have the misfortune to be born twice."[10] And upon learning that she's to be sold to a new master, she begins "to doubt seriously" that life is a gift, as the old witch who taught her everything used to say.

Life would only be a gift if each of us could choose the womb that carried us. But to be deposited inside a wretch, an egoist or a self-centered bitch who makes us pay for the misfortunes of her own life, or to belong to the cohort of the exploited and humiliated, those whose name, language and religion are imposed upon them, oh what a martyrdom![11]

In the face of the endless atrocities she is obliged to witness, Tituba takes to "imagin[ing] another course for life, another meaning, another motive." "Life had to be given a new meaning," she thinks. Nonetheless, she continues to feel ambivalent about motherhood; she hesitates and questions her convictions. Back in her native Barbados and once more free and able to practice as a healer, living out of the way in a makeshift cabin, Tituba contemplates a tiny newborn girl she has just saved, resting on her mother's breast, and fears she was wrong to refuse motherhood for herself. When she falls pregnant again, she decides to keep the child, but also to fight for change in the world ahead of its birth. As we may predict, the confrontation does not turn out well for her.

These days, despite only occurring in situations of great panic and distress, infanticide elicits general horror in our society, which judges the mother who carries it out as a monster, without thinking to investigate the circumstances that lead to such extreme action or to admit that a woman may refuse motherhood, even at such a price. In the winter of 2018, in the Gironde, South-West France, thirty-seven-year-old Ramona Canete faced a charge of five infanticides. These were babies born as a result of marital rape: "I do express my refusal, I cry during intercourse, I cry after intercourse," the accused woman said. And yet her husband was only called as a witness.[12] In the US, in 1974, Joanne Michulski, thirty-eight

years old, used a butcher's knife to behead the two youngest
of her eight children on the lawn of her suburban house. She
was judged to be unstable and was committed to a mental
institution. Her husband stated that she had never been violent with them before and that in fact she had seemed to love
them very much. He only added that none of their children
had been "wanted." The pastor who lived next door testified
that the young woman had appeared "quietly desperate" from
the moment the family had moved in.[13] "Instead of recognizing the institutional violence of patriarchal motherhood,
society labels those women who finally erupt in violence as
psychopathological," according to Adrienne Rich's analysis.[14]
In 2006, a French feminist collective recorded the testimony
of an anonymous woman, who described how she had twice
given birth alone and then suffocated each baby. She had been
married at eighteen and, at twenty-one, already had three
children, with whom she lived at home, day in, day out. "I
felt like a kind of drawer: you pop a child in and then, soon
as it's empty, you pop in another one, and there you are."[15]
When she tried not to engage in sexual intercourse, her husband beat her. "I was not to have my own desires, I had all
I could possibly wish for, apparently: I had food to eat every
day, I had children who went to school. He didn't want to
know if I hoped for something different, that was the least of
his worries."[16] She used all kinds of methods to try to abort
her pregnancies—and, indeed, succeeded nine times—but
it hadn't always worked. "It's an inhuman situation but, in
the moment when you are doing it, it's the only solution you
have."[17] The collective that published her story warns against
the misconception that, with the advent of legal contraception

and abortion, France would see the end of unwished-for pregnancies being carried to term.

Improving one's lot, or simply making one's life liveable, includes the option to have as many children as one would like, or not to have any at all. Jules Michelet emphasizes the social violence of the era that created the witch. According to Michelet, for the "pact with the Devil" myth to arise, "there was needed the deadly pressure of an age of iron . . . it was needful that Hell itself should seem a shelter, an asylum, by contrast with the hell below."[18] In this context, the serf became "exceedingly afraid of worsening his lot by multiplying children whom he could not support," while women lived in fear of pregnancies.[19] Throughout the sixteenth century, "the desire, the need for barrenness grew more and more."[20] On the other hand, the priest and lord would have been keen to increase the number of their serfs. In the conceptual world shared by both oppressors and oppressed at this time, the sabbath appears as the symbolic location of this clash of wants and wishes. It offers the poor the fantasy of somewhere to turn in their flight from the injunction to procreate. Indeed, the demonologists agreed, saying that "no woman ever came away [from a sabbath] pregnant": "Satan makes the harvest grow, but he makes women infertile," as Michelet sums it up.[21] In the real world, it is female healers who are most closely engaged in practices intended to limit births, and this is one key reason for the ferocity of the opposition they encounter.

"Now hell itself felt like a refuge": long after Michelet's time, we find the same reversal in Alexandros Papadiamantis's novel, *The Murderess* (1903). Khadoula, an old peasant woman, midwife and healer, the daughter of a witch, is horrified by the fate of women in her society: not only do the girls go from one slavery to another, from bondage to their parents to bondage to their husbands and children, but their families must ruin themselves in order to pay for their dowries. She therefore cannot help feeling relieved when she attends the burial of a baby girl from her community: "On returning to the house of mourning in order to attend the wake held after the funeral and called the 'consolation,' Khadoula could find no consolation. She was simply overjoyed at the good fortune of the innocent baby and its parents. And sorrow was joy and death was life; and all things were not as they seemed."[22] She muses, "What service can one render to the poor! . . . The best one could do for them would be to give them the barrenwort if one had it (God forgive me!). Even the malewort would do . . ."[23] And, gazing at her own little newborn granddaughter, Khadoula mutters bitterly, "It is meant to suffer and to make us suffer."[24] Losing her head, she ends up strangling the baby, and then embarks on a crazed spree of slaughter. Despite the horror of his heroine's actions, Papadiamantis follows her into her exile, far from human society, a return to the natural elements that offer comfort, up until the inevitable revelation of her guilt.[25]

Reaching for a New Way

Before the great plague of 1348, which killed around a third of Europe's population, the Church had stayed relatively indifferent to the question of birth rate; ideally, it would even have preferred to convert the masses to abstinence. This was soon to change. At the end of the sixteenth century, Franciscan theologian Jean Benedicti advocated an unlimited birth rate, assuring families that, as for the birds, "God would provide."[26] The population of Europe was set to explode over the course of the eighteenth century, but this did not hold back the campaigns of pro-birth advocates, despite their less than glorious motivation. Toward the end of the nineteenth century, in France—where the fertility rate had plateaued a century earlier, bucking the general European trend—pro-birth advocates agitated "'in the name of social peace, national interest and the protection of the race': competition for jobs obliged working families to keep their mouths shut; a plentiful supply of soldiers was needed for the war; and immigration from the colonies presented a real threat to national identity."[27]

By virtue of an apparent paradox that's easily disentangled, concern for humanity's well-being and respect for life are actually to be found among those who accept or promote limiting births. Witchfinders did not hesitate to torture those suspected of being pregnant, nor to execute very young children or force them to witness their parents' suffering.[28] In our own time, nothing is more deceitful than the "pro-life" label assumed by militant anti-abortionists, a large proportion of whom are also in favor of the death penalty and, in the US, the free circulation of guns[29] (there were more than 15,000 deaths by shooting in the US in 2017[30]), and there is no sign of their marshalling such ardour to protest against wars, nor against pollution, which it is estimated was responsible for one death in six around the world in 2015.[31] "Life" does not inspire them to action except when it comes to wrecking women's lives. A pro-birth policy is about wielding power, not about care for humanity. Besides which, it only applies to the "right" kind of women: as the historian Françoise Vergès has shown, in the 1960s and 1970s, while refusing to legalize abortion and contraception on the mainland, the French state encouraged these practices in its overseas dominions; in La Réunion, an island off the east coast of Madagascar, white doctors carried out thousands of forced sterilizations and abortions.[32]

Choosing to break the chain of the generations offers a way of bringing a fresh perspective to your own circumstances: a chance to reshuffle the cards of the powers at work, to loosen the vise of fate and give more attention to the here and now. In the US, in the 1990s, researchers Carolyn M. Morell and Karen Seccombe showed that the choice to remain childless was not confined to a minority of upper-class women: among those Morell interviewed, three quarters came from poor or working-class backgrounds. All had forged careers for themselves and they directly attributed their social rise to their decision not to have children. One of the women, Gloria, a forty-three-year-old doctor, said, "If I had been nice and complacent and pleasing I would probably be living in Florida, with six kids. Probably a high-school dropout, married to a mechanic and probably not doing very well economically, probably wondering how I'm going to pay my next bill. [. . .] But that's not what I chose to do."[33] Sara, forty-six, who grew up in a district in South Philadelphia where there were many Jewish immigrants from Eastern Europe, described this as "a ghetto-like experience:"

> I had the belief that there had to be more than I could see and hear going on around me [. . .] It wasn't uncommon for me, even at eight or nine or ten, to take my fifteen cents and literally disappear for the day and take

a trolley car into the center city and then walk to Rittenhouse Square and take the bus and go to the University of Pennsylvania library to just *look* and listen.[34]

In 1905, an anonymous American social worker who called herself "A Childless Wife" wrote: "Whenever I learned the reason of woman's submission it was always based upon the fact that she had children and no money, the existence of the one precluding the obtaining of the other. [. . .] I discovered that enough money, rightly earned, can buy freedom, independence, self-respect and the power to live one's own life."[35] Refusal of motherhood is not necessarily the preserve of white women, either: among African-American women born between 1900 and 1919, a third remained childless, a higher proportion than among white women.[36]

This rebellion against the current state of the world and the kind of life most of us ought to be content with is also key to Corinne Maier's indictment of the status quo. She execrates the successive straitjackets of school and the workplace—restrictions we are, moreover, meant to be grateful for. She deplores the fact that having children effectively "transfers to the next generation" the question of what makes our lives meaningful. "We live in a society of ants, in which working and nesting shape the ultimate prospects of the human condition. If work is the opium of the masses, does that make children our consolation? A society in which life is limited to earning a living and reproducing is one that has no future, for it has no dreams."[37] For Maier, procreation represents the deadlock at the heart of the current system, to the degree that it induces us to perpetuate a way of living which leads directly to ecological catastrophe and which guarantees our compliance (because we have children to feed, bills to pay, etc.). The writer Chloé Delaume—placed center stage by Camille Ducellier in her 2010 film *Sorcières, mes soeurs* ("Witches, my sisters")[38]—concurs, intoning: "I am the nullipara, never will I make a child. I abhor bloodlines and their toxic fictions, the notion of inheritance describes only the relationship of a virus to its most recent carrier." And also: "To stave off the fear in your belly is all that bothers you, to fill it with embryos: an act of tranquilization, for a people that survives only thanks to its antidepressants."[39]

I am alarmed at how, despite considering myself a gentle and serene person, returning to the issue of procreation, and the reasons I refuse to do it, rapidly puts me in a towering rage—yes, anger dominates again . . . Resistance to having children may be one way to hold society responsible for its lapses and failures, to refuse to pass the buck, to say there's no more room for compromise—which no doubt explains the unease this causes others. But this "no" is only the obverse of a "yes": it follows from seeing that the human enterprise could have turned out so much better, from a rebellion against what we are doing with our lives and with the world. And from the feeling of being better able to hold firm, to steer between the burdens and traps of our shared destiny by means of a life without a child. This option offers an extra reserve of oxygen, a further store of resources. It also authorizes excess and letting go: an orgy of freedom and time for exploration, in which you can roll and roll till you're breathless, without fear of going too far, but with the intuition that interesting things begin precisely here, where you would otherwise feel obliged to stop. By my logic, not giving life to others allows us to enjoy our own lives fully. And, to date, this decision has cost me only a single argument with a friend: a bitter dispute which overtook us without warning following a turn in the conversation, and from which, despite our efforts, our friendship has not really recovered. Born the same year as my father, this friend remains heavily influenced by his Catholic upbringing, although this is far from being his main interest (or we would not be friends), and this background most likely explains his reaction. What's more, in the heat of debate, his argumentation quickly tends to reveal its religious bedrock. So, with a wrathful finger raised high above us, he lobbed me lines like, "Hope is not to be parceled out willy nilly!" But there you are: sometimes choosing not to procreate may actually offer our best chance of not "parceling out hope."

The Subtle Alchemy of (Not) Wanting a Child

This attitude makes me almost completely exceptional and an embarrassment to the society I live in. In France, only 4.3 percent of women and 6.3 percent of men say they do not want a child.[40] Contrary to what we may imagine, the number of childless women decreased consistently throughout the twentieth century, with "permanent non-reproduction" (whatever the reason) now at 13 percent.[41] Even though its birth rate dropped for the first time in 2015, then again in 2016 and 2017, France still holds the European record for the highest rate—along with the Republic of Ireland.[42] One explanation for this may be the provision of childcare for the very youngest children, so sparing French women the choice between work and motherhood which women must face in Germany, for example.

On the other hand, the burgeoning range of books about life without children, seen in the last few years in the US, can be explained by the fact that the birth rate there reached a historic low in 2013—not that this is necessarily a disaster, mainly thanks to immigration. The proportion of American women between forty and forty-four who have never given birth went from 10 percent in 1976 to 18 percent in 2008, and this across all communities.[43] Writer Laura Kipnis predicts that the birth rate will continue to drop "until there is a better social deal for women—not just fathers doing more childcare but vastly more social resources directed at the situation, including teams of well-paid professionals on standby (not low-wage-earning women with their own children at home)."[44] In Europe, apart from in Germany, it's broadly in the south (in Italy, Greece and Spain) that childlessness is increasing, principally thanks to the devastating economic instability caused by European Union policy, as well as by the absence of appropriate mitigating measures and childcare systems.[45] Among women born in the 1970s, nearly one in four may stay childless.[46]

We could try to distinguish two categories—people without children because they don't want them, and people with children because they want them—but it's impossible to maintain a clear division between the groups. Some people have no children due to economic barriers or to the circumstances of their private lives, although they would have wanted them; and vice versa: others bring children into the world whom they hadn't planned to have, especially as abortion is still frowned upon in many cultures. Even if they're not against the right to abortion, couples may be unwilling to make use of it if they have the economic and emotional stability to

allow an unplanned pregnancy to go to term. Besides, in view
of ubiquitous pro-family propaganda, we may presume that
a large number of parents have given in to societal pressure
rather than to an impulse of their own. "I sincerely believe
that these days the desire for a child is about 90 percent social
and 10 percent subjective and spontaneous," says Sandra, one
of the voluntarily childless women interviewed by Charlotte
Debest.[47] (These percentages are of course open to debate!)
Nonetheless, we may assume that there is in every person
an initial desire or non-desire for children—whatever may
be the future fate of this desire or non-desire—and that we
then shore up these notions with more or less explicit arguments. Our different dispositions arise from a complex and
mysterious alchemy that moves independently of all prejudice. Having had an unhappy childhood, we may aspire, sym-
bolically, either to repair the damage or to halt it where we
can. Of a cheery and optimistic temperament, we may wish
to remain without offspring; depressive, we may yet wish for
them. It is impossible to predict where the great roulette of
feeling will stop for each person. "One person's motivations
for parenthood—such as wishing for a role, or for influence,
identity, intimacy, pleasure or immortality—can be another's
reasons for not becoming a parent," as Laurie Lisle observes.[48]
What's more, human beings are capable of great wonders, but
also of unbearable horrors; life is beautiful but hard, such that
it is at the very least intrusive and presumptuous to judge for
others whether they should stick with the beautiful or the
hard, and whether they should choose to pass this on or not.

Some would like to see themselves and their partner reflected in a new person and/or they are seduced by the pros-

pect of daily life with children, whereas others wish to live their lives alone or to devote themselves fully to life with their partners. Having chosen this last configuration, in 2015 psychotherapist and writer Jeanne Safer said she had spent the last thirty-five years with her husband in "rare intellectual and emotional intimacy."[49] Some will wish to augment their lives, to welcome what may come, taking on board the joyous or less-than-joyous chaos of what follows; others will choose a more focused, more collected and calmer path—these are only two different modes of intensity. For myself, without even going into the debates over the ecological impact of a drop in the birth rate, I could not add another member to a society that has so spectacularly failed to establish a harmonious relationship with its natural environment and that seems so determinedly set on destroying the latter completely. Knowing myself to be a pure product of this consumer society, and that therefore my children could hardly count on my help in adapting to the environmental-crisis paradigm, only further confirms my position. I also recognize my feeling in this comment from American novelist Pam Houston: "I wanted nothing to do with diapers made out of petroleum products, wanted to take no responsibility for one more dream home being built on wild land."[50] But when I see Hamza, a friend's child, who is coming up for seven, pedalling delightedly toward the beach along a path on the island of Yeu, with his little helmet on, my heart melts: while this vision doesn't make me change my mind, it reminds me that the world's beauty is still real and helps me understand those who decide there is still time to share it with a child, instead of remaining fixated on the looming disaster.

There is room for every view, it seems to me. I only struggle to understand why the one I subscribe to is so poorly accepted and why an immovable consensus persists around the idea that, for everyone, to succeed in life implies having offspring. Those who flout the rule will be told what it's no longer acceptable to tell gay people, to wit: "What if everyone did the same as you?" Even in the social sciences, you come across the same obtuse mindset. When sociologist Anne Gotman interviewed men and women about their "wish not to breed," she presented their statements within a web of her own critical comments, all more or less insidiously angled to discredit them. For example, she diagnoses "a troubled relationship to otherness" or reproaches her interviewees for "neglecting the grounding aspect of the genealogical and anthropological principle of perpetuation of the species"—whatever that may mean. Upon writing, "How can we dispute that children take up time and therefore take time away from work, from social and personal life?" she immediately adds, "But is this really what's at stake?"[51] And when one woman tells her, "I don't want a child, I don't see what the problem is,"[52] she metamorphoses into an amateur psychoanalyst and starts guessing that the second part of the statement "could be read like the admission of a question . . ." Every page of her book drips with disapproval. She accuses those involved of "posing as victims" and of being "precious" about recognition of their choice.[53]

A No-Think Zone

With 7.5 billion human beings on the planet, any danger of extinction looks far from imminent—or, at least, any danger of extinction *for lack of births*. As actor and comedian Betsy

Salkind points out, "When God said be fruitful and multiply, there were only two people."[54] In the West, at least, contraception is widely available, and a child can no longer be considered an indispensable economic advantage—quite the opposite. What is more, we are living in an era characterized by loss of faith in a better future (or even in a future at all), on an overpopulated planet that is poisoned with a wide range of pollutants, where exploitation is rife, and, in the West, we are under serious threat from fascism. I can't help thinking of that cartoon by Willem from 2006: it shows a middle-class family in a well-to-do, warm and comfortable room; to the right, the house looks onto a ravaged outside world, littered with abandoned cars and ruined buildings, where skeletal people crouch among rats. On the doorstep, with a generous wave, the father presents this desolate scene to his petrified daughter and son, saying, "One day, all this will be yours!" And yet, admit to the slightest hesitation about launching someone into such an environment, and everyone starts to squawk in horror. Of course, there will always be many reasons for wanting children, but this desire should not be taken entirely for granted. Have we forgotten to apply a crucial update to our assumptions?

An extraordinary intellectual laziness and spectacular absence of consideration surround this issue, sheltering behind the dubious excuse that it comes down to "instinct." People can't seem to stop handing out recipes that are intended to work for everyone, observes American feminist essayist Rebecca Solnit—and these recipes regularly fail to deliver. "Nevertheless, we are given them again and again." She notes, "The idea that a life should seek meaning seldom emerges;

not only are the standard activities [of marriage and chil-dren] assumed to be inherently meaningful, they are treated as the only meaningful options."[55] Solnit deplores the herd mentality that locks so many people into lives that conform entirely to social prescription and yet "are still miserable." She reminds us, "There are so many things to love besides one's own offspring, so many things that need love, so much other work love has to do in the world." It's this lack of imagination that Michèle Fitoussi inadvertently revealed in her furious critique, in *Elle* magazine, of Maier's book *No Kid:*

> There emerges from all this merely the overblown rehashing of a lazy ideology, already in evidence in Maier's previous work [*Bonjour paresse* ("Hello idle-ness"), on boredom at work and ways of resisting it]. The right to pleasure as the sole item of faith—and that we should eliminate all that stands in its way. [. . .] Thus rid of life's little slings and arrows, all our days will be devoted to blissed-out amusements or the contemplation of our navels while nibbling on ginger biscuits [?]. Without love or humor; the two elements are essential for happiness but, unfortu-nately for Maier, they are sadly lacking here.[56]

Once more, as with *I Married a Witch*, the insistence on "love" enables guardians of the status quo to silence all critics of their dominant position.

Not having a child means knowing that, when you die, you will leave behind nobody birthed by you, partly moulded by you and to whom you would have handed down a sense of family and the enormous, sometimes overwhelming baggage of stories, situations, sorrows and treasures accumulated by previous generations—everything that you yourself inherited. You may expect to be mourned by a partner, by siblings and/ or friends, but that isn't at all the same thing. This may be the only aspect of the decision that is truly difficult to accept. "I only regret that I won't have someone to think of me as I think of my mother," says Dianne in *Families of Two*, a book made up of interviews with such two-person families.[57] Yet this doesn't mean you will have no legacy. The same imaginative block prevents us from seeing that creating a legacy—aside from the fact that children may not necessarily take yours on board, or not in the way you mean them to—can take many forms: each person's path through life is a succession of dominoes knocked onward, and each knock leaves its mark, one we are not always best placed to map for ourselves. In the same book, two voluntarily childless Americans describe how their decision to leave their jobs and cycle around the world for a year was prompted by a conversation with cyclists encountered on a coastal path, who would themselves never discover the consequences of their encounter: "We never know how we are affecting other people!"[58] For most of us, children are only the most visible manifestation of our sojourn on Earth, and the only one we are enjoined to count like this. Besides, even our children often have far more than two begetters. For example, aren't you just a little responsible for the existence of the child born somewhat later, with someone else, to the partner whom you left, or for the one conceived by two friends whom you introduced?

Despite the now widespread accessibility of contraception,

it apparently remains unthinkable that one may love and desire a person without wishing to have a child with them. The women who say they don't wish to be mothers are therefore repeatedly told this is because they haven't yet "found Mr. Right." And the mysterious notion that the only valid sexual encounter is a potentially reproductive one appears to persist, perhaps because this offers the only possible *evidence* of sexual activity, proving thereby that the male protagonist is a "real man" and the female a "real woman." This view is rubbished by a nicely provocative retort usually attributed to Pauline Bonaparte: "Children? I prefer to be there at the beginnings of a hundred than to finish a single one of them."[59] We cannot exclude the possibility that we may sometimes be having children in order to prove that we are having sex (a high price to pay for a bit of grandstanding, if you ask me). Or, otherwise, to prove we are not gay, thereby revealing ourselves as quietly homophobic.

The Last Bastion of "Nature"?

For heterosexual couples, procreation and, more specifically, motherhood represent the last realm where, even among progressives, the "Nature" argument, which we have learned to distrust in almost every other circumstance, still calls the shots. We know that, down the centuries, the most bizarre—and most oppressive—theories have been justified by the "obvious and unquestionable" proof apparently furnished by "Nature." For example, in 1879, Gustave Le Bon confirmed that "The brains of many women are closer in size to those of gorillas than to the more developed brains of men. This inferiority is so evident that no one could gainsay it for a moment: only the degree of difference is worth any discussion."[60] With time, the absurdity of this kind of thinking has become abundantly clear. These days, we avoid attributing any particular disposition or specific behavior to any physical feature. In progressive circles, for example, no one will tell gay and lesbian people that their sexual practices are problematic, that they are attracted to the wrong people and that their organs haven't been designed for use in this way; no one would ever venture: "Excuse me, but did you misread the manual? Nature actually says . . ." And yet, as soon as we're on the topic of women and babies, it's a free-for-all: the result is a carnival of biological Freudian banana skins, if I may put it this way. Suddenly you find yourself surrounded by fervent advocates of the very narrowest biological determinism.

They have a uterus: this is the truly irrefutable proof that women *ought* to have children, right? We appear not to have advanced an inch since the eighteenth century, when the entry for "*Femme*" ("Woman") in Diderot and d'Alembert's *Encyclopedia* comprised a description of a woman's physical appearance and the conclusion that "all these facts demonstrate that the purpose of women is to have children and to feed them."[61] We continue to believe unshakeably that women are programmed to want to be mothers. In earlier times, this was put down to the independent volition of their uterus, a "formidable animal," "possessed with the desire to create children," "lively, resistant to reason, working in the interests of fearsome desires to dominate over all."[62] The self-motivating womb has now relinquished its place in the collective imagination to that mysterious organ known as the "biological clock," which no X-ray has yet managed to locate, yet whose relentless ticking is easily detected by putting your ear to the belly of any woman between thirty-five and forty. "We are used to thinking about metaphors like 'the biological clock' as if they were not metaphors at all, but simply neutral descriptions of facts about the human body," observes essayist Moira Weigel.[63] The term "biological clock" was first used to refer to women's fertility in 1978, in a *Washington Post* article titled "The Clock is Ticking for the Career Woman."[64] In other words, this expression was an early harbinger of the imminent anti-feminist backlash, and its dazzlingly successful integration into the female anatomy makes it a unique phenomenon in the history of evolution—it would have given Darwin pause for thought. Since women's bodies give them the option of carrying a child, of course Nature would prefer that women also change the resulting infant's nappies, once born, that they attend all meetings with pediatricians and, while we're on the subject, that they mop the kitchen floor, do the washing-up and remember to buy loo roll for the next twenty-five years. This is known as "maternal instinct." Yes, Nature orders precisely this, and not, for example, that, in order to thank women for taking on the major task required for perpetuation of the species, society do its best to compensate them for the inconveniences they thereby suffer; nothing of the sort. If you thought that might make sense, you haven't really understood Nature.

Antediluvian notions still cluster around women who have not had children. The persistence of epithets like "fulfilled" and "glowing," attributed as a matter of course to future mothers—although, if you listen to the women themselves, experiences of pregnancy can be widely divergent—implies agreement with the equally persistent, contrasting belief in the spinsters whose bodies are shriveled and dried out by the emptiness of their womb. This is to ignore the fact that, as Laurie Lisle describes it, even empty, the uterus is "an active organ with its menstrual and sexual sensations."[65] Furthermore, let's be clear that, when it isn't occupied, the uterus takes up little space, so the notion of a cavity draped with cobwebs and swept by bleak and whistling winds becomes patently fantastical. Yet we attribute to childbearing the virtue of fulfilling women's erotic and emotional needs, and, thereby, to regulating urges that might otherwise become uncontrollable. To dodge motherhood is therefore to sidestep a process of purification and domestication, to avoid the only redemption available to a body that has been the focus of so many questions, fears and revulsions over the centuries. "Marriage and motherhood are the antidotes that will sublimate a necessarily flawed body," as David Le Breton writes.[66] To refuse these antidotes is to go on sowing confusion, to invite suspicious or pitying looks. And yet, here too, individual experiences contradict the assumptions. Having accumulated health problems throughout my life, I am deeply relieved not to have had to share with a child, by carrying it first in my body and then in my arms, the physical resources I can still marshal.

Once, at a conference where I had just finished arguing for women's achievements to be dissociated from their motherhood, the next speaker, a doctor specializing in infertility, began by declaring solemnly that my words would have been "dire" for his patients to hear. I was stunned. I felt, on the contrary, that my argument ought to be of some use to them, should they ultimately fail to fall pregnant: they would have to surmount the pain of not realizing their wish, but this need not be compounded by a sense of incompleteness or failure as women. Many doctors will freely lecture those who do not want children, saying they "should spare a thought for those who can't have any." But "motherhood is not a communicating vessels scenario," as Martin Winckler reminds us in *Les brutes en blanc* ("The brutes in white"), his book on medical malpractice in France. Of course, a woman who is struggling to fall pregnant may feel envious toward those who reject this option, but two seconds' reflection are enough for anyone to see the irrational thinking here: one woman having a child for the sake of another who is unable to would only double the misery. Any other view is tantamount to seeing women as interchangeable representatives of some single female being and not individuals with their own distinct personalities and wishes.

This view is, however, very widespread, if we accept the remarkable resistance generated by this basic truth: learning that you are pregnant is wonderful when you want a child, but a heavy blow when you don't. Yet the articles we find online describing the first signs of pregnancy are predicated on the assumption that *all* women reading them wish to be pregnant, whereas in reality a fair number of them must be reading amid gut-twisting anxiety. "You have stopped using your usual method of contraception and you are waiting. But with each cycle the wait seems to go on so long . . ." assumes, for example, *Aufeminin.com* ("*Comment détecter un début de grossesse*"—"How to spot your early pregnancy"); the related topics are called such things as "*Booster sa fertilité: quatre-*

vingts aliments à privilégier" ("Boost your fertility: twenty-four foods to favor") and *"Les meilleurs positions pour tomber enceinte"* ("The best positions for getting pregnant").

One of my friends was at one point very afraid she might be pregnant by her lover. For several reasons, it was nevertheless almost impossible that she could actually have been pregnant. A dear psychiatrist friend interpreted her anxiety as the manifestation of a subconscious desire to have a child with this man, with whom she was very much in love. But my friend saw things differently: the idea of being pregnant inspired such terror that she panicked as soon as she couldn't be completely certain that she wasn't. "I'd love to entertain the theory of some subconscious ambivalence—very, very subconscious, in this case . . . But can we be sure that the default norm, for every woman, is to want a child?" she asked me, perplexed. Good question—yet it's one that, for many, should not need to be asked. Winckler describes his alarm when, one day, colleagues told him, "Fair enough, but when you prescribe an IUD or an implant, you do realize it is *an aggression imposed on women's unconscious desire to fall pregnant?* At least the ones who take the pill can forget to take it and fulfill their suppressed urges!" (Emphasis in original.) And one young woman reported that her gynecologist told her, "If it hurts during your period, that's because your body wants a pregnancy."[67]

In Swedish novelist Mare Kandre's *Quinnan och Dr. Dreuf* ("The Woman and Dr. Dreuf"), the eminent (and transparently anagrammatized) gynecologist recommends, in order to calm the torments exhausting his patient's delicate intellectual capacities, that she try the universal remedy of motherhood, known for its "great sanctity" and its "purifying action upon the female psyche."[68] He almost falls out of his armchair when the young flibbertigibbet replies that she doesn't want children, saying:

> My dear young lady, ALL women want them! [. . .] for certain reasons, woman is and generally remains broadly unaware of her feelings, of her desires and of her actual needs. [. . .] her true feelings must, in general, be interpreted by an analyst of my caliber so that the woman is not left to be completely led, even swallowed up by her feelings, so that she doesn't altogether miss her vocation, the source of the disorder and thereby at the root of the most complete chaos thus far experienced in the civilized world!

In support of his words, the doctor hands his client a dusty volume of the works of his mentor, the late Professor Popokoff. He makes her decipher a passage where Popokoff writes, "in their heart of hearts all women want to have children"—before snatching it back on being struck by the thought that she may have her period. He thunders:

> You surely don't mean you consider yourself superior to medical science! Our knowledge of women has taken centuries of intense research in the morgues and asylums to reach this conclusion. Countless experiments have been conducted, theories have been tested over and over on pigs, toads, tapeworms and goats. You cannot imagine the level to which these unarguable facts have been cross-checked!

How, indeed, can we remain unconvinced?

More unexpectedly, even a feminist of Erica Jong's caliber may share this assumption. Looking back on the women's movement in the US in the 1970s, Jong explains the failure of Betty Friedan's followers (wives and mothers) and Gloria Steinem's supporters (single, without children) to come together as follows: "Women who had rejected family life despised women who had embraced family life. Perhaps the hatred was partly sour grapes. The urge to have children is so strong that you renounce it in yourself only at great cost."[69] This is a bizarre declaration. If we must dig up old trails of disdain, hatred and bitterness in this story, they are more likely to be found on Friedan's side, for she accused Steinem of discrediting the movement by bringing in the hussies, paupers and lesbians. Many personal accounts corroborate that Friedan was a difficult, even rancorous figure, whereas Steinem lives and breathes serenity, so the two women are rather poorly chosen if we want to talk about prejudice around automatic expectations of a desire for motherhood and the fulfillment that achieving it may bring. That such untruths can be published demonstrates the dogma's potency.

Similarly, preparing an article in France in 2002, psychiatrist Geneviève Serre interviewed five voluntarily childless women, from a fundamentally skeptical standpoint. She wrote, "The fact that several of the women had been pregnant, sometimes several times, and that they'd taken the decision to abort, may offer grounds to suppose that there was some desire for a child but that this desire had been ignored."[70] Pregnancy as the manifestation of a subconscious wish for a child: does this also operate for women who have been raped? Or for those where abortion is illegal, who risk their lives to rid themselves of an embryo? If we must allow for some ambivalence or some subconscious desires, in the case of my friend with her horror of pregnancy, we cannot exclude the theory of a fleeting aspiration to normality: it isn't easy to row against the flow one's whole life. On this point, one voluntarily childless young woman described her persistent sense of "appearing like a circus freak."[71]

A man who doesn't become a father is avoiding a social function, whereas women are thought to play out the realization of their innermost identity through motherhood. Logically, if the desire for a child were biologically founded, we should be able to detect some biological anomaly among those who don't feel it. And, should it be lacking, we could recommend that women consult a doctor; alternatively, having internalized the norm, women will self-diagnose. You'll be expected to take steps for yourself, to work on yourself, until such time as the desire for a child results. At this point, we come to the same paradox that lies at the heart of the beauty industry: to be a "real woman" means putting blood, sweat and tears into achieving something that's meant to come naturally. When it comes to procreation, the psychoanalytical and psychiatric discourse turns out to be surprisingly effective in taking up the baton of the consensus on nature, lending a vague air of scientific authority to the worst clichés. Having identified among her interviewees qualities she describes as "masculine," including "independence, efficiency, discipline, interests such as politics," Serre writes, "This self-sufficient, independent masculine side may stand in the way of a femininity that's more passive, more receptive in the sense of accepting life's gifts, which is likely to be necessary in accessing motherhood."[72] Mothers, you lazy and dependent creatures who are content to float in the great mystery of life and leave politics to men: you have selected the nineteenth century, please hold the line.

In the Clearing

Women who refuse motherhood are also faced with the prejudice that they must therefore hate children, like the witches who dined out on small roasted bodies during sabbaths or cast fatal spells on their neighbor's child. This is doubly exasperating. First, because it is far from true in most cases: it can even be a strong sympathy with children that makes you refrain from having your own, while others may choose to have them for deeply dubious reasons. Lucie Joubert comments ironically, "What could make procreation more enticing than the terrifying prospect of long years spent in a retirement home without visits or entertainment? It's a nightmare that some guard against by having eight children, one for each day of the week, plus one extra—you can never be too careful."[73] The number of children who are abused, beaten or raped may also have us wondering if everyone who has them really loves them. Besides, we do have a right not to seek out children's company and actually to loathe them outright, even if this means mercilessly relieving our friends of their delusions and giving that image of sweetness and devotion they call "Woman" a thorough trampling. On this point too, in any case, there's no way to emerge looking good. Tired of the arch looks and the comments elicited as soon as they show any fondness toward a child or give one a cuddle ("you look so natural like that," "you'd make a wonderful mother," etc.), some women may prefer to display a thoroughgoing dislike, even if this means coming across as monstrous. But, it's true, we may like children and like to spend time with them—and yet not want them for ourselves. "I also cook really well, and I've no interest in opening a restaurant!" as Jeanne, heroine of the comic strip *Et toi, quand est-ce que tu t'y mets?* ("How about you, when are you going to start trying?"), neatly puts it.[74]

Writer Elizabeth Gilbert proposes three categories of women:

> There are women who are born to be mothers. There are women who are born to be aunties. And there are women who should not be allowed to be within ten feet of a child. It is very important that you figure out which one of those camps you belong in, because tragedy and sorrow results [sic] from ending up in the wrong category.[75]

Gilbert herself belongs to the "auntie camp." In a French women's magazine in 2006, one young woman demonstrated the miracles the "auntie" types may achieve. As a child, she had gone on holiday with a friend, to stay with her friend's aunt. Upon arriving, she discovered that the aunt in question was Sabine Azéma—one of the few French actresses who is open and serene about her choice not to be a mother. This holiday with "Auntie" Sabine was repeated several years in a row:

> Sabine lent us a little camera and encouraged us to write scenes that we would then shoot. We spend hours looking for costumes in the market. Sabine has booked a little car, but, as she hates driving, she

gets stuck for hours behind a lorry and we shriek with laughter. We are not children, she isn't a grown-up, it's magic. Monsieur Hulot-style hols, not a whiff of McDonalds but lots of *Arsenic and Old Lace*-ish tea-rooms and our hotel garden rather than the crowded town square. Sabine gives us extraordinary presents: spinning tops from New York, English pencils. More than anything, she brings us her sense of joy.[76]

There is a richness in the range of possible roles to play that we tend to underestimate. One day, while in her forties, Gloria Steinem was interviewed by Joan Rivers, host of *The Tonight Show*. Rivers said, "You know, my daughter has been the biggest joy in my life and I can't imagine not having her. Don't you regret not having children?" to which Steinem replied, "Well, Joan, if every woman had a child, there wouldn't be anybody here to tell you what it's like not to have one."[77]

Plenty of women have revealed why the meaning they wished to give their lives was incompatible with motherhood. Chantal Thomas, a lover of freedom, solitude and travel, expresses it very simply: "Nothing in that whole business ever appealed to me, neither the pregnancy, the childbirth, nor the daily requirements of feeding a child, of taking care of it, of raising it."[78] If you read Simone de Beauvoir's autobiography, *The Prime of Life*, what is particularly striking about the young Beauvoir is her uncompromising, unbounded appetite: she devours books, she stuffs herself with films, she is obsessed with becoming a writer. The same voracious appetite drives her physically too. Appointed to a teaching position in Marseille, she discovers walking. As soon as she can, she goes on a walking trip, gobbling up the kilometers, intoxicating herself with land-scapes and sensations, not always bringing the appropriate kit, never allowing herself to stop (despite a few warning signs) for fear of accident or attack; she leaves behind many of the friends who try to join her. Beauvoir treasures her freedom, as evidenced by the delight with which she describes, in a few lines, the charm of the series of rooms she rents. From her student years in Paris and thereafter, she adores living alone:

> I could get home with the milk, read in bed all night, sleep til midday, shut myself up for twenty-four hours at a stretch, or go out on the spur of the moment. My lunch was a bowl of borsch at Dominique's and for supper I took a cup of hot chocolate at La Coupole. I was fond of hot chocolate, and borsch, and lengthy siestas and sleepless nights: but my chief delight was in doing as I pleased. There was practically nothing to stop me. I discovered, to my great pleasure, that "the serious business of living" on which grownups had held forth to me so interminably was not, in fact, quite so oppressive after all.[79]

It is impossible not to see that a pregnancy would have nipped in the bud this joyous impulsiveness, this passion, and would have taken Beauvoir far from all that she loved and valued. Later in the book, she explains her avoidance of motherhood, a topic on which she had "so often been taken up," like this: "my happiness was too complete for any new element to attract me. [. . .] I never once dreamed of rediscovering myself in the child I might bear. [. . .] I never felt as though I were holding out against motherhood; it simply was not my natural lot in life, and by remaining childless I was fulfilling my proper function."[80] As for the feeling of disconnection some women have, a friend of mine confirmed the truth in this, confiding that, when she had an abortion at the age of twenty, the operation remained entirely abstract for her: "It was as if I'd had my appendix out."

Then there is Gloria Steinem, who opens her autobiography, *My Life on the Road*, with these words:

> This book is dedicated to:
>
> Dr. John Sharpe of London, who in 1957, a decade before physicians in England could legally perform an abortion for any reason other than the health of the women, took the considerable risk of referring for an aborting a twenty-two-year-old American on her way to India.
>
> Knowing that she had broken an engagement at home to seek an unknown fate, he said, "You must promise me two things. First, you will not tell anyone my name. Second, you will do what you want to do with your life."
>
> Dear Dr. Sharpe, I believe you, who knew the law was unjust, would not mind if I say this so long after your death:
>
> I've done the best I could with my life.
>
> This book is for you.[81]

In Steinem's case, far from being a betrayal of her own mother, her decision not to prolong the succession of generations constitutes an attempt to do justice to her mother, to recognize her legacy and to honor her family history. Before Steinem's birth, her mother, Ruth, who had started out in journalism, had, at one time, been on the point of abandoning her husband and first daughter, and leaving to try her luck in New York with a friend.

> If I pressed and said, "But why didn't you leave? Why didn't you take my sister and go to New York?" she would say it didn't matter, that she was lucky to have my sister and me. If I pressed hard enough, she would add, "If I'd left, you never would have been born."
>
> I never had the courage to say: *But you would have been born instead.*[82]

After her parents separated, young Gloria lived alone with her mother, who fell into depression. As soon as she was able, Steinem escaped to New York and made her own dreams come true instead. In homage to her mother, she writes, "Like so many women before her—and so many even now—she never had a journey of her own. With all my heart, I wish she could have followed a path she loved."[83]

While working on this chapter, rummaging one day among some papers that had belonged to my father, I came across a faded blue notebook inscribed with the words "*École supérieure de commerce de Neuchâtel*" ("Neuchâtel: Faculty of Economics and Business"). Inside, I found nothing more businesslike than a long list of literary quotes, all in my father's very particular handwriting, which was, like him, elegant and angular. He had copied out the contents page of a journal called *Le livre de demain* ("The book of tomorrow"), with texts by the likes of Maurice Maeterlinck and Edmond Jaloux. His own father's early death, when he was only twelve, and the turmoil this brought into his life, had deprived my father of the literary studies he had dreamed of. So cultured and so curious, he had been obliged to study business—for which he had no particular bent. He was then able to make a very good living, but he never managed to go back to the career he had wanted, and nothing could alleviate his regret, the pain of his untapped talents. As for me, long before fully understanding my father's heartbreak, I had been immersed in a world where nothing was more real or worthy of interest than books and writing. It may be that our parents sometimes pass on passions so deeply felt that they leave room for nothing else—especially when they haven't been able to pursue them as they would have wished. Perhaps there is some urge for compensation which cannot tolerate half measures—a need to mark out a clearing amid the forests of the generations, to set oneself up there and forget the rest.

An Unacceptable Word

All of this remains unacceptable for many people. In a book where elsewhere she judges that "women without children are mistakes," that they're in fact "their own widows," actor Macha Méril felt it reasonable to address the spirit of Simone de Beauvoir as follows:

> Super-smart Simone, on this point you have committed the sin of bad faith. You too would have liked to have children, but choices you took and that demon

Sartre deflected you. With your American lover [the
writer Nelson Algren], you were within an ace of allowing your womanly body to open up to motherhood. You would have been no less brilliant, nor your
brain have spun less rapidly.

(Lucie Joubert, who quotes these words, comments: "Her
brain, no, but her pen might have slowed a little—who can
say?")[84] In 1987, Michèle Fitoussi (the *Elle* magazine journalist who was so enraged by Corinne Maier's book *No Kid*)
published her own book, *Le ras-le-bol des superwomen* ("The
superwomen have had enough"), which focused on the challenges of balancing family and work, and on the unfortunate
consequences of women's emancipation. Yet it seems out of
the question, from her point of view, that some women should
be allowed to simplify their lives by removing one of the elements from the equation. Or at least, not *that* element.

When we are not doubting the "good faith" of voluntarily
childless women, we are trying to make them into substitute
mothers: female teachers are playing mother to their students; books are female writers' offspring, etc. In an essay in
which she thinks through ways of "challenging the stigma of
childlessness," Laurie Lisle devotes some time to discussing
symbolic motherhoods; apparently this may answer a genuine
personal need, but, if we are to believe the online reaction,
the tendency to insist on this angle has outraged many female
readers who do not feel the same.[85] One such dissenting voice
comes from Clothilde, who is voluntarily childless: as a tutor
at nursing college, and especially in her interactions with students, she wants "to unlearn mothering . . ."[86]

From the received common-sense perspective, any self-realization that is not motherhood appears not only as a substitute for it, but as a poor imitation. This is nicely illustrated in Anne Fontaine's film *Coco Before Chanel* (2009), about Gabrielle Chanel's early years in fashion. The young heroine is in love with a man who dies in a road accident at the film's end. We see young Coco in tears, then we jump to watching her first professional triumph. At the end of a fashion show, the audience claps and cheers, while she remains sitting in a corner, staring sadly into space. In conclusion, the voice-over tells us that Chanel went on to become a huge success, but that she never married and never had children. We are given the impression that, in the wake of this bereavement, she must have lived like a nun, and was solely concerned with her career due to having lost the love of her life. Whereas, in fact, Chanel had a rich and busy life: she had friends and lovers, some of whom, at least, she seems to have loved. There is something manipulative—or, more likely, the laziness of cliché—in leading viewers to think of her career as a kind of consolation for her personal loss. She had begun to design clothes well before her lover's death, driven by a deep creative impulse, and evidently this work brought her immense satisfaction.

Whenever she sees them hesitate, Elizabeth Gilbert encourages her interlocutors to ask about her non-motherhood; it's important to her and she likes to discuss it. In contrast, Rebecca Solnit is infuriated at being asked about it so often:

> Part of my own endeavor as a writer has been to
> find ways to value what is elusive and overlooked, to

describe nuances and shades of meaning, to celebrate
public life and solitary life, and—in John Berger's
phrase—to find "another way of telling," which is
part of why getting clobbered by the same old ways
of telling is disheartening.[87]

She wrote her article on the subject in the wake of a lecture she gave about Virginia Woolf. To her great surprise, the
audience discussion rapidly turned to whether Woolf, celebrated author of *Mrs. Dalloway* and *To the Lighthouse*, ought
to have had children. In 2016, French writer Marie Darrieussecq had the same unpleasant surprise. Invited to talk about
her new translation of Woolf's *A Room of One's Own* on the
France Culture radio channel, she was asked the same question. She began by patiently responding that Woolf's sufferings were certainly deep-rooted, but that nothing suggested
her lack of children had played a part in them. When the
interviewer pressed her on the point, Darrieussecq lost her
temper: "Really this is beside the point! Excuse me—I'll be
polite about it—but really this is too much! Do people ask
such questions of a male writer without children? *I couldn't
care less!* For me, this is really to reduce Woolf to the sum
of her female body, and this is not at all what she's doing
in this essay."[88] . . . These clashes are further confirmation
of Pam Grossman's view in the introduction to her celebration of "literary witches," among whom Woolf takes her due
place, that "women who create things other than children are
still considered dangerous by many."[89] And best beware: even
being Virginia Woolf cannot exonerate you for not being a
mother. Any readers who are considering not reproducing,

or who may have neglected to get on with it, be warned: it's no good locking yourself away and writing masterpieces in a sad attempt at deflecting attention from this grave oversight, which has of course made you very unhappy, even though you don't know it. If you must write masterpieces, do it for other reasons—for the pleasure; otherwise, rather devote the leisure moments of your scandalous existence to reading novels in peace under a tree, or to whatever else you'd like to do.

The trauma caused by the 1970s' feminist movement lies behind all kinds of myths. For example, not one bra was publicly burned at the time and yet the whole world remains convinced that, as Susan Faludi writes, "the bonfires of feminism nearly cremated the lingerie industry."[90] Similarly, the movement was sometimes accused of contempt toward motherhood and of making women who aspired to it feel guilty. While this may be true of the behavior of some individuals—which is indeed regrettable—it is not true of the discourse of the time. In the US, researcher Ann Snitow has found no trace of any supposed "hatred of mothers" in contemporaneous texts.[91] As for the ephemeral National Organization of Non-Parents (NON), founded in 1972 by Ellen Peck, there were no links between NON and the feminist movement. In fact, there was very little, if any, feminist argument in favor of not having children. One notable exception was the "Statement on Birth Control" conceived by the Black Women's Liberation Group of Mount Vernon, New York, in 1968. In reaction to the opinions of some black men who felt that contraception implied an insidious form of genocide, they answered that, on the contrary, it meant "the freedom to *fight* genocide of black women and children," for those who stayed childless were the more empowered.[92] In France, women demonstrators chanted, "A child if I want, when I want": "The radicalism of the 'if I want' was mitigated by the 'when I want,'" in Christine Delphy's analysis. "The campaign always foregrounded the birth-control options of the time and the number of births; it never focused on the principles behind this. Plainly, the feminist movement never dared to articulate the idea that a woman may not want a child at all."[93] For Charlotte Debest, "the turbulence of the new social and psychoanalytical ideas of the 1970s did, some-how, lead to the astonishing injunction: 'Do as you wish but do become parents.'" Women are particularly vulnerable to this paradoxical "injunction to want a child." And they are all the more sensitive to it because, as one (voluntarily child-less) woman remarked to Debest, they have a tendency "not to distinguish between what they want and what is asked of them."[94] Jeanne Safer describes how one day she came to real-ize that she didn't want to have a baby: she "*want[ed] to* want to have a baby."[95] The "freedom of choice" we are meant to have achieved is thus exposed as largely an illusion.

The outcome of this cultural situation is a total absence of support for women who abstain from childbearing. One of Debest's interviewees says, "I don't know how possible it is to serenely not want a child."[96] This fragile and practically invis-ible legitimacy prompts women to wonder, as soon as some-thing goes wrong in their lives, whether the cause of their misfortune may not have its roots in their lack of progeny. I see this in myself: if I stub my toe on a piece of furniture (I'm hardly exaggerating), I automatically assume it must be my due punishment. More or less consciously, I am forever *awaiting my punishment* for allowing myself to live the life I wanted. On the other hand, whatever small fix she's in, hardly any mother will stop to wonder if her decision to have children has anything to do with it. An anecdote from Chantal Thomas shows this dynamic at work:

> A woman came over to me, just to tell me how her miserly daughter-in-law had schemed to have her driven out of her own house, in Brittany. Noticing that her story did not upset me, she went on the attack: "And you? Are you satisfied with your children? Do you get along well with them?" "I don't have any children." (Silence and a long look.)—"That must be terrible," she said, and turned her back on me.[97]

When I was fifteen, and already sure then that I didn't want to be a mother, I found my resolve somewhat shaken on seeing Woody Allen's 1988 film *Another Woman*, in which the heroine, played by Gena Rowlands, is a fifty-something philosophy professor. At the end of the film, she collapses and sobs, "Maybe I should have had a child." It took me a while to realize that this scene was not the reflection of an objective, implacable reality, and that Woody Allen was not necessarily an exemplary feminist.[98] And yet, on encountering voluntarily childless women, people still regularly threaten, "You'll regret it one day!" They are betraying some very weird thinking. Can we force ourselves to do something we haven't the least wish to do solely in order to head off a hypothetical regret hovering in the distant future? Such an argument ties these women right back into the system they are trying to escape, the unbreakable cycle of anticipation which is induced by a child's presence and through which hopes of guaranteeing the future can eat up the present: take out a loan, work yourself to death, fret about the inheritance you'll be passing on and how you'll pay for their studies . . .

Be all this as it may, and though it may upset Woody Allen, it seems that the decision not to have children almost never, in the long run, leads to the torment so often promised. Geneviève Serre was obliged to recognize, despite her prejudice, that the women she met felt "no lack and no regrets."[99] Pierre Panel, an obstetrician, notes that, among the patients who have come to him for a sterilization, the incidence of regret is "tiny." "The regrets we do hear of tend mostly to come from patients who have undergone—and I describe it advisedly as *undergone*—a tubal sterilization before legalization,[100] that is, in the context of decisions effectively taken more by the doctor involved than by the patient herself."[101] Where there are regrets, these may be genuine, of course. But researchers are also proposing a theory of *compelled* regret: "Plainly, this is because women have been told throughout their lives that, for as long as women have no children, they cannot be complete, that they feel a lack or sense of being undervalued when they grow older," Lucie Joubert concludes. And she adds: "Say we change the message; we could see the specter of these regrets vanish for good."[102] What if society were to legitimize women's freedom to be who they wish— then what? "I don't want to be pushed to get married, to have kids, to work, do this, do that. I just want to be a person," says thirty-seven-year-old Linda.[103]

The Last Secret

There is the rare, almost nonexistent regret, about which we nonetheless talk all the time; and then there is the regret that seems much more prevalent, but which it is forbidden to mention: the one that sometimes follows motherhood. We can indulge in purple prose on the horrors of parenthood as much as we like, but only on the condition that we always, always conclude: despite everything, it makes us so happy. It is precisely this rule that Corinne Maier gleefully demolishes in *No Kid*:

> If I didn't have kids, I'd be halfway through a round-the-world trip with all the money I'd earned from my books. Instead, I am on house arrest at home, serving meals, forced to get up at seven every day, to have absurd lessons recited at me and to keep the washing machine going. All this for kids who take me for their skivvy. Some days I do regret it, and I don't mind saying so.

And further on:

> Who knows what I could have become if I'd not had children, if I were less embroiled in keeping it all going, the shopping to do and the meals to provide? I'll admit I'm just waiting for one thing: that my children will pass their baccalaureates so I can at last give more time to my little creative amusements. I'll be fifty by then. After that, when I'm grown up, my life will really begin.[104]

Maier's transgressing this taboo unleashed the vitriol of Michèle Fitoussi: "This wish to have someone remove the progeny who exhaust us and ruin our lives—who among us hasn't felt that? At *Elle*, the most acerbic pens have filled many pages with this stuff, but with the required humor and talent to help the medicine go down."[105] "Humor" and "talent," here, are code words for "moderation" and "conformity." Letting off steam is only allowed when firmly marshalled in service of the conventional view. Yet Maier is not alone in daring to step out of line. "I had a child against my own better judgment," the actor Anémone claimed in 2011. She had resigned herself to taking a pregnancy to term after going through three abortions, two of which took place in poor conditions. Her two greatest goals being solitude and freedom, she explained that she would have been "much happier" without children (she had two). "You have to expect a good twenty years of them," she said. "After the cuddly little baby, there's the child who's all bony and who you have to sign up to school and take to classes of this, that and the other. It's exhausting, life goes by and it's not your own life."[106] The journalist Françoise Giroud, similarly, says of her son, "From the day he was born, I went about with a rock tied to my neck."[107]

"This woman should be dragged out into the street, her teeth should be remove [sic] with a claw hammer, and then every child in the town should be lined up and made to cut a piece off of her with a knife. Then she should be burned alive." This is one of the anonymous attacks posted on a German discussion forum and directed at Israeli sociologist Orna Donath, author of a survey bringing together the voices of women who regret becoming mothers.[108] Corinne

Maier's stance—inflicting practically unfiltered on her children the public revelations of her regret at having brought them into the world and the burden they represented to her—scandalized many readers. Here, we see the opposite: the women who contributed to Donath's study are all anonymous, although this has evidently not diminished the hostility of its reception. And while not all reactions were quite so aggressive, there was nonetheless a rush from all quarters to reject Donath's findings. On French radio, for example, one speaker declared that the interviewees' views were surely due to the conflict situation they were living in—even though the Palestinian occupation and its repercussions on Israeli society go unmentioned among the reasons for the women's regrets. Others assumed that Donath interviewed the mothers of young children, who, in a few years' time, with greater perspective, would feel better about their children—yet some of the interviewees were already grandmothers. On the German social networks, where in 2016 this study caused heated debate under the hashtag #regrettingmotherhood, one mother of two adolescents berated the study's participants, saying:

It's a real shame that these women seem unable to find enrichment through contact with their children, that they can't learn to grow, to discover deep new feelings with them, to manage to see the world with fresh eyes, to find new appreciation for the little things in life, to find new meaning in the notions of respect, care and love, but also to discover experiences of great joy. In fact, it's about putting your ego aside and showing humility.

She finishes with the words: "LOVE IS NON-NEGOTIABLE!"[109] When exactly did "love" become a gag on women's mouths? Doesn't love deserve better? Do women not deserve better?

"Society will accept only one response from mothers to the question of motherhood: 'I love it,'" Donath concludes.[110] But regret does happen—and, as with all secrets, when unspoken, it festers, or breaks out in moments of crisis or conflict. And it must be wishful thinking to imagine that children cannot feel it or guess at its presence. Many of the American writers—men and women, gay and straight—who wrote about their refusal to have children in the essay collection *Selfish, Shallow, and Self-Absorbed* describe being unable to believe in idealized representations of the family after witnessing their own parents'—and especially their mothers'—frustration and bitterness. Danielle Henderson explains that, "Through [her mother], I learned that motherhood has no guarantees."[111] Michelle Huneven describes how her own mother, who "clearly had wanted children," found herself at a loss in their actual presence. A trifle would enrage her, "a child's question, a book out of place." When Huneven was a teenager, her mother would be constantly bursting into her bedroom to accuse her of some misdemeanor or other. One day, when her mother was ill with diabetes and curled up in bed, her husband beside her, she spotted her two daughters in the doorway and called out, "Who are these goddamn children? [. . .] Make them go away. I don't want any children. Get rid of them." And Huneven, then aged ten, claims to have found some relief in this: "Finally, what I'd long suspected had been spoken."[112] Giving a context to this feeling, a setting for its expression, may help to temper it, to channel and so reduce as far as possible the pain that it may cause. The women involved could confide in someone close to them, or even open up to their children directly, at a well-chosen moment. To say to your child, during a calm conversation, "You know, I love you deeply, I am so happy to have you, but I'm not sure I was perfectly cut out for this role," is not at all the same as yelling at your child that they're ruining your life and you wish they'd never been born. It could even disperse an obscure anxiety your kids may feel that some failing on *their* part, some imagined disappointment or shortcoming, could be the cause of your regret.

Orna Donath herself has no wish to be a mother, and she has become used to the endless assurances that she will regret her choice. "Regret is used as a threat to push women who do not wish to be mothers into motherhood even when abortion is not an issue," according to her analysis.[113] Astonished that no one seemed to see that one may, on the other hand, regret having given birth to one or more children, Donath decided to investigate. Her own position created an empathic connection and a certain mutual understanding with the women who responded to her call-out: their shared aspiration to be "nobody's mom" gave them common ground. Similarly, she observes, some women who cannot have children, although would like to, will surely feel stronger affinities with mothers who are happy to be so than with women who are voluntarily childless. This leads her to note that our family status may not say much about our deeper identity. Broadly, she refuses to set mothers up in contrast to non-mothers: the American edition of her book opens with an homage to her recently deceased grandmother, Noga Donath, who loved being a mother and with whom Orna held long discussions, each listening to the other with curiosity and goodwill, seeking to understand the other one, wishing them happiness and glorying in their achievements. Adrienne Rich also wrote that "The 'childless woman' and the 'mother' are a false polarity, which has served the institutions both of motherhood and heterosexuality. There are no such simple categories."[114]

The subject of Donath's study is specifically regret and not ambivalence. The women she spoke to say that, if they could go back, they would not choose motherhood again. Although motherhood is meant to turn "flawed" women into "fulfilled" ones, among Donath's interviewees, the opposite has happened. "If a little leprechaun came and asked me, 'Should I make them go away like nothing happened?' I would say yes without hesitating," says Sophia, who has two young children. "It's just an unbearable burden for me," says Sky, mother of three teenagers. All these women love their children; what they do not like is the experience of motherhood, what it is doing to them and to their lives. "I wouldn't want them not to be here. I just don't want to be a mother," Charlotte concludes. Sophia explains further:

> Without a doubt, I really am a wonderful mother. [. . .] I mean, I'm a mother whose children are important to her; I love them, I read books, I get professional counsel, I try to do my best to give them a better education and a lot of warmth and love. [. . .] But still, I *hate* being a mother. I *hate* being a mother. I hate this role. I hate being the one who has to place

boundaries, the one who has to punish. I hate the lack of freedom, the lack of spontaneity.

Anémone too made this distinction: "When I have them in front of me, I can't look at them and feel sorry I have them, that wouldn't make sense, but I do regret becoming a mother."[115] Tirtza, whose children are in their thirties and are parents themselves, realized her mistake from the moment of her first baby's birth: "I immediately saw that it is not for me. And not only is it not for me: it is the *nightmare* of my life." Carmel, a mother of two adolescents, had a similar experience: "That day I started to understand what I had done. It intensified over the years." From this collection of evidence, Donath concludes that, while some women experience postpartum depression without this having any effect on their deep desire to be mothers or any compromising effect on their future happiness, among others, the birth of a child is a shock from which they cannot recover. Donath calls for wider recognition of this experience and that we allow women to be more open about what they are living through.

Some of the women question the conditioning they received, the generally accepted "truths" about parenthood: "It's like saying, 'A child's smile is worth everything.' It's bullshit. It's not true at all," according to Sunny, a mother of four. But, among the few benefits they do find in motherhood, there is the sense of being part of society, of fitting in with social expectations. They feel that they have "fulfilled their duty," as Debra puts it; at least they are left in peace. Brenda, who had three children, remembers her happiness after each birth: "The closeness and intimacy with the children, the sense of belonging, the pride in yourself—you've realized a dream. It is other people's dream, but you've still realized it." Many of the interviewees admit that, although they realized this wasn't for them when their first child was born, they nonetheless went on to have more due to social pressure. Rose, a mother of two, says she would never have done it if she had known better what to expect and if she had had "a supportive environment that could accept this type of decision." Here, we find the precise reverse of the situation described by Géraldine, the young woman who told Charlotte Debest she thought it almost impossible "to serenely not want a child."[116] On one side we have a nonsensical and painful decision, only somewhat mitigated by the accompanying social approval; on the other, a decision made in accord with one's own wishes, one that may be part of a happy life, yet is undermined by the more or less veiled disapproval communicated by those around us. "As a woman who chooses to be childless, I generally have just one problem: other adults," says Danielle Henderson.[117]

Ultimately, given the current cultural norms, only one kind of woman can pursue her life with absolute peace of mind, enjoying both her own satisfaction and society's approval: the woman who has one or more children she wants to have, who feels enriched by this experience and has not paid too high a price for it, whether thanks to her comfortable financial circumstances, to a working life that is fulfilling but still leaves time for family, to a partner who does their share of the educational and domestic tasks, to a wider circle—of relatives and friends—that helps out, or thanks to all these things at once. (If it is thanks to her easy financial situation, there remains a strong possibility that our exemplar's happiness also relies on her domestic employee or nanny's demanding and often badly paid job.) Other women are all condemned to some kind of greater or lesser torment, and to envying each other, and so widening the divisions between them. Adrienne Rich describes her conversation with a "brilliant" and childless scholar of her own generation as follows:

> She describes her early feelings when she used to find herself at conferences or parties among faculty wives, most of whom had or would have children, she the only unmarried woman in the room. She felt, then, that her passionate investigations, the recognition accorded her work, still left her the "barren" woman, the human failure, among so many women who were mothers. I ask her, "But can you imagine how some of them were envying you your freedom, to work, to think, to travel, to enter a room as yourself, not as some child's mother or some man's wife?"[118]

Women know how very difficult it is not to find ourselves, at least occasionally, systematically wanting what we do not have, and so not knowing very well where we stand.

All the women whose voices we read in Orna Donath's book are at times troubled by guilt and relieved at last to have a chance to speak out. They are terrified at the idea that their children might learn of their confessions. Pregnant with her third child, Maya also insists that she is a good mother, and declares, "No one can guess it [that she doesn't love being a mother] about me. [. . .] And if one can't tell this about me, then it's impossible to know it of anyone else." Some women

are determined never to mention these feelings to their children, certain that they could never understand and might be
horribly hurt—but not all women. Thus Rotem is delighted
by the book's publication because she feels it's important to
share the idea that parenting need not be an essential step in
life, precisely for the good of her own daughters: "It doesn't
matter to me—I already have two children—but I want my
daughters to have this option."

Through these mothers' experiences, Donath invites us
not only to conclude that society should be making motherhood less difficult, but also that the expectation laid on women
to become mothers is overdue a rewrite. Some women's regret "indicates that there are other roads that society forbids
women from taking, by *a priori* erasing alternative paths,
such as nonmotherhood." If we were to restore these forbidden paths, it is not guaranteed that the sky would fall on our
heads. Perhaps we might even avoid many tragedies, much
pointless suffering and much wasted energy. And we might
see the flourishing of brand-new routes toward happiness.

3

The Dizzy Heights

SHATTERING THE IMAGE OF THE "OLD HAG"

One summer evening a few years ago, I was dining with my friend D on a restaurant terrace, where the tables were closely packed together. D is a kind of virtuoso conversationalist: passionate, generous, perceptive, gifted with a prodigious and almost unlimited capacity for listening. But, in the heat of a discussion, and perhaps also because she is used to addressing her students from a lectern, she tends to forget to keep the volume down—which can be a touch embarrassing when, in aid of the most effective analysis, she is recapping the latest developments in your personal life, thus offering your romantic problems to the wisdom of a bunch of strangers. That evening, a couple is dining beside us. The woman holds back barely ten minutes before erupting: "Excuse me, Mademoiselle! This is too much! We can't hear ourselves think!" My friend instantly responds with profuse apologies and, subdued, focuses hard on her plate. Yet, a few moments later, she looks up at me, radiant once more. Eyes bright, she whispers triumphantly: "She called me 'Mademoiselle!'" And I know exactly what she means. We are both in our early forties, which is to say in a period of our lives when, as intellectual women with stable professional lives, whose jobs are fulfilling and who have the means to eat well, to look after ourselves and to exercise, we still have a right to the odd "miss" to spice up the usual diet of "mrs" which has become the general rule. I also notice when they come my way—how could I not? A man is called "mister" from the age of eighteen or earlier until the end of his life; for a woman, there must always come this moment when, in all innocence, people encountered in her daily life join forces to tell her that she no longer appears young. I remember being upset and even offended by my first "madames." They gave me a shock. It took me a little while to persuade myself it wasn't an insult and that my value was unrelated to my youthfulness. However much I scoffed at Alix Girod de l'Ain's candid admission of an attachment to her grocer's blandishments, I too had grown used to that most precious privilege which youth lends a woman. Without my realizing it, my youth had become deeply meshed with my sense of my own identity, and I was struggling to give it up.

I am dragging my feet as I write this chapter. Some part of me does not feel like facing up to the question of age quite yet: after all, I think, I'm not even forty-five. As the American actor Cynthia Rich remarked in the 1980s, "we learned early on to pride ourselves on our distance from, and our superiority to, old women."[1] It isn't easy to unlearn these life lessons. I am gradually coming to understand how little thought I have given to the prejudice and fear that age provokes in me. We often say that aging and death are taboo in our society—except it is only *women's* aging that is infra dig. When the rather slick English magazine *Sabat*, which celebrates contemporary expressions of witchcraft, brought out an issue on "the crone," foregrounding the power of older women, the cover only featured women who were essentially young, with smooth faces and firm bodies— one of them a typical fashion-magazine model from the Elite modeling agency.[2] With all their thousands of fashion images, week after week, month after month, women's magazines invite readers to identify with models of between sixteen and twenty-five, so leaving *out* of the spotlight the age and appearance of a large proportion of those same readers.

In 1984, Barbara Macdonald, the author of foundational texts on ageism, and also Cynthia Rich's partner, described how she found herself facing a new kind of invisibility as she grew older: "I had lived my life without novels, movies, radio, or television telling me that lesbians existed or that it was possible to be glad to be a lesbian. Now nothing told me that old women existed, or that it was possible to be glad to be an old woman."[3] Macdonald was particularly saddened and infuriated on realizing that this atmosphere of silence and prejudice did not let up in feminist circles—far from it. At their gatherings, she was always the oldest, which made her wonder where the other older women were, all those with whom she had campaigned in her youth. At Cambridge, Massachusetts, in her sixties, she had frequented a feminist café-cinema whose walls were decorated with posters of women including Virginia Woolf, Mary Wollstonecraft, Gertrude Stein and Emma Goldman. Of the other habituées, Macdonald wrote, "The younger women there have no place in their heads to fit me into, have no idea what I come for as no other woman my age comes, yet I am nearer the age of most of the women on their posters from whom they draw their support."[4]

Macdonald relates an excruciating experience. Aged sixty-five, standing around at the beginning of a feminist night march in Boston, she suddenly spotted one of the monitors speaking to Rich (who was twenty years younger), and apparently talking about her. The monitor was worried that Macdonald would not be able to keep up with their pace and wanted to put her in a different part of the marching formation. Macdonald was furious. Because the young woman assumed she might not be able to judge her own capacities, so did not address her directly, she was humiliated. The repeated apologies of the mortified monitor, who quickly realized her mistake, could not repair her mood. Macdonald was discouraged: having felt throughout her life, as a woman, like a problem in a world of men, she now felt, as an older woman, like a problem in a world of women. She wondered, if she could not find her place there, among women marching, where else she would be able to find it . . . [5]

Macdonald also makes a revealing comment about a list featured in a 1979 issue of *Ms.* magazine: "80 Women to Watch in the '80s." Of the women listed, only six were in their fifties and one in her sixties: "That's invisibility," she remarks. Even for the forty-somethings in the list, the message was discouraging: they could deduce from it that they too would turn invisible within the next ten years. But worse was to come: it emerged that the magazine had asked older women to make the selection, and it justified this approach by quoting one of these selectors saying, "established women have the responsibility to boost others." But, to Macdonald, "her statement smacks of maternal self-sacrifice and invisibility."[6] On a broader level, Rich and Macdonald call for feminists to free themselves of the markers and roles inherited from the patriarchal family. Rich observes that, when two women are talking freely, they would be stunned to silence if one were to recall, "She could be my daughter," or the other, "She could be my grandmother." And she distrusts the very concept of "sisterhood." "The brands say that we will continue to be good servants—to police ourselves and to police each other, as good servants always do. We will hold each other to our roles. We will deny each other the subversive power that lies in possibilities."[7] Indeed, I recall my own pained surprise on spotting a very lazy strapline to a recent portrait piece on Gloria Steinem in the French press: "Mamie fait de la résistance" ("Granny does resistance").[8] Not only was it incorrect, for Steinem is nobody's grandmother—and this points to the poverty of our vocabulary for such a female figure—but it reduced Steinem to a condescending stereotype, and one to which she bears no resemblance at all. "Each time we see such a woman as 'grandmother,' we dismiss the courage of her independence; we invalidate her freedom," Cynthia Rich writes. "We tell her, in the face of her own choice, that her real place is in the home."[9]

Always Already Old

In 1972, the American intellectual Susan Sontag wrote a brilliant article on "The double standards of aging" for men and women. In it, she describes one of her friends who, on her twenty-first birthday, moaned, "The best part of my life is over. I'm not young any more." At thirty, the same friend is certain that, this time, it "really is the end." And, ten years later, she told Susan (who hadn't been there) that her fortieth birthday had been the worst of her life, but that "although she has only a few years left, she means to enjoy them while they last."[10] And so I see myself once more, the evening of the party I threw for my own twentieth, unable to talk to my guests about anything other than my distress at the idea of being old from then on—the life and soul of the party I must have been, that night! I can no longer recreate the headspace I was in that evening, but I remember it very clearly. In recent years, two major voices on this issue, Thérèse Clerc, founder of the Maison des Babayagas, a retirement home near Paris that is run by and for women, and the writer Benoîte Groult (both died in 2016), have brought the question of aging to the fore in French feminism.[11] But we must also discuss the sense of looming obsolescence that overshadows *every* woman's life and is specific to women: we can hardly imagine a man rolling on the floor at his own twentieth's festivities, whimpering that he is old. "Journalists have been asking me since I was, like, 22, 'Are you afraid of aging?,'" actor Penelope Cruz confirms.[12] Macdonald had already said, back in 1986, "The message young women get from the youth culture is that it's wonderful to be young and terrible to grow old. If you think about it, it's an impossible dilemma—how can you make a good start in life if you are being told at the same time how terrible the finish is?"[13]

A substantial aspect of women's anxiety about their expiry date relates, of course, to their ability to have children. And, on first glance, their fears do seem to be justified by the biological facts: greater difficulty in becoming pregnant after thirty-five and greater risks of infant deformity after forty are only the most salient points. Nonetheless, Martin

Winckler dares to call out many doctors' excessive alarmism, saying, "At thirty-five, eighty-three women out of a hundred can have children, and at forty, it's still at sixty-seven in a hundred! This is far from the disastrous picture painted by so many doctors!"[14] What is more, cases of famous men becoming fathers late in life—such as Mick Jagger, whose eighth child was born in 2016, when he was seventy-three and already a great-grandfather—create the illusion that age makes no difference to men. But their fertility also declines with time: it peaks around the age of thirty to thirty-four, then gradually diminishes; by age fifty-five to fifty-nine, men are half as fertile as at their peak fertility. Delays in conception and even the risks of miscarriage, genetic anomalies and genetic disease in the fetus all increase with the age of the father.[15] Of course, a woman should be in relatively good health in order to have a healthy pregnancy and birth, but, after the birth, it is best if both parents are fit and ready to look after their child or children. Focusing only on the mother's age amounts to reinforcing the old patriarchal pattern, in which the heaviest burden of children's care and education falls solely to their mother. (Jagger's two youngest children are in fact being brought up by their respective mothers, from whom he was already separated by the times of the births. His contribution amounts to buying each a place to live and sending them a maintenance allowance in line with his worth.[16]) In short, the idea—which has no equivalent for men—that we can only be a true, and truly fulfilled, woman if we have children creates an additional pressure on women, and it's a "man-made" phenomenon, not a biological one.

But women's anxiety around age also relates closely to

their physical appearance. To a degree, the ubiquitous cult of youth affects both men and women; men may also suffer from prejudice around age. But the way society views each party is very different. A man is never disqualified on the sex and romance front due to his age, and when he starts to show signs of aging, he stirs none of the pitying glances or repugnance encountered by aging women. We go into raptures over the tanned and handsome face of Clint Eastwood, who is eighty-seven as I write this. A study has shown that, in Hollywood, female stars tend to find their earnings grow up to the age of thirty-four, then rapidly decrease, whereas their male equivalents reach their maximum earnings at age fifty-one and maintain stable incomes thereafter.[17] During the Democratic primaries for the 2008 US presidential elections, conservative columnist Rush Limbaugh went to town on the prospect of Hillary Clinton's presidency: "Do the American people want to watch a female president age before their very eyes?"[18] Compare how, through Barack Obama's two mandates, the world watched with affection as the American President went gray, and appreciated the elegance with which he did so (calling it "the White House effect"). Perhaps Limbaugh himself did not feel much affection for Obama, but at least he never felt inclined to weaponize the president's visible aging against him.

"Men don't age better than women, they're just allowed to age."[19] The late, great Carrie Fisher retweeted this when, in 2015, viewers of the latest episode in the Star Wars saga were scandalized to see that Leia was no longer the intergalactic, bikini-clad brunette bombshell of forty years ago (some even tried to ask for their money back).[20] We do sometimes mock men who dye their hair: after François Hollande's election to the French presidency, his predecessor Nicolas Sarkozy crowed to his supporters, "Do *you* know any men who dye their hair?" Five years later, the socialist President's former communications adviser was still swearing the claim was untrue, attempting to spare his former boss this shame. But no one thinks it ridiculous that the majority of women dye their hair. In 2017, in France, 2 percent of men over forty-five said they dyed their hair, compared with 63 percent of women.[22] At the time Sontag was writing her article, Pablo Picasso, who was to die a few months later, was photographed in shorts in his studio and frolicking in a bathing suit alongside his last girlfriend, Jacqueline Roque, who was forty-five years younger than him. And Sontag wrote, "Society allows no place in our imagination for a beautiful old woman—a woman who might be like Picasso at the age of ninety, being photographed outdoors on his estate in the south of France, wearing only shorts and sandals."[23]

A Fool's Bargain

Women's early expiry date is also reflected in the age differences we see in many couples. In France, in 2012, among those sharing a home, the man was older (if only by a year) in eight out of ten couples.[24] In 19 percent of couples, the man was five to nine years older, whereas the opposite situation applied in only 4 percent. True, the proportion of couples in which the woman is older is growing: 16 percent of those that got together in the 2000s, compared to 10 percent of those forming relationships in the 1960s. But, since the 1950s, the number of couples with an age gap of ten years or more has almost doubled, increasing from 8 percent to 14 percent.[25] Some men will happily admit to their preference for youthfulness. A forty-three-year-old recently separated photographer confides, for example, that "The idea of starting a relationship with a woman of my own age puts me right off. Once, on Tinder, I raised the slider up to thirty-nine, but really I couldn't do it."[26] The writer Frédéric Beigbeder, who, at forty-eight, married a woman of twenty-four, claims that "the age gap is the secret for the couples that last." He has written a novel about the relationship between J. D. Salinger and the young Oona O'Neill, who later married Charlie Chaplin, who was thirty-six years her senior. At seventy-four, the Swiss writer Roland Jaccard (who was also one of the founders of the right-wing magazine *Causeur*) co-wrote, with his girlfriend Marie Céhère, an account of how they met. She was fifty years younger than him. He claims to have "observed that women were aging in record time, and worse than men."[27] And when the magazine *Esquire* had an epiphany and decided to celebrate forty-two-year-old women,[28] whom they declared to be not as repulsive as previously thought, the website *Slate* responded with an ironic ode "In Praise of 56-year-old Men . . ." which was the age of the journalist behind the *Esquire* article.[29]

The world of cinema plays its part in normalizing this situation. In 2015, American actor Maggie Gyllenhaal protested publicly after being considered too old, at thirty-seven, to play the lover of a man of fifty-five.[30] Several American media platforms produced graphs showing the routinely vast age gaps on the silver screen, which are much greater than in real life. They tended to read this as a sign that cinema remains a male-dominated industry, where men are able to play out their fantasies.[31] *HuffPost* did the same for French cinema and published similarly revealing graphs—particularly when it came to well-established actors such as Daniel Auteuil, Thierry Lhermitte and François Cluzet—although the gaps were slightly smaller than in the US film industry. It concluded: "We could not find a single major star of French cinema for whom most of his partners were women of his own age.[32] Presenting the Golden Globes ceremony in Hollywood, in 2014, comedian Tina Fey summed up the plot of *Gravity,* in which George Clooney and Sandra Bullock play astronauts, like this: "It's the story of how George Clooney would rather float away into space and die than spend one more minute with a woman his own age."[33]

When, much more rarely, a woman has a partner who is younger than her, far from passing without comment, the age gap is thoroughly chewed over in the gossip mill. The woman will be called a "cougar," a derogatory term implying she is predatory, for which the nearest male equivalent, "silver fox," is, in contrast, complimentary. A friend told me that, at his daughter's primary school, a girl with a crush on a boy in a class below hers was called a cougar. In 2017, the world of politics offered a perfect illustration of this difference in treatment. Twenty-four years older than her husband the President of France, Brigitte Macron was the target of incessant "jokes" and sexist remarks. On one front page of satirical paper *Charlie Hebdo* (10 May 2017), a cartoon by Riss, with the title "He'll do miracles!," showed the new president of the Republic proudly pointing to his wife's rounded belly: the same old way, always and forever, of reducing women to their reproductive usefulness and of stigmatizing menopausal women.[34] By contrast, Donald Trump was the object of numerous jibes attacking (generally with good grounds) almost every aspect of his life, but never the twenty-three years that separate him from his wife Melania.[35]

Books published by women over the last few years shine a harsh light on the degree of misogyny, violence and coercion that can arise in outwardly loving relationships. The heroine of Camille Laurens' depressing novel *Celle que vous croyez* ("The woman you thought"), who is approaching fifty, reinvents herself on Facebook as a seductive single of twenty-four. The publisher presents the book as the story of a woman "who cannot bring herself to give up desire."[36] I can't decide which assumption intrigues me more in this statement: the idea that, at forty-eight, you ought to avoid embarrassing everyone and stop trying to have a love life, or the one whereby "not giving up" turns out to mean cutting your age by half. Whichever you go for, the novel's true subject seems to me to be the abject levels its universally repugnant male protagonists will stoop to. Then there's geographer Sylvie Brunel, who wrote a book drawing on her own story: in 2009, while she was heading up the sadly notorious Ministry for Immigration and National Identity, Brunel's husband Éric Besson, with whom she'd had three children, left her after twenty-six years of marriage, for a twenty-three-year-old student.[37] Brunel enumerates all the women who have similarly been rejected around her, such as Agnès, whose husband declared, when she turned forty-five, that she was nothing but a "fat cow," before maneuvering to expel her from their house so he could begin a new life there with another woman, twenty years younger.

Brunel wonders if the liberation of woman has turned out to be more liberating for men: before divorce became widespread, she notes, they would take mistresses without leaving their wives, which at least guaranteed the latter a degree of material security. Keen to be free, her own ex-husband left her all their assets, but Brunel observes that, for many women, separation entails a sudden and drastic impoverishment: "I know an incredible number of women who've not only been left by their husbands, but have had to confront the dishonesty of partners who've suddenly become penny-pinching, egotistical and hostile, who arrange for their own bankruptcy yet refuse even to provide for the most basic needs of their children"[38]—children for whom the ex-wives naturally retain responsibility. In general, these wives have been carrying out all the domestic and educational work, and have also ended up neglecting or even sacrificing their careers. Brunel describes how Besson never learned to use their washing machine and how, when he won local elections, his constituents used to stop *her* in the street to tell her their problems, using the magical opening formula: "Knowing your husband is very busy . . ." Blandine Lenoir's 2016 film *Aurore* shows the same situation, but in a less well-heeled setting. In it, Agnès Jaoui plays a woman of fifty, a mother of two girls, who has for many years looked after the accounts at her husband's small company. There is no evidence of these years of work—no pension allowance, in particular—for her husband, who then went on to leave her and start another family, never felt the need to issue her payslips. When she walks out of the restaurant where she's been a waitress, she finds herself entirely alone and without resources. The separation becomes a moment of truth, in which the imbalance at the heart of so many couples is revealed and the winner takes it all. In France, 34.9 percent of single-parent families, roughly 2 million people, live below the poverty line, compared to 11.8 percent of people in couples. Eighty-two percent of those single parents are women.[39]

Ever ready to justify inequalities as the result of genetics and simply to ignore the influence of culture, evolutionist thinkers will explain that men are programmed to distribute their genes among the widest possible range of young women, which means women presenting outward signs of fertility, and that the discarding of premenopausal women is just a collateral effect of the demands of perpetuating the species: a sad outcome, but one we should be resigned to.[40] Here, too, however, the existence of just one man who loves and desires his menopausal partner—and of course there are in fact many such men—is enough to disprove this theory, unless we are desperate to diagnose a genetic defect among these men. We may more usefully see in this situation the persistence of our old patriarchal order. In France, up until 2006, the legal age of marriage was eighteen for boys, but fifteen for girls.[41] For sociologist Eric Macé, the age gap among couples today represents a remnant of times "when women were socially defined through reproductive unions," in which, as he aged, the man "increased in economic and social power," whereas the woman "would lose her bodily capital: her beauty and fertility."[42] This order of things is apparently not as far behind us as we thought. Now free, in theory, to earn a living and, like men, to accumulate economic and social power, women are often prevented from doing this by the fact that they are still left with sole responsibility for their children, which is to say by the fact that they are still "defined by their reproductive union." Hence, while still a good thing, easy access to divorce allows men to leave their middle-aged wives for other women whose "bodily capital" remains intact.

Studying the use of the age criterion on the dating website Meetic, Marie Bergström, another sociologist, observed that, from the age of forty onward, after a separation, the proportion of male users looking exclusively for younger women increases. She explains this by noting that it is usually a man's ex-wife who has custody of their children and that the men carry less of the burden of the children's day-to-day education than their exes. For example, a divorced man of forty-four describes how, when they met, his new partner was at first worried by his living far from her home. He assured her this wouldn't be a problem, for "nothing kept him" in the town he was living in, even though he was the father of two teenagers. "For love, I could even have crossed oceans," he said . . . "Separation makes men young again," Bergström concluded. "Single and without children to look after, they are ready for new beginnings and seek out women who, 'equally' young, are likely to share their ambitions." Interestingly, we also find this feeling of youthfulness among single women without children, such as this forty-nine-year-old writer who, wishing to meet a new partner, set her minimum age criterion at thirty-five and the maximum at fifty: "But I was even uneasy with that. I was looking at the pictures of men in their fifties and they looked so old!"[43]

The inequality between the sexes on issues of age is both one of the easiest to spot and one of the hardest to challenge. We cannot *make* people find the signs of a woman's aging beautiful, you will be saying. At the time Sophie Fontanel was treating her Instagram followers to the slow whitening of her coiffure, I found myself stuck ruminating over one of the comments beneath the pics. It read, "Let's be honest here: this looks awful." (Fontanel is smart enough to know that aggressive comments say more about those who write them, about their self-hatred, than about their objects.) How can we be so oblivious to our conditioning, to the prejudice and the long history of imagery that shapes our gaze and forges our ideas of what is beautiful and what is ugly? Those anonymous trolls who harass feminists on Twitter often say the latter are "ugly:" "All rebels are 'ugly,'" according to David Le Breton's analysis.[44] And the American philosopher Mary Daly has observed that "the beauty of strong, creative women is 'ugly' by misogynistic standards of 'beauty.'"[45] To age is to lose your fertility, your seductive powers and your role as the care provider for a husband and children—at least according to the dominant criteria; it makes you a rebel, however unintentionally. To age is to awaken the fear that a woman always inspires when she exists "not only to create and nurture others but to create and nurture her Self," as Cynthia Rich writes.[46] The aging female body acts like "a clear reminder that women have a self that exists not only for others." Given these conditions, how could this body not appear ugly?

The broadly accepted opinion is that wide age gaps in couples and women being abandoned when they reach their mid-to-late forties are something of an inevitability. The broadly accepted opinion is that it's something of an inevitability. The ordinariness of the scenario helps to make it acceptable. "My husband left me for a younger woman. *Ha, ha, ha,*" pronounces Erica, the heroine of Paul Mazursky's 1978 film *An Unmarried Woman*—bitterly. But we can't go banning men from leaving women they no longer love, nor should we put up with feminists giving themselves an even worse rep by sticking their noses into other people's relationship choices. After all, as Woody Allen said of his relationship with Soon-Yi Previn, the adopted daughter of his ex-wife Mia Farrow and thirty-five years younger than him, "the heart wants what it wants."[47] Besides—and more seriously—the age difference that favors men within couples is so profoundly inscribed in our customs that it encompasses widely differing situations. Even when the gap is very big, we cannot exclude the possibility that some of these couples exist simply because society allows them to, without each partner's age being a determining factor in the appeal they hold for the other. It's impossible to declare that the men involved are dominating bastards and the women are submissive idiots or opportunists—aside from anything else, this would require my falling out with around 80 percent of my friends, if not with myself too, and I'm not keen to do that. And yet . . . the phenomenon could do with closer scrutiny.

An Eternal Freeze-Frame?

The American series *Broad City* portrays the adventures of two young, broke New Yorkers, Ilana and Abbi. At the start of one episode first broadcast in October 2017, Ilana spots Abbi's first gray hair and trumpets her envy: "You are becoming a witch: a dope and powerful fucking witch!" Abbi does not share her excitement. Later in the day, as if privileged with a new aura, she does indeed seem to meet a witch, but she also bumps into her ex-boyfriend out walking with his partner and their child. Depressed, she cracks and goes to a dermatologist to get Botox injections. (Meanwhile, Ilana is consulting a high priestess of sex therapy because she has not been able to reach orgasm since Trump's election.) The dermatologist is fifty-one, but looks twenty years younger. She cheerfully explains, "It's hard to be beautiful these days. It is my full-time job, but, for most other women, it's their second full-time job, where you're *losing* money." Alarmed by the rather extreme before-and-after photos of women that adorn the surgery walls, Abbi begins to regret going there. Before making her escape, she tells the dermatologist, "I think you're really beautiful, and I think you would be even if you didn't do all this crazy shit to your face." At this, the dermatologist bursts out laughing, before stopping short, in horror: "Oh no. I laughed . . ." and patting her face anxiously. (The episode ends with a great sabbath meeting in the middle of Central Park, bringing together Ilana, the sex therapist and other witches. Abbi brings the dermatologist along too.)[48]

In an attempt to spare themselves the sad fate of the abandoned and humiliated ex-partner, and more generally the opprobrium associated with age, women who can afford it do indeed work hard to keep their appearance as unchanged as possible. They are accepting an absurd challenge. They must pretend time is not passing, and therefore look the only way society dictates it is acceptable for a woman over thirty to look: like a young woman who has been pickled alive. The greatest ambition we may foster is to be "well preserved." Of course, celebrities feel the pressure more than most. At more than sixty years old, Inès de la Fressange has maintained her lean body, her smooth-skinned face and the helmet of chestnut hair she had when she first trod the catwalk for Chanel, forty years ago. The top models of the 1990s may genuinely spend their entire lives (and a good portion of their fortunes) making sure that, every time they appear in public, the world says "Wow! She hasn't changed!" This must have been the intention behind the Versace show of September 2017, in which Carla Bruni, Claudia Schiffer, Naomi Campbell, Cindy Crawford and Helena Christensen came together once more, all dressed in the same design of a super-skintight gold dress, revealing their figures to be just as slender and their legs as chiseled as ever. Donatella Versace explained that she took her inspiration for this show from a 1994 campaign in which Crawford had posed with her peers in exactly that dress. On social media, some saw the occasion as the return of "real women." But Sophie Fontanel commented:

It's funny in the first place, really, to call women who have been almost entirely remastered by aesthetic treatments "real." I say that without ill will, for everyone should do as they wish and can. It's just that this viral image gives us a very topsy-turvy view of women—to see women who have changed as little as possible in twenty-five years: no wrinkles, no flab, no white hair, as if changing were the one thing absolutely to be avoided.

Fontanel concluded: "The representation of women at fifty, in all their beauty and freedom, remains uncharted land."[49]

In polar opposition to this vicious cycle, American photographer Nicholas Nixon has been taking a black-and-white portrait of his wife, Bebe Brown, and her three sisters, Heather, Mimi and Laurie, annually since 1975. In this way, he calmly documents their aging, showing each woman as an object of interest and affection, allowing the viewer to imagine each woman's interior world, their relationships to each other and the events they have lived through. "We are bombarded by images of women every day—in entertainment, in advertising, in art, on social media—but depictions of women who are visibly aging remain too rare," observes journalist Isabel Flower, writing on Nixon's project. She continues:

> Stranger still, women whom we know to have aged are often made to appear as if they have not, suspended in a state of quixotic youthfulness, verging on the bionic. But Nixon [. . .] is interested in these women as subjects, not just as images, and he's committed to documenting the passage of time, not defying it. Year by year, his portraits of the Brown sisters have come to mark the progress of all of our lives.[50]

Interesting fact: in 2017, the American magazine *Allure* announced that it would henceforth ban the description "anti-aging," used of beauty treatments and cosmetics, from its pages. "If there's one inevitability in life, it's that we're getting older," wrote its chief editor, Michelle Lee:

> Every minute. Every second. [. . .] Growing older is a wonderful thing because it means that we get

a chance, every day, to live a full, happy life. [. . .] Language matters. When talking about a woman over, say, 40, people tend to add qualifiers: "She looks great . . . for her age" or "She's beautiful . . . for an older woman." Catch yourself next time and consider what would happen if you just said, "She looks great." [. . .] I'm not going to lie and say that everything about aging is great. [. . .] But we need to stop looking at our life as a hill that we start rolling uncontrollably down past 35.[51]

A grab bag of platitudes? Perhaps—but sometimes these platitudes can become an issue of life or death. In Switzerland, in 2016, the assisted-suicide group Exit helped an octogenarian to die who had no incurable condition, and this led to an inquiry. Her doctor explained that this "extremely flirtatious" old lady "could not stand growing old."[52] As it was confirmed that she was entirely sound of mind, the case was closed. But would we see a man request assistance to die for this reason?

In her book *Une Apparition* ("An apparition"), Sophie Fontanel sets out her philosophy: "Women are not condemned to remain exactly as they were in their youth. They have the right to enrich themselves with a new look, a new kind of beauty."[53] (And she specifies: "I would not call this a duty; every woman will do as they see best." Similarly, I am striving to show here what society expects of us and what it forbids, but I do not mean that we should all, always, oppose it systematically. Being a woman is no simple thing, and each of us will make our own decisions—which are always amenable to change, in one way or another—as best we can and wish.) Even a fearless and exemplary feminist like Benoîte Groult did not take on board that beauty and youth can be quite separate things: "Worrying about one's beauty is not in itself antifeminist," she insisted, under pressure to explain her facelift—and given what she has described of the miserable fate reserved for aging women of her milieu, her choice is understandable.[54] In contrast, Fontanel insists on this distinction: "I do not seek out youth, I seek out beauty," she writes.[55] As for me, looking back through photos of my twenty-five-year-old self, I do feel an initial twinge of regret for my baby-smooth skin and completely brown hair. But, at the end of the day, I prefer my gray locks. I look less ordinary. Ignoring the often confused or disapproving views others may have, I like the idea of letting my hair metamorphose slowly, developing its own new tints and lights, with the softness and glow they lend it. The idea of smothering this distinctive feature with an off-the-shelf dye depresses me. And besides, I like the feeling of confidently entrusting myself to the embrace of time as it flows, instead of tensing against it, trying to resist.

Our anxious obsession with preserving the appearance of extreme youth effectively establishes a gulf between the categories of young woman and old woman. White hair is all the more powerfully associated with aging and infertility for being seen almost exclusively among older women; and yet, it's not rare for it to begin appearing in your late twenties or even earlier. In autumn 2017, Sarah Harris, fashion editor for British *Vogue*, who is well known for her long gray hair, posted a surprising photo of herself on Instagram, with her newborn daughter in the crook of her arm—an unusual association of the signs of aging with signs of fecundity. Harris has said that she found her first gray hairs at sixteen and stopped dyeing her hair in her twenties.[56] But, more than anything, the delusional diktat of eternal youth—one of the many circles it's been left up to us to square—condemns women to live never-never lives, in thrall to our own shame. In 2007, American writer Anne Kreamer published a book about accepting her white hair. The realization had come to her at forty-nine, after years of dyeing her hair without a second thought, upon seeing a photo in which she was posing between her blond daughter and a white-haired friend. She got a shock:

> I felt like I was a black hole between gaily dressed Kate and about-to-burst-into-laughter Aki. My uniform of deep, dark mahogany hair and dark clothing sucked all light out of my presence. Seeing that person—that version of myself—was like a kick to my solar plexus. In one second, all my years of careful artifice, attempting to preserve what I thought of as a youthful look, were ripped away. All I saw was a kind of confused, schlubby middle-aged woman with hair dyed much too harshly. [. . .] Kate looked real. Aki looked real. To me, I looked like I was pretending to be someone I wasn't.[57]

For Fontanel, too, it was the obligation to pretend that began to feel depressing—she "could no longer stand to see herself colored up by post-production," she says.[58] The restriction was spoiling everyday life: every time she emerged from water while on holiday, instead of enjoying the pleasure of bathing and sunshine, she was afraid people would see the white roots in her wet hair. Women's obligation to look young forever now seems to her a subtle way of neutralizing them: we force them to cheat, then we turn their cheating into grounds to denounce their fakeness, the more easily to dismiss them.[59] And indeed, if actresses don't want to attract hate-filled comments about their aging looks, they may feel driven, instead, to run the alternative risk of ridicule should their cosmetic surgeon turn out to be somewhat heavy-handed. (Susan Sontag defined actresses as "highly paid professionals at doing what all women are taught to practice as amateurs."[60])

When Women Start to *Talk Back*

After all, we have to consider: what if all this effort actually achieves nothing? "Pretending to be young and being young are two different things, and anyone who looks closely will know the difference," as Anne Kreamer notes.[61] There is something perverse in making women run a race that they've all already lost. What's more, even if a woman manages the feat of preserving her thirty-year-old appearance or, according to general opinion, "still" looks great "for her age," the temptation for her partner to find a new life with a younger model often seems to be irresistible. The opening shots of *An Unmarried Woman* show an apparently ideal couple: after seventeen years of marriage, well-off New Yorkers and parents of a teenage daughter, Erica and Martin, are still bound by great mutual understanding. They have a fulfilling sex life; they laugh and talk things through. But Erica's world suddenly crumbles when her husband dissolves into tears and admits he has fallen in love with a woman of twenty-six. Erica's preservation of her youthful body hasn't made the slightest difference. In real life, even Sharon Stone, without a doubt one of the most famous women to make a serious attempt *not to grow old* and whose exploits in this realm were often relayed by popular press outlets, saw her marriage founder and her husband pick up a younger woman. Jane Fonda similarly was left by her second husband for a woman twenty years younger. And, after his separation, at the end of an eighteen-year relationship, from the sublime Monica Bellucci—who is two years older than him—actor Vincent Cassel found his next partner in a model thirty years his junior.

In her book, Sylvie Brunel describes her impression, when her husband left, of not recognizing the man with whom she had shared her life, of finding herself face to face with a stranger. Indeed, when a man in middle life exchanges his partner for a younger one, in retrospect this can cast doubt on the motivations that until then had kept him in the first relationship. The woman who is left may wonder if all he desired about her was her youthfulness, if what he enjoyed was principally all the work she did for him, along with the status he gained through their partnership and through fatherhood. But one question demands an answer first of all: what if this man can only love a woman whom he dominates? This set-up implies a double abuse: of the woman who is rejected, but also, more subtly, of the new partner. Talking about his relationship with Soon-Yi Previn, Woody Allen specified that he did not consider equality a prerequisite in a couple: "Sometimes equality in a relationship is great, sometimes inequality makes it work."[62] Even if the degree of inequality isn't always huge, and while happily it is not always deliberate, an age difference increases the likelihood that the man will have the advantage from at least one perspective, be it social, professional, financial or intellectual. It may therefore prove that some men are interested less in a woman's youthful body than in what it indicates: a partner of lower standing and with less life experience. (The exclusive erotic focus on younger bodies is based on a false assumption, for, once again, it is well known that, even at forty-five plus, men's bodies are often considered desirable.)

In the current schema for men's upbringing and socialization, as we have said, "there is no Princess Charming." On the contrary: men learn to mistrust love, to see it as a trap, a threat to their independence, and to see the couple almost as a necessary evil.[63] Women are conditioned to wait for the love that will make them happy, that will bring them the wealth and pleasure of shared intimacy, that will show them who they truly are. So they show their readiness to make any sacrifice, to the extent of masochism, in order to "make it work." When a woman enters a relationship wanting it with all her being, while the other partner is dragged into it reluctantly, all the ingredients for a fool's bargain come together. (Sylvie Brunel describes how Éric Besson humiliated her publicly—at their wedding—by rejecting loud and clear the commitment to fidelity ordinarily made between spouses.) Even when they take part with good grace and give the impression of full involvement, men who have assimilated their conditioning will still remain single at heart, in the sense that they never entirely buy into the shared life their partners aspire to. They will accept it as a task, a nuisance, a risk. They just want a peaceful life. Psychology guides that claim to teach women the art of communicating with men without annoying them, haunted as they are by the figure of the "nag," are categorical on this point. For example, one suggests: "When he comes home, exhausted after a long and demanding day at work, don't throw yourself at him with a hundred questions on the things that matter to you, such as the future of your relationship and the nature of his feelings for you."[64] By which the woman should understand that it was *she* who asked to be there, and she, therefore, who must make the greater effort. (For the same reason, we should avoid asking men to prepare the dinner or take out the rubbish; or, should we dare, only do so with the employment of many circumlocutions, and much cooing and flattery.)

It follows that, for men, an aging partner is problematic in that she no longer passes for a representative of the generic category of "young woman," with all the qualities of a fresh, inoffensive ingénue that we more or less consciously associate with it—not always correctly, I should add. With time, a woman's individuality will have come to the fore. She will have gained experience, if not confidence. Now, the tolerance threshold is low: a woman who is self-assured, who asserts her opinions, her desires and dislikes, is very swiftly written off as a harpy, a virago, by both her partner and her peers. (One girlfriend told me how, when she happens to correct or contradict her partner in front of their friends, it never goes unremarked; when the opposite occurs, their friends don't even notice.) Valerie Solanas described the consequences of the muzzle thus permanently imposed on women like this:

Niceness, politeness, "dignity," insecurity and self-absorption are hardly conducive to intensity and wit, qualities a conversation must have to be worthy of the name. Such conversation is hardly rampant, as only completely self-confident, arrogant, outgoing, proud, tough-minded females are capable of intense, bitchy, witty conversation.[65]

A man who is not interested in give and take between equals will prefer to turn to someone younger. He is more likely to find unconditional admiration from such an audience, and that's more flattering than the gaze of the woman who knows him intimately, having lived with him for ten, fifteen or twenty years, even if she still loves him. In my book *Beauté Fatale* ("Fatal Beauty"), I supported the theory that those who go for younger women are mostly just trying to live within a mental comfort zone, and I quoted these comments by Francesca Magugliani—a close collaborator of John Casablancas, who founded Elite modeling agency—on Casablancas' relationships: "When you reach eighteen, you start thinking and becoming intelligent. The day the girl matured and had a mind of her own, it was finished. John wants adulation. They'd start talking back to him."[66] This psychological comfort involves an "erotics of ventriloquism"—in which the dominant partner projects their feelings and desires onto the other partner—which is so widespread that we generally mistake it for eroticism full stop.[67] Unquestionably a shady character, in 2016 Casablancas was the subject of a hagiographic biopic which was celebrated by women's magazines across the board. Titled *The Man Who Loved Women*, it could more accurately have been called *The Man Who Loved Under-Eighteens*. Singer Claude François acknowledged similar tastes: "I like girls up to seventeen, eighteen; after that, I start to steer clear. Do I have affairs with some over-eighteens? Of course I do, luckily. But, after eighteen, I get wary because they start to think, they're not natural anymore. Sometimes it starts even earlier."[68]

If the witch-hunts particularly targeted older women, it is likely because they displayed an unbearable degree of confidence. Confronted by their neighbors, by priests or pastors, even before judges and torturers, these women *talked back*; as Anne Barstow writes, they "talked back in a time when they were increasingly expected to be submissive."[69] They were better able to do so, being unconstrained by a father, husband or children. These were women "given to speaking out, to a bold tongue and independent spirit."[70] It is no surprise that such unwelcome, even feared speech could be taken for wicked enchantment. For the historian John Demos, the primary motivation of witchcraft accusations against women of middle or advanced age in New England was their "uppity" attitude, especially in regard to their husbands. Back then, if you fitted the stereotype of the nag—still alive and kicking today!—you were dicing with death. In sixteenth-century England and Scotland, women's insolence could be punished by use of the "scold's bridle" or "witch's bridle:" an iron frame that enclosed a woman's head and secured her tongue with a bit that was often covered in spikes, such that any attempt to move her tongue or mouth would cause the "bridled" woman to be appallingly pricked.

Watchwomen of the Borders

More broadly, what seems most problematic about women's aging is their *experience*. This is what led so many old women to the pyres: "Spellcraft was an art. [Witches] had had to work at their lessons, to learn their knowledge, to gain experience: older women therefore naturally appeared more suspect than younger ones," Guy Bechtel explains.[71] Disney classics such as *Snow White and the Seven Dwarfs* and *Sleeping Beauty* "depict generational clashes between old witches and young beauties, pegging a woman's worth on fertility and youth— never hard-won wisdom," observes Kristen J. Sollée.[72] This has to be one reason why white hair is accepted on men but ill received on women: the experience the color denotes is considered reassuring and attractive in men, but threatening in women. In France, indignant that people felt free to criticize his appearance (poor thing!), right-wing politician Laurent Wauquiez denied having dyed his hair gray in order to appear more experienced and to inspire greater confidence, as *Le Monde* alleged.[73] The mere fact that such a suspicion was plausible speaks volumes.

"Hag" was not pejorative in its original usage: it described "the wise woman who sat on the hedge—the boundary between the village and the wild, the human world and the spirit world," in Starhawk's explanation.[74] With the witch-hunts, this once valued and sacred knowledge and power came to be seen as dangerous, fatal even. Analyzing Hans Baldung's sixteenth-century painting *The Three Ages of Man and Death*, the central figure of which is an old woman, historian Lynn Botelho observes:

> It is the marks of sex and sexuality on an old body that draw viewers in, while simultaneously causing them to look down and away, where their gaze con-

fronts the figure of an owl, whose association with the night, darkness and evil was well known. The panel's background confirms the owl's dark meaning. It is stark, dead, and destroyed, with moss-covered dead trees, war-ravaged fortifications, and a clouded and veiled sun; it is the old woman who anchors this scene of decay and destruction, almost as if she has caused it.[75]

The disqualification of women's experience represents an immense loss to and mutilation of our collective knowledge. Urging women to change as little as possible and censoring the signs of their maturing means locking them into a debilitating schema. A moment's thought reveals the insane idealization entailed by our cult of youthfulness. One of the reasons I have avoided motherhood is that nothing on earth could persuade me to guide a new person through those terrible ordeals known as childhood and adolescence; I could not stand to relive them through my child, to see my child tested by the same trials, the same tasks, to come up against the same setbacks due to awkwardness, naivety and ignorance. Childhood is characterized by fabulous capacities of perception and imagination—to which we may hark back for the rest of our lives—but also by truly distressing vulnerability and impotence. There is a pleasure in taking stock of all that we have understood, learned and achieved over the years, and in sensing the exponential increase of our ease in the world.

Of course, time's passing also lays us open to unhappiness, disappointment and regret. But if we are lucky enough not to have experienced major tragedy—or, sometimes, even if we have—age will bring us perspective, and, with it, room for maneuver: the capacity to work as we wish in our lives. I think of everything in me that has been appeased, balanced and tamed, everything I have purged, living with ever fewer scruples and hesitations, happy at last to have a free hand, able to get to the heart of things. Every occasion, every encounter resonates with the preceding occasions and encounters and deepens their importance. Friendships, loves and thoughts grow, develop, are refined and enriched. Time's passing feels to me like that moment when, on a mountain hike, you're approaching the summit and you become able to picture the landscape you will see when you reach the highest point. Of course, there is no summit to time, we all die before we get there, but the mere sensation of its closeness is exhilarating. To go on forever playing out the helplessness and vulnerability of early youth allows us to pass in a society that condemns confident women—but this forces women to give up the greatest sources of potency and pleasure in life. A few years ago, a *Marie Claire* article entitled "Plus belles à quarante-cinq ans qu'à vingt-cinq!" ("More beautiful at forty-five than at twenty-five!") presented a rather bizarre argument. Women in their fifties struggle to believe they are ever more attractive to men, the journalist explained, then added: "The greater their self-doubt, the more they move us. Now, as we know, when it comes to seduction, vulnerability is a deadly weapon . . ." At all ages, it seems, the key is to preserve your capacity to pass as a poor defenseless little thing.

Despite the censure of society, with age we do gain a strength which sometimes allows us to reconfigure life's trials. In 1978, suffering from breast cancer at the age of forty-four, "the very years when women are portrayed in the popular media as fading and desexualised figures," African-American poet and essayist Audre Lorde commented:

> Contrary to the media picture, I find myself as a woman of insight ascending into my highest powers, my greatest psychic strengths, and my fullest satisfactions. I am freer of the constraints and fears and indecisions of my younger years, and survival throughout these years has taught me how to value my own beauty, and how to look closely into the beauty of others. It has also taught me to value the lessons of survival, as well as my own perceptions. I feel more deeply, value those feelings more, and can put those feelings together with what I know in order to fashion a vision of and pathway toward true change. Within this time of assertion and growth, even the advent of a life-threatening cancer and the trauma of a mastectomy can be integrated into the life-force as knowledge and eventual strength, fuel for a more dynamic and focused existence.[76]

The years bring a sense of clarification superbly expressed by Gloria Steinem in *Revolution from Within*, which was written when she was approaching sixty. She describes fleeting encounters with younger versions of herself, in familiar New York streets that she has been roaming for decades.

> She can't see me in the future, but I can see her very clearly. She runs past me, worried about being late for

an appointment she doesn't want to go to. She sits at a restaurant table in tears of anger arguing with the wrong lover. She strides toward me in the jeans and wine-red suede boots she wore for a decade, and I can remember the exact feel of those boots on my feet. [. . .] She rushes toward me outside a lecture hall, talking, laughing, full of optimism.

Fortified by the time that has passed since then, Steinem observes this former self with mixed feelings.

I used to feel impatient with her: Why was she wasting time? Why was she with this man? at that appointment? forgetting to say the most important thing? Why wasn't she wiser, more productive, happier? But lately, I've begun to feel a tenderness, a welling of tears in the back of my throat, when I see her. I think: *She's doing the best she can. She's survived—and she's trying so hard.* Sometimes, I wish I could go back and put my arms around her.[77]

The Figure of Choice for Abjection

While older women are indeed feared for their experience, it is also the case that the aging female body inspires genuine revulsion—and this helps lift the lid on the revulsion inspired by the female body at any age. Sylvie Brunel, as she appears in her book, and the character of Aurore, protagonist of the eponymous fictional film, both discover the horror their physical aging seems to induce. On one visit to her ex-husband, who is looking after the two little girls he has with his new partner, Aurore has to take off her jumper because of a sudden hot flush. She begins to explain, but he stops her short and covers his ears in order not to hear the word "menopause." Sylvie Brunel describes how an editor to whom she outlined her book project replied, "I think you have nothing to gain by talking about that. You will damage your image . . . There are some words that shock, that's all. 'Menopause' is like 'hemorrhoids:' a topic we don't talk about . . ." And when one of her friends wonders whether to follow a menopause-symptoms treatment that could bring increased risk of cancer, her gynecologist responds, "Better to have cancer than the menopause. At least we can treat cancer."[78]

One way to interpret the scenario of the woman rejected in midlife is to understand that her partner can no longer bear to see in her, as if in a mirror, the signs of his own aging. Or perhaps he leaves his middle-aged wife so that he is free to rejuvenate himself via a new partner: "Loving the next generation is a kind of vampirism," according to Frédéric Beigbeder, for example, who takes pride in his "Dracula side."[79] But we may also consider a different theory: he sees his wife's aging, but not his own. "Men have no bodies"—so says Virginie Despentes, who, in my opinion, we should be taking at her word.[80] Men's dominant position in economics and politics, in love and family relationships, but also in the artistic and literary worlds allows them to be absolute subjects and to make women into absolute objects. Western culture decided early on that the body was repulsive—and also that it was female, and vice versa. Theologians and philosophers projected their horror of the body onto women, and were thereby able to disavow the claims of their own bodies. Saint Augustine explains that, in men, the body reflects the soul, but that this isn't the case for women.[81] Saint Ambrose concurs, asserting that man is soul while woman is sensation.[82] In the tenth century, Abbot Odo of Cluny robustly challenged his peers: "We who are loath to touch vomit and dung, even with our fingertips, how is it we love to embrace in our arms this sack of ordure?" Both the distrust and the archaic views here are alive and well today. As in earlier times, "there are almost no bodies that are not female" in the artistic, journalistic and advertising images that surround us, as David Le Breton observes.[83] And our evergreen taste for perfect physiques does not prevent a widespread revulsion toward the female body—on the contrary. As if echoing Odo, on 21 December 2015, during a rally on the presidential campaign trail, Donald Trump remarked on Hillary Clinton's brief absence when she took advantage of an ad break to go to the toilet: "I know where she went—it's disgusting, I don't want to talk about it. No, it's too disgusting. Don't say it, it's disgusting."[84] (Americans: you had a narrow escape! You just missed being led by someone who uses toilets.)

For Jean Delumeau, "repugnance toward the 'second sex' was increased by the spectacle of the decrepitude of a being closer to the earth than men were, and therefore more rapidly and more visibly 'perishable' than he who could claim to embody the soul."[85] The degree to which Delumeau himself buys into this reasoning is hard to gauge, but we can see that, logically, it is absurd. However much men "claim to embody the soul," they remain as "close to the earth" as women, and their decay is no less rapid or visible. The only additional power they have is that of making it so that their decay is not counted against them. In the private sphere, in the street, at work and in Parliament, men can signal loud and clear the pleasure or displeasure occasioned them by the sight of women's bodies or clothes, their weight or their age, without their own body or clothes, weight or age ever coming under fire. In order to attack Clinton over her need, occasionally, to answer a call of nature, Trump must be able to pretend, at least implicitly, that he himself has neither bladder nor guts. It must take an unbelievable nerve to pull this one—but it's a temerity handed on a plate to Trump by nearly two millennia of misogynist culture. This is a pure example of the arbitrary power permitted by a dominant position: men don't have bodies *because*. End of.

Delumeau points out that "the Renaissance and the Baroque period have bequeathed, particularly from the pens of aristocratic poets such as Ronsard, De Bellay, Agrippa d'Aubigné, Sigogne, Saint-Amant, etc., a wretched portrait of the typical ugly old woman, who was most often presented as a skeletal carcass."[86] Ronsard did not hesitate to recommend his reader "drop the old one" and "pick up a new one."[87] His poem "Contre Denise Sorcière" ("Invective Against Denise, a Witch"[88]) is nothing but a long litany of insults addressed to an old lady from the Vendôme who had been accused of witchcraft and whipped naked. "In the West, female old age becomes the preferred figuration of abjection," writes Antonio Domingues Leiva. Women's demonization in sermons and ministries establishes a "code of hideousness from which a straight line can be traced directly to the feminicide of the sixteenth century." This "code of hideousness" is still in force. In a sociological inquiry into "the social world of old women," published in 1979, in the US, one of the respondents described, for example, how a group of children, at whom she had smiled upon meeting them in the street, shouted back, "You're ugly, ugly, ugly."[89]

Why should a woman's white hair so often lead people to presume that she is "letting herself go"—if not because her hair instantly recalls the image of a witch dressed in rags? Analyzing how a group of old women were described in a local press article, in Boston, in 1982, Cynthia Rich picked out that, according to the journalist, one of them had "well-cared for gray hair"; would this detail have seemed necessary if the hair had been blond or brown?[90] Sophie Fontanel describes how, when she stopped dyeing her hair, one of her friends was as horrified as if she "had stopped washing."[91] In her case, the assumption of neglect is all the more revelatory for being so far from the truth: we are talking, here, about an elegant and well-turned-out woman, with taste, someone who works in fashion . . . During the period of her transition between dyed hair and white, the short-circuiting of this antediluvian assumption often plunged passers-by into confusion:

> Disconcerted, eyes would rush to my roots. Then, just as suddenly, they would jump from my hair to my clothes, as if some indicator might be there, some overall "laxness" I might have adopted. Some explanation. But if they observed my attire, as it were, they saw well-pressed clothes and a fair dose of vanity. I had given up nothing more than the dye.[92]

The immediate association of women's aging with death is still hanging on with remarkable tenacity, as shown by this unexpectedly aggressive rant that an Italian journalist addressed to Fontanel:

> You do realize that, when we die, our hair and nails keep growing, and that makes things . . . It's terrifying. It's a real horror story. Three centimeters of white hair leap out at you if you should ever happen to open the coffin lid a few days after burial. Well, having said that, you'll say no one ever opens the coffin, or it's very rare, thank God. But you, you're planning to go walking around with the coffin lid open, in full view of all and sundry![93]

Similarly, a friend speculated that the reason she disliked seeing her mother with white hair could be because that prompted thoughts of her death. But who thinks about death when they see Richard Gere or Harrison Ford?

Frequently, too, in literature and visual art, we find a dramatic juxtaposition between images of seductive women and images of decay and death. Delumeau notes "the ongoing presence and long standing of the iconographic and literary theme of the apparently comely woman whose back, breasts or belly are already rotting."[94] In the nineteenth century, Charles Baudelaire takes up this theme in his poem "Une Charogne" ("A Carrion"). Out walking with his lover, the narrator comes upon a decomposing animal, which he describes with a flurry of self-indulgent details. His first thought is to see in this object the future fate of the woman at his side—certainly not his own:

And yet you will be like this excrement,
This horrible stench,
O star of my eyes, sun of my being,
You, my angel, my passion.[95]

This association has not yet disappeared from our lives today. We still indulge in a kind of quasi-automatic narrative reflex, as in this scene from season six of *Game of Thrones* (2016). In the privacy of her candlelit bedroom, Melisandre, the "red witch," who has used her charms to make several of the men in the series submit to her, takes off her necklace and contemplates her true self in the mirror: she is a bowed and sad-eyed old woman, with only a few white hairs left, drooping breasts and a sagging belly. We may find these confrontations seem to stave off our worst fears; they offer a kind of relief, even triumph, for this body whose withering we anticipate or notice is losing its attractions and with them the power that it used to wield over the male subject. But they also suggest that aging reveals women's fundamental darkness and malignity. "We seem to think that nature always shows in the end—that women, though beautiful in their youth, will sooner or later come to look like what they truly are: people whose hearts are ugly," Bechtel comments.[96]

Desire Demonized

Older women's sexuality also gave rise to particular fears around the time of the witch-hunts. No longer having the formal right to a sex life—since they could no longer have children and were, in many cases, widowed—yet experienced and still interested in sex, these women appeared as immoral and threatening forces in the social order. They were assumed to be bitter—for they had lost the respected status that went with the role of the mother—and envious of younger women. In the fifteenth century, as Lynn Botelho writes, a direct connection is established of "post-menopausal women with witches and, in turn, their association with anti-fertility."[97] These older women are seen as "oversexed [. . .] sexually insatiable and [not to] be satisfied by mere mortal men."[98] In *In Praise of Folly*, Erasmus gives an eloquent description of this type: "our old Women, even dead with age, and such skeletons one would think they had stoln out of their graves, and ever mumbling in their mouths 'Life is sweet'"[99] Once again, we find the stamp of this imagery reflected in the horrified words of Fontanel's Italian journalist: "How do you see your sex life? Can you picture yourself riding some guy with your witchy hair? Men are already afraid of women; but if we go about frightening them right off, poor things, we shouldn't be surprised if one day they can't get it up at all!"[100]

These hellish visions beg the question of whether another meaning may not be hidden behind the term "letting yourself go," so frequently associated with white hair. In November 2017, the women's magazine *Grazia* put Sophie Fontanel on its cover, marking a step in the right direction. But, on the pages inside, an article of advice on hair care encouraged women tempted to copy Fontanel's dye-less look to "choose a short, structured style with geometric lines, otherwise you risk looking somewhat unkempt."[101] It's a classic line to take. The aim is to minimize the extent of this offensive mop of hair, but also to impose a clear distinction between two categories of women: on one side, those who may retain their sensuality, their desire for seduction, thanks to their blond, chestnut, red or brown hair, whether natural or dyed; on the other, those who are "giving up" and must indicate this with their hyper-restrained haircut. We can assume that a white mane revives the notion of the sabbath and of witches giving free rein to their desires, breaking away from all constraints. A few years before this article, another magazine was alternatively insisting on "discipline": "Gray is pretty in a neat cut and for well-disciplined hair (although it need not be short). Curly heads, however, should keep up the dye job."[102]

"Disheveled, disobedient or unruly hair is an alleged telltale sign of witches," writes Judika Illes, an American writer on the esoteric. "Even if she tries to keep her hair under control, a witch's hair will spring out from beneath a headscarf or refuse to remain in a braid."[103] In *The Witches of Eastwick*, when at last Jane Spofford (Sarandon) fully accepts her powers and desires, she allows her impressive head of frizzy ginger hair, previously held back in a tight plait, to cascade over her shoulders. With her white, untamed hair, remarkable both for its color and its freedom, singer Patti Smith—who goes on practicing her art without the least concern for looking pretty, restrained or delicate, as is generally expected of women—is the epitome of a modern witch. In 2008, the *New York Times Magazine* could not help asking this living legend of rock why she never used conditioner—a question of *smoothing out* the tangle, I suppose.[104] In the same way that "sad," used of a single person, may often actually mean "dangerous," could "letting herself go" in fact really mean "liberated," even "uncontrollable"?

In his description of the foolish old women (the French

translation offers "*vieilles amoureuses*"—"old lover-ladies"), Erasmus went on to describe how, "to set themselves off better, they shall paint and daub their faces, always stand a tricking up themselves at their looking-glass, go naked-necked, bare-breasted, be tickled at a smutty jest, dance among the young girls, write love-letters, and do all the other little knacks of decoying hot-blooded suitors."[105] Still today, when a well-known woman of forty-plus takes a younger lover, even if she is far from appearing like the very old women described above, the vocabulary chosen by the popular press plainly insinuates that the man is a kind of gigolo: there is talk of Sharon Stone, Demi Moore, Robin Wright or Madonna's "toy boy." As it happens, while married to Demi Moore (who was sixteen years his senior), actor Ashton Kutcher starred in a sex comedy film called *Spread*—or *Toy Boy*, for most of its European markets. Yet we do not accuse—at least not openly—the younger partners of famous older men of venality, even though these men take much less care over the youthfulness of their appearance than their female counterparts.

When, at fifty-one, Monica Bellucci admitted finding something "very erotic" about the "potency" emanating from older men such as Mick Jagger, *Paris-Match* magazine was flabbergasted: "Are we to understand from this that your libido is as strong as it was when you were twenty?"[106] And the world tottered on its axis at the very idea. Given that the dominant line tells us women are no longer attractive after forty-five—at the very maximum—we must naively assume that, at this age, women's libido vanishes in a puff of smoke. This amounts to folding the desire women feel together with the desire they are meant to arouse: ventriloquized eroticism,

once more. And it explains the persistence of the taboo
around older women's sex lives, which is all the more unfair,
as Sontag noted, given that women tend to come later to sexual fulfillment than men:

> not for innate biological reasons but because this cul-
> ture retards women. Denied most outlets for sexual
> energy permitted to men, it takes many women *that*
> long to wear out some of their inhibitions. The time
> at which they start being disqualified as sexually at-
> tractive persons is just when they have grown up sex-
> ually. The double standard about aging cheats women
> of those years, between thirty-five and fifty, likely to
> be the best of their sexual life.[107]

In 2000, in Portugal, a former cleaning lady, Maria Ivone
Carvalho Pinto de Sousa Morais, lodged a complaint at Lis-
bon's administrative court. Five years earlier, when she was
in her fifties, a surgical disaster had left her with difficulty
sitting and walking, intense pain and gynecological problems
that ruled out any kind of sex life. The court ruled in her favor
and granted her compensation, the total of which was reduced
the following year by the Supreme Court. The basis for this
reduction was as follows:

> With all due consideration for the injuries caused
> to the plaintiff, we believe that the sum granted in
> compensation is excessive. It has not in fact been con-
> firmed that the plaintiff has lost her capacity to carry
> out her domestic tasks [. . .] and, taking into account

her children's ages, she is likely only to be looking after her husband, which excludes the necessity for a full-time hired help in the home. [. . .] Furthermore, we must not forget that at the time of the operation, the plaintiff was already fifty, had given birth twice, and at this age, not only is sex no longer as important as in her youth, but her interest in it will be diminished with her age.

In the summer of 2017, the European Court of Human Rights concluded, on the contrary, in the plaintiff's favor. Of the seven European judges, two (from Luxembourg and Slovenia) remained in opposition, which provoked an acerbic confrontation between them and their two female colleagues (from Ukraine and Romania).[108]

Creating Another Law

"We were madly in love. I have rarely known such an intense physical passion. As soon as we met again, we would devour each other, literally. We could spend days on end without leaving my bedroom . . ."

In the 2005 film *Aurore,* the heroine, having become a professional cleaner, is hired to work at a retirement home run by women—the Maison des Babayagas, in Montreuil, although it isn't named in the film. Faced with many set-backs and disappointments in her personal life, one day, while cleaning the floor, she cracks and begins to cry. One of the residents, played by a genuine "baba yaga," Arghyro Bardis, known as Iro (who died shortly after filming), tries to console her. The two women have a long conversation, during which the older woman, who is more than seventy, retells a memory of love. "When was this?" asks Aurore, dreamily. We too expect this to be a memory cherished from a now-distant youth. Bardis's reply: "Three years ago. Such happiness we had. And then life came between us . . ." Aurore's delighted surprise is written all over her face. When, later, she goes on her way, walking down the road in the shelter of her umbrella, she smiles to herself. While, up to this point, she had been fielding rejection after rejection, always coming up against prejudice that excluded her, from this moment she unwittingly opens a door onto a world governed, as she discovers, by other laws—a world of fantasy, freedom and generosity, the existence of which she hadn't even imagined possible.

In 2006, the feminist activist Thérèse Clerc, who was bisexual, appeared in Jean-Luc Raynaud's superb documentary *L'Art de vieillir* ("The art of growing old"), which profiled five elderly French retirees, asking for their thoughts on aging, sex and death. "They're my fabulous sexual adventures," she explained, wickedly, three years later. "We showed it to some secondary-school students last week: they were dumbstruck. I said to them: 'Listen, children, how can this really bother you so much?' Believe me, we couldn't get away with anything. That said, the old people who saw it were happy enough . . ."[109] Clerc also features in a sequence in Camille Ducellier's 2010 film *Sorcières, mes soeurs*, in which she masturbates before the camera. That was when she was eighty-three. Not only was she calmly asserting her sexuality, her life force, but in one static shot her beautiful face fills the screen—and it's stunning. She exposes the thoroughgoing stupidity of all the hateful images imposed on us by the generations of misogynist priests, painters and hacks who have monopolized women's verbal and visual representation for far too long. "To be a witch is to be a subversive in the eyes of the law," she says, in her deep voice. "It is to create *another law*."

The heroine of Paul Mazursky's film *An Unmarried Woman* also discovers a secret portal hidden in the world of her programmed obsolescence. Crushed by her husband Martin's exit to live with his new twenty-six-year-old sweetheart, little by little, Erica regains her spirit. She grows tougher, starts going out again, and, after all the years of sex with only her husband, she decides to try out sex without feelings—except she then accidentally stumbles upon true love. In the gallery where she works, she meets Saul, a whimsical and charismatic painter (played by British actor Alan Bates). And the lovers begin a fascinating pas de deux. (Jill Clayburgh, who plays Erica, entirely deserved her Best Actress award at Cannes that year.) They play, they embrace, they circle and discover each other—and fight with each other too. Over several scenes, they seem to be walking a tightrope: an argument brews, then breaks out, and we feel their affair could be cut short. Then, each time, they come back together at the last moment. With a look, a prank, a smile, they rebuild a complicity that looks irresistible. After one of their skirmishes, Erica grumbles, "Men!" To which Saul, naturally, instantly replies, "Women!" With acrobatic nimbleness, together they discover a liberty that allows them to vault over the traps and burdens set up by the conventional concepts of women and men, but also in the situations they negotiate—the dinner at which Erica introduces Saul to her teenage daughter, for example. In comparison, the couple formed by Martin and his new young partner suddenly looks quite banal, pathetic and limited. If her husband's leaving her first seemed like the end of the world, hurtful and humiliating as it must have been, it did give Erica the opportunity of a genuine rebirth. To claim, as some people do, that combatting the sexism in so many situations would require us to make only puritan films, boring films with worthy messages, not only must you be seriously lacking in imagination, but you must also have missed the entire realm of cinema to which *An Unmarried Woman* belongs.

In a very different mode, Joseph L. Mankiewicz's Hollywood classic *All About Eve* (1950) offers a delightful lesson in undermining the rule of patriarchy. A doyenne of the New York scene, Margo Channing (played by Bette Davis) is a gutsy actor with a witty and flamboyant personality. At the height of her glory, she takes young theater fan Eve Harrington under her wing and introduces her to her inner circle. She soon realizes her mistake. The modest and bashful admirer fades away to reveal an unscrupulous hussy who is quite determined to steal everything Margo has: her roles, naturally, but also her partner, Bill Sampson, who is an actor too.[110] And Margo is vulnerable: she has just turned forty and already anticipates a decline in her career. What's more, Bill, whom she loves very much, is eight years younger than her. We can all predict what will happen next. Eve turns out to be a talented actor, able to bring a freshness to her work that Margo can no longer guarantee. It would fit with the natural order if Eve were to triumph and send her rival to the scrapheap—indeed, Eve admits to this goal in an interview, in only marginally more decorous terms. She and Bill could then form a more classic couple, with glittering future prospects, ready to seduce both press and public. Margo is petrified—and unable to hide it. She has angry outbursts, storms around, gets drunk, causes scandal upon scandal and exhausts Bill with scenes of pre-emptive jealousy. We assume that, by going on this way, she will precipitate the blow she hopes to avoid: fed up, he will take refuge all the sooner in the arms of young Eve. Meanwhile, Bill tries to reassure Margo, insisting he still loves her, yet he cannot appease her sense of insecurity. He accuses her of paranoia, which is only half true: her rival is indeed pursuing a merciless campaign, and all indicators point to its eventual success. In a rare moment of calm, confiding in a friend, Margo sighs over this temperament that makes her go "swooping about on a broomstick and screaming at the top of [her] voice." She realizes she has overreacted when she sees Eve, "so young—so feminine and helpless": all Margo would so like to be for her lover, she says. All considered, it seems impossible for the witch, the "harridan," to succeed against this apparently sweet and inoffensive young woman. Margo refuses to believe that her relationship with Bill could turn out to be stronger than society's unbending rules; she is too afraid of her own wishful thinking. Yet, when Eve makes her play for him, Bill rebuffs her with amused contempt. And when the couple meets again, Margo at last accepts his marriage proposal. Eve will still have the dazzling success she dreamed of in front of the cameras, yet without causing the downfall of her predecessor—and, in the process, Eve has sold her soul.

Sometimes, life makes prejudice a liar. Even a deeply unconventional writer like Colette seems to have accepted the idea that old age for women is about a hopeless decline that turns them into repugnant creatures. Her novels *Chéri* (1920) and *The Last of Chéri* (1926) recount the relationship between nearly fifty-year-old Léa and Chéri, a young man who—although he still loves her—after a few years leaves her to marry a younger woman. The affair ends badly. Six years after their break-up, on a whim, Chéri drops in on Léa, whom he can't seem to forget. When he sees her again, he is traumatized by her transformation.

> A woman was writing at a small table, facing away from him. Chéri was able to distinguish a broad back and the padded cushion of a fat neck beneath a head of thick gray vigorous hair, cut short like his mother's. "So I was right, she's not alone. But who on earth can this good woman be?" [. . .]
>
> The gray-haired lady turned round, and Chéri received the full impact of her blue eyes.[111]

Aging has the power to strip women's identity away entirely, to empty them of their substance: it has replaced the Léa he once knew with an unfamiliar, asexual creature.

> She was not monstrous, but huge, and loaded with exuberant buttresses of fat in every part of her body. [. . .] The plain skirt and the nondescript long jacket, opening on a linen blouse with a jabot, proclaimed that the wearer had abdicated, was no longer concerned to be a woman and had acquired a kind of sexless dignity.

During their encounter, Chéri silently begs her, "Stop! Show me your real self! Throw off your disguise! You must be somewhere behind it, since it's your voice I hear." A few weeks later, in a room papered with photos of the young Léa, Chéri kills himself.

Of course, we may feel that the tragedy revealed through Léa's new appearance is not so much that of female aging as that of her abandonment, her disappointment in love. It also reveals the mistake Chéri made in leaving her: had he been braver and less cynical (he married for money), his lover might not have aged in this way. It is her suffering and disappointment, not age alone, that has so transformed her. During the weeks of wandering between this brief, disastrous last encounter and his suicide, Chéri also thinks regretfully of all the time irrevocably lost due to his error: had he stayed with Léa, "it would have meant three or four years to the good; hundreds and hundreds of days and nights gained and garnered for love." But both novels are nonetheless haunted from the start by the horror and fear evoked by the figure of the old woman. In the mornings, during the last days of their relationship, Léa used to take care to put her pearl necklace on before Chéri woke, to hide the looseness of her neck skin. Coming upon an ugly and grotesque old biddy of their circle, flanked by a blank-eyed and very young escort, she feels as though she is confronting her own future. But then, in this cruel, superficial and worldly society, where no one is let off the hook, aging is an inexcusable sign of weakness.

However you read her books, things fell out much less tragically in Colette's personal life. A little before she turned fifty, she began a relationship with Bertrand de Jouvenel, her husband's seventeen-year-old son. Then, at fifty-two, she met Maurice Goudeket, who was thirty-six and who became her third husband. They lived together until Colette's death, in 1954, at eighty-one.[112] In short, while age robbed Léa of her identity, her creator remained fully herself, in possession of all that made her worthy of love. We also have as many images of the older Colette as we do of her in her youth, and they are no less delightful: she is shown writing in bed in her Paris apartment, surrounded by her cats, with windows open over the Palais-Royal gardens, still savoring all that life could offer, despite the various physical problems that besieged her.

These days, women's chances of aging in good health and good economic conditions are seriously compromised by their inadequate pensions, which are on average 42 percent less than men's. This can be explained by women's greater tendency to work part-time and to stop work to look after children—the "mums' glass ceiling" remains intact.[113] But there is no need for this inequality to be augmented by another: their persuasion that age diminishes their value. The potency of the stereotypes and prejudice can become deeply demoralizing, but they do present opportunities to forge new ways forward. And, in turn, to taste new experiences: the joys of insolence, of adventure and invention, of admiring those who *are* ready to live their lives to the full—and of not wasting your time with the rest. Prejudice of this kind is an invitation to reveal our iconoclasm, in the original sense of the word: to show our readiness to shatter the old images and, with them, the curse they have inflicted.

At the end of her article, Sontag wrote:

Women have another option. They can aspire to be wise, not merely nice; to be competent, not merely helpful; to be strong, not merely graceful; to be ambitious for themselves, not merely for themselves in relation to men and children. They can let themselves age naturally and without embarrassment, actively protesting and disobeying the conventions that stem from this society's double standard about aging. Instead of being girls, girls as long as possible, who then age humiliatingly into middle-aged women and then obscenely into old women, they can become women much earlier—and remain active adults, enjoying the long erotic career of which women are capable, far longer. Women should allow their faces to show the lives they have lived. Women should tell the truth.

Almost a half-century later, this proposal remains available to all the women who wish to take it up.

4

Turning the World Upside Down

WAR ON NATURE; WAR ON WOMEN

From several perspectives, you could call me stupid.

In all circumstances, and for as long as I can remember, if you need a silly question asked or a completely off-point answer or a ridiculous comment commented, for any and all occasions, I'm your woman. I sometimes notice an incredulous gaze alight on me and realize that the gazer must be thinking, "But I thought she wrote books . . . ?" or "Jeez, they'll hire anybody at *Le Monde diplomatique* these days . . ." I come away as ashamed as if I'd stumbled and executed a spectacular banana-skin slide, ending in a crash before a gaping audience (something of which, moreover, I am *also* entirely capable). This aspect of myself exasperates me all the more for remaining stubbornly beyond my control. Usually, half a second after the words are out of my mouth, I am as bewildered as my interlocutor—but there's no taking them back. I can't help it and, after almost forty-five years of these regular feats of public confusion, I have concluded that I just have to live with them. It isn't easy.

On the one hand, these stupid moments doubtless emerge

from some aspects of my own character. A total lack of practical sense, allied with a deficit of theatrical experience. Also, something of a dilettante attention span, a degree of distractibility that can fascinate observers and becomes even worse when I forget to put my glasses on, the visual haze augmenting the mental fog in which I swim. And a timidity that leads me to fluster easily and does not lend itself to quick reflex decisions. A general disposition to better grasp and analyze the elements of a situation when at greater distance from it, rather than in the moment . . . In short: I am slow on the uptake. But I do believe there's also a strongly gendered dimension to my stupidity. I am impulsive, emotional, occasionally naive. I am a walking sexist cliché, a genuine scatterbrain, the archetype of the irrational little lady. I am useless in all the areas women are meant to be useless. At the lycée, I almost had to retake a year because of my science grades. I have no sense of direction. If I had a driving license (thank the Lord, I haven't), I'd be a sitting target for my local garage to flog me the most baroque and expensive repairs. In my professional life, I maintain a relationship of intense mutual mistrust with economics and geopolitics—in other words, with the most typical male bastions, those lying closest to our centers of power.

It took me a while to understand that intelligence is not an absolute quality, but can include enormous variations depending on the contexts in which we exercise it and the people we have before us. Different circumstances and interlocutors have the power to reveal or attract drastically different aspects of ourselves, to stimulate or to inhibit our intellectual capacities. Society assigns women and men very different and differently valued realms of competence, such that women more often find themselves feeling stupid. It is women who run the greater risk of appearing deficient in the more prestigious fields, the ones considered to really count, whereas the fields in which women are more likely to have developed some skill are neglected, disdained or are sometimes altogether invisible. Women do therefore have less confidence in themselves. Our uselessness is a self-fulfilling prophecy. Sometimes, I say stupid things out of ignorance, but sometimes, too, I say them because my brain blocks, my neurons are scattering like a flock of starlings and I'm panicking. I am trapped in a vicious circle: I can sense my interlocutor's condescending or contemptuous reaction, so I say something outrageous, thus confirming their judgment, in my own as well as their eyes. The interlocutor in question may be a fellow journalist, but could equally be the washing-machine engineer who, hardly inside my door, asks me something about the machine's functioning and, before I've had time to open my mouth, repeats the question roughly and impatiently, as if fully aware of having an idiot to deal with (and yet, for once, I was about to answer sensibly). Sexism appears at all levels of the social scale, offering us, in glorious stereo, a constant reminder of our deep-rooted dimness. And I should be making ready for my later years, for, apparently, the only thing stupider than a woman is an old woman. Cynthia Rich describes how, if she went to a hardware shop with Barbara Macdonald, and Macdonald asked the salesperson a question, he would address his reply to Rich (then in her forties, while Macdonald was in her sixties).[1]

After centuries of scientific and religious men, of doctors, politicians, philosophers, writers, artists, revolutionaries and public entertainers ringing every possible change on women's congenital stupidity and hopeless intellectual incompetence, and justifying this as required with the most ill-founded ravings about our anatomical weak points, it would be very surprising if we did not feel somewhat inhibited. In a striking litany summing up the conventional discourse on women down the years, American writer Susan Griffin writes:

It is decided that the minds of women are defective. That the fibers of the brain are weak. That because women menstruate regularly the supply of blood to the brain is weakened.

All abstract knowledge, all knowledge which is dry, it is cautioned, must be abandoned to the laborious and solid mind of man. "For this reason," it is further reasoned, "women will never learn geometry."

There is a controversy over whether or not women should be taught arithmetic.

To a woman who owns a telescope it is suggested that she rid herself of it, that she "stop trying to find out what's happening on the moon."[2]

Griffin owes her reflections on "the laborious and solid mind" and the ban on geometry to Immanuel Kant, while the reference to the telescope comes from a tirade addressed by Chrysale to Philaminte in Molière's play *The Learned Women* (1672):

You should burn all this useless lumber, and leave learning to the doctors of the town. Take away from the garret that long telescope, which is enough to frighten people, and a hundred other baubles which are offensive to the sight. Do not try to discover what is passing in the moon, and think a little more of what is happening at home.[3]

The two sources shouldn't really be read as of equal weight; the second one is spoken by a fictional character, and there's no need to rehash the debate about Molière's misogyny here. That said, some of his images seem to be enjoying long afterlives. While I was immersed in reading all these texts, an advertisement for an online retail site was showing images of a woman's brain in cross section, with her thoughts written inside: "Astronomy isn't really my thing. But my neighbor's anatomy is another matter . . ." They were selling telescopes for €49.99.[4]

These assumptions also show why women continue to have "things explained" to them by supremely arrogant men—as explored by Rebecca Solnit in the duly celebrated title essay of her collection *Men Explain Things to Me* (2014). Her piece was prompted by an occasion in 2008. At a fashionable party, a man had talked to Solnit about an apposite book that had recently been published and of which he had read a precis in the *New York Times* . . . without realizing that he had its author in front of him. He was so confident that, for a moment, Solnit almost believed she might have missed the publication of an important book on the same subject as her own. She writes:

This syndrome is a war that nearly every woman faces every day, a war within herself too, a belief in her superfluity, an invitation to silence, one from which a fairly nice career as a writer (with a lot of research and facts correctly deployed) has not entirely freed me. After all, there was a moment there when I was willing to let Mr. Important and his overweening confidence bowl over my more shaky certainty.[5]

First thing the next day, she wrote her article in one go, and, as soon as it appeared online, it ignited like a powder trail. "It struck a chord. And a nerve."[6] Among the many responses Solnit received, there was one from a middle-aged man living in Indianapolis, who wrote to say he had "never personally or professionally shortchanged a woman" and to reproach her for "not hanging out with 'more regular guys or at least do[ing] a little homework first.'" After which, he gave Solnit "some advice about how to run [her] life, and then commented on [her] 'feelings of inferiority.'"[7]

We end up assimilating this view of ourselves, the fact of our own idiocy, our personal incompetence. When perfectly nice, innocent tourists ask me for directions in the street, if I'm at all uncertain, I answer that they'd do better asking someone else—but then, usually as soon as they're off again, I realize I could easily have shown them their way. "Sense of direction," "economics"—as soon as a term of this ilk begins to flash in my head, I panic, just as I used to with the word "maths." A few years ago, researchers from the University of Provence asked two groups of primary-school students to recreate from memory a fairly complicated geometric design. For one group, they called it a "geometry" exercise; for the other group, it was a "drawing" exercise. In the first group,

the girls did less well than the boys. In the second, free of the
terrifying shadow of maths—and working, therefore, without prior expectation of failure—the girls did better than the
boys.[8] Toward the end of secondary school, I too had a brief
opportunity to be free of these paralyzing limitations which
I had come to see as irremediable. I had one teacher who was
passionate about her subject, as patient as she was caring and
a million miles from the self-important loudmouth types I
was used to. Thanks to her, two years before the Maturité
(the Swiss equivalent to secondary-school graduation exams),
I became almost *good at maths* and managed a very respectable
grade in the exam. In the oral section, after running through
my demonstration without a hitch, I gave the right answer to
a slightly tricky question, and she exclaimed, "Bravo!" It was
twenty-five years ago and I have never forgotten that "bravo,"
so improbably meant for me, next to a blackboard covered
in sums. Revelation: my stupidity was not set in stone! (In
2014, Iranian mathematician Maryam Mirzakhani became
the first woman to receive the Fields Medal, the equivalent
of the Nobel Prize for maths.)

"Excellent at *what?*"

Alongside the subjects I gave up as a lost cause, there were always others where I felt more competent, with some cause for
pride—after almost failing in my science subjects, I won the
prize for translation from Greek at Maturité. But I'd become
convinced that these were subaltern fields, which justified my
status as a nice little intellectual satellite, condemned forever to maintain my distant orbit around the Planet of True
Knowledge, playing my own little tune. Gradually, however,

I began to question this generally accepted truth. These days, I still thoroughly regret a few of my weaknesses. For example, despite what is often suspected of me (and all intellectuals), I am far from contemptuous about practical things and I'm sorry to be such a klutz at them. But, if we go beyond domestic practicality, I am increasingly emboldened to challenge the dominant criteria for evaluating intelligence.

As a reader, I fell in love with *Le Monde diplomatique* newspaper for its literary and philosophical articles, for its eye on our times and society, for its political commitment, its bylines from top intellectuals and its sophisticated and unconventional illustrations. I saw in it a poetic approach to journalism that appealed a great deal. When I began to work there, I was disconcerted by the passion shown by so many of my colleagues for figures, maps and tables, all elements whose presence I had so far hardly noticed. Not only do these remain impenetrable to me, but, on the rare occasions when I linger over them and a flash of understanding zigzags through the darkness of my brain, I don't feel any fulfillment in my thirst for knowledge. I don't deny their utility or value, nor the fact that they are much appreciated by a section of our readership, but there are also many people, and I count myself among them, to whom these signs say nothing, and who prefer other ways of comprehending the world that are no less rich. At first, I was ashamed, but more recently I have come to terms with this. Generally speaking, as I grow older, I increasingly see the limitations to our definitions of knowledge; I see the blind spots and the weaknesses of those who patronize me. I dispute—at least inwardly—both the absolute value of my stupidity as it appears to them and the absolute value of their intelligence for me, even while, for them, it all goes without saying. Which is understandable: why should they burden themselves with these subtleties when they have the good fortune to operate on the right side of the intelligence bar? Maybe this is why I write books: to create spaces where I can be competent (at least, where I hope I am); to shine a light on subjects that may not previously even have been understood or identified as issues, by asserting their relevance and their value.

When we speak of women's place in academia, we tend to talk about the proportions of female students or professors, or that certain disciplines are almost exclusively taken up by men. We deplore sexism—on the part of students and teachers—just as we deplore the lack of self-confidence that prevents girls from choosing to work in physics or computer science. But too often I think we forget to question the actual content of what is taught; we neglect the fact that, for young women, going to university implies adopting varieties of knowledge, methods and codes that, for centuries, have been almost entirely created without them—when not actually *against* them. If you raise this problem, you will be suspected of essentialism: do you mean to suggest that women have different brains, that they might have a "specifically female" way of approaching knowledge? That, if they had had some input, we might have included little hearts in our maths formulae, perhaps? Whereas, in fact, this accusation of essentialism can be turned against the accusers: it is precisely because women and men do *not* constitute fixed essences suspended in an abstract space, but rather two groups that maintain relationships adopted within the movement and turmoil of history, that we cannot consider "university knowledge" to be objective and so endow it with any absolute value.

We often say that history is written by the winners. For example, for some years now, every October, Columbus Day has offered an occasion for ever more effective challenges to the official history, showing how, in the expression "discovery of America," the very word "discovery" is problematic, and recalling that an iconic explorer for some people is a bloody invader for others. In a way, women too have been history's losers—and their history has been bloody, as these pages alone demonstrate. Why should they be the only losers with no right to a *point of view*? Of course, women's condition will never coalesce into a single point of view. Some male historians might adopt a feminist approach, just as some female historians may reject readings of the witch-hunts in feminist terms. Even so, can we claim that our belonging or not to the group in question has no impact on our approach? As we are reminded, the fact that the discipline of history was created by men has not been without effect on the treatment of the witch-hunts, or rather, to start with, their non-treatment, for they were for a long time quite simply ignored or mentioned only in footnotes. Yet another example: on reading Erik Midelfort's assertion that, in societies uncomfortable with the notion of women living alone, the witch-hunts played a "therapeutic" role by purging society of the single and "eccentric" women it could not accept, Mary Daly raised two questions. First, whether we would dare to use the same adjective about the persecution of Jews in the pogroms or about the lynchings of black people. And then: therapeutic for whom . . . ?[9]

In *Revolution from Within*, her "book of self-esteem"

from the early 1990s, Gloria Steinem quoted from a study
of 200,000 American middle-school students; among the
young women, there was a substantial tendency to increased
self-deprecation during their transition to university, whereas
their male peers' self-esteem was either maintained or increased. Many academics at that time were deeply resistant
to attempts to diversify their canon in order to give greater
space to women's and minorities' works. They shot down
all that was "politically correct" or "PC"—an acronym that
Robin Morgan (one of the founders of WITCH) commented
could just as well be called "plain courtesy." They claimed to
be guardians of "excellence." "As if the more important question were not 'Excellent at *what*?'" Steinem added.[10] In her
view, academics were resisting so hard because they knew this
change would require not only bringing women and minorities into the course programs and into all their other teaching structures, it would also mean "learning to see with new
eyes—to question the very idea of 'norms' against which all
other experience is judged."

I have always felt that my dissatisfaction with the he-
gemony of the "hard sciences" and with a certain way of
approaching the world—a cold, clean-cut, objective, over-
viewing gaze—had to do with my nature as a woman, but,
unable to be specific about the connection, I have avoided
putting it into words. The shadow of essentialism was holding
me back, still. I didn't want to end up defending a "female"
way of seeing and doing things; besides, I could clearly see
that not all women were like me, just as I could identify some
men who shared my own intellectual sensibility. So, I have
made do with pursuing an idea that I return to almost obses-

sively throughout my books, whatever their focus—I would probably even find a way to slip it into a book about crustaceans' reproduction. What I try to express over and over is a critique of this cult of rationality (or, rather, of what we take for rationality), which seems so natural that we often give up identifying it as such. This cult determines both our way of viewing the world, of organizing our knowledge about it, and how we act in and on it, how we transform it. This leads us to conceive the world as a collection of separate, inert and unmysterious objects—understood in terms of their immediate usefulness, which it is possible to know objectively—which should be chopped up for conscription in the service of production and progress. Our cult can still trace its roots back to the all-conquering science of the nineteenth century, even though quantum physics has since arrived to sow upset amid this optimism (assuming it isn't simply arrogance). Quantum physics speaks instead of a world in which each mystery solved only reveals further mysteries, and where, in all likelihood, this quest will never reach an end. This is a world where the objects are not in fact separate, but interdependent; where we are dealing with flows of energy, with processes, rather than with stable, identifiable objects; where an observer's presence has an effect upon the process that follows; where, far from being able to rely on immutable rules, we observe irregularity, unpredictability, inexplicable quantum "leaps." All this leads Starhawk to suggest that modern physics confirms the witches' early intuitions. Physicist Bernard d'Espagnat proposed that, bearing in mind the resistance of matter and the world in general to any complete or final understanding, it would not be absurd to look to art for fleeting insights into what remains and always will remain beyond our understanding: a conclusion whose dizzying consequences for our habitual organization of knowledge is only just becoming imaginable.[11]

Even though we are still struggling to take the implications of these discoveries on board a century later, they clearly give the lie to a world view that took hold in the seventeenth century, especially with René Descartes, who, in a famous line from his *Discourse on Method*, dreamed of seeing men "render ourselves lords and possessors of nature."[12] In his key study, geographer Augustin Berque analyzes the problems arising from a Cartesian approach.[13] Sinologist Jean-François Billeter retraces the path of what he calls this "chain reaction": the progress of the Cartesian view throughout the planet, beginning in the West in the Renaissance period, via a coolly calculated commercial vector and misrepresented as the height of rationality.[14] And literary historians Michael Löwy and Robert Sayre have shown how, although now often dismissed as a band of overexcited, dandified night owls, the Romantics understood the fundamental systems error that has come to dominate our lives. Even while aiming to explore and legitimize alternative psychic realms, the Romantics did not espouse a refusal of reason; rather, they sought "to counter instrumental rationality—in the service of domination over nature and over human beings—with substantive human rationality."[15]

All of these thinkers have helped me to clarify my misgivings about this civilization in which we live and breathe: about its association with a conquering, crowing, aggressive world; its naive and ridiculous belief in the possibility of separating mind from body, and reason from emotion; its blind, almost allergic narcissistic reaction to anything that is other than itself; its habit of disfiguring its territory with urban architectural aberrations, and of calling for sledgehammers to kill every gnat going (not to mention the decision to kill the insects in the first place); its over-sharp edges, its too-bright lights; its intolerance of all that is shadowy, fluid, mysterious; the general impression of moribund commercialism that this civilization gives off.[16] These writers nurture a sense of regret, not for what has been, but for what could have been. Up to now, I had not found a satisfactory way of joining this obsession up with my feminism, despite being convinced there was a connection. But, by setting the accepted history of the witch-hunts alongside their interpretation by so many women writers, all has become clear.

The Death of Nature

Caliban and the Witch, the title of Silvia Federici's book, refers to a character in Shakespeare's play *The Tempest,* a deformed and dark-skinned creature, the son of a witch, as ugly morally as he is physically hideous, whom the sorcerer Prospero describes as a "poisonous slave" and "thing of darkness." Caliban represents the slaves and colonized peoples whose exploitation, like that of women, enabled the initial accumulation of capital necessary for capitalism to flourish. But the enslavement of women ran in parallel to yet another enslavement, to which it was perhaps even more closely connected: that of nature. This is the thesis developed in 1980 by the ecofeminist philosopher Carolyn Merchant in *The Death of Nature,* a work conceived as complementary to that of Federici.[17] Merchant examines how, during the Renaissance, the intensification of human activities, requiring vast quantities of metal and wood, as well as great expanses of arable land, which altered the Earth's physiognomy to a previously unseen degree, also entailed an equally massive recasting of our mental horizons.

The old view conceived the world as a living organism, often figured as a nurturing maternal presence. Since antiquity, particular opprobrium was reserved for excavatory mining, which, in texts by Pliny the Elder, Ovid and Seneca, was considered an act of aggression driven by greed (for gold) or blood thirst (for iron ore). In the sixteenth and seventeenth centuries, lust was added to the roster, and such mining was denounced by poets including Edmund Spenser and John Milton, who described it as a rape of the Earth. The imagination of the time saw "a direct correlation between mining and digging into the nooks and crannies of a woman's body."[18] The mine itself was analogous to the vagina of Mother Earth, and the cavities where metals lay hidden became her uterus. Having gradually grown untenable, these ancient views were replaced by others that, in stripping out our sense of the world as a *living* body, dissipated all such old scruples and would eventually allow untrammeled exploitation. Similarly, the new commercial frenzy demanded unheard-of quantities of wood for building wharves, bridges, locks, barges and ships, but also for the production of soap, beer barrels and to make glass. This gave rise to the first hint of concern for managing nature in its guise as a "resource": in Venice, in 1470, a law was passed that henceforth the town's arsenal, and not its other authorities, would organize oak felling. Merchant sums up the new scene that emerged:

As European cities grew and forested areas became more remote, as fens were drained and geometric patterns of channels imposed on the landscape, as large powerful waterwheels, furnaces, forges, cranes and treadmills began increasingly to dominate the work environment, more and more people began to experience nature as altered and manipulated by machine technology. A slow but unidirectional alienation from the immediate daily organic relationship that had formed the basis of human experience from earliest times was occurring.

The mechanistic view which took over allows for a "certain and consistent" knowledge of the world; the natural disorder of organic life gave way to "the stability of mathematical laws and identities."[19] From now on, the world is viewed as dead and its matter as passive. The model of the machine and especially that of the clock is applied in every arena. In his *Discourse on Method*, Descartes likens animals to automata. Thomas Hobbes—who had probably heard about the first calculating machine, invented by Blaise Pascal in 1642—compared reasoning to a simple series of additions and subtractions.

In this period, we see a phenomenon that Susan Bordo calls a "drama of parturition": a forced rupture from the organic and maternal world of the Middle Ages in order to step forward into a new world where "precision, clarity and detachment" rule.[20] The human being emerges here "as a decisively separate entity, no longer continuous with the universe with which it had once shared a soul." Bordo sees in this a "flight from the feminine, from the memory of union with the maternal world, and a rejection of all values associated with it," replaced by an obsession with maintaining distance and demarcation.[21] Guy Bechtel expressed it in other terms: the "machine for creating man anew" was just as much a "machine for killing women as they once were."[22] With this arises a "super-masculinization of rational thought," a cold and impersonal "distinctively male cognitive style."[23] This interpretation, Bordo stresses, should in no way be dismissed as a twentieth-century feminist fantasy: "the founders of modern science consciously and explicitly proclaimed the 'masculinity' of science as inaugurating a new era. And they associated that masculinity with a cleaner, purer, more objective and more disciplined epistemological relation to the world."[24] The English scholar Francis Bacon proclaimed it "a masculine birth of time."[25]

The entire relationship between people's sense of themselves and the world around them is overturned. The body is rethought as separate from the soul—and repudiated: "I am not this assemblage of members which is called the human body," as Descartes wrote.[26] Bordo reminds us that disdain for the body—often compared to a prison or cage—in Western philosophy goes back to ancient Greece, even though, as she explains, for Plato as for Aristotle, the body and soul were inextricably joined, the soul able to leave the body only at the moment of death.[27] Descartes marks out new territory here: he turns body and soul into two fundamentally different substances. For him, the human mind "is altogether different from the body."[28]

No longer perceived as a nourishing bosom, nature then

became a wild and disorderly force which had to be tamed. And the same went for women, as Carolyn Merchant shows. Women were said to be closer to nature than men and more sexually excitable (the project of repression was so effective that, these days, women are considered to have a *weaker* sexual appetite). "The witch, symbol of the violence of nature, raised storms, caused illness, destroyed crops, obstructed generation and killed infants. Disorderly women, like chaotic nature, needed to be controlled."[29] Once curbed and domesticated, both women and nature could be reduced to their decorative function, to become "psychological and recreational resources for the harried entrepreneur-husband."[30]

Generally considered the father of modern science, Francis Bacon strikingly illustrates the parallels between these two subjugations. For a dozen years, he was a valued adviser to the King of England, James I, and occupied various roles in the King's inner circle, notably that of attorney general. Author of an influential treatise on demonology, James I had modified legislation upon acceding to the English throne: henceforth, all practice of witchcraft, not only that which had been used for murder, would be punished with death. For Merchant, Bacon's writings implicitly advocate applying to nature the same methods as were used on suspected witches. The imagery he drew on to envisage his goals and scientific methods derives directly from the courtrooms—and the torture chambers—where he had spent so many hours. He advises submitting nature to interrogation to make it give up its secrets: we must not believe, he wrote, that "the inquisition of nature is in any part interdicted or forbidden"; on the contrary, nature must be "bound into service," "put in constraint" and "moulded" by the mechanical arts.[31] Our language still bears the mark of this conquering stance, the hangover of a virile and aggressive sexed approach: we speak of "a penetrating mind" and of "hard facts"—by which we mean indisputable facts.[32] We even find this in the work of a philosopher-ecologist such as Aldo Leopold, who wrote that "a conservationist is one who is humbly aware that with each stroke he is writing his signature on the face of his land."[33]

At last broken in, by the nineteenth century, nature could be depicted in the form of a docile woman, no longer resisting the assaults of science. For example, a famous piece by French sculptor Louis-Ernest Barrias called *Nature Unveiling Herself Before Science* (1899) shows a bare-breasted woman gracefully removing the veil that covers her head. Seeing it today, it's hard not to think of the French propaganda posters produced during the Algerian War that encouraged Algerian women to take off their headscarves (with slogans such as "Are you not pretty? Unveil yourself!"), as well as of the 2004 statute which banned the wearing of headscarves in French schools. It is apparently intolerable that women—especially indigenous women—and, by the same logic, nature, should hide anything at all from the patriarchal and Western gaze. The practice of shaving those suspected of witchcraft from head to toe—body hair as well as head hair—to enable their comprehensive inspection can be seen as a harbinger of this requirement that everything be visible, the better to be controlled.

Dreuf, Popokoff and the Rest

Mare Kandre's Dr. Dreuf conducts his practice from an address on Scoptophilia Street; "scoptophilia," also called the "scopic drive," is described by Sigmund Freud as pleasure taken in observing a person as an object, along with a feeling of control. The street lies in the fictional town of Tris. Night is falling as Kandre's story begins. The doctor is in his office, a small dusty room; the shelves of his library are decorated with yellowed glass jars in which float "a few wombs suspended in formaldehyde and some female breasts," as well as an aborted female fetus.[34] The gynecologist's housekeeper has already begun to prepare his dinner. The penultimate patient of the day has just arrived and lain down on his couch. It's her first session. She is called Eva and has come to consult "this man who enjoys great renown, unquestionably an expert" because she suffers from a strange condition: she is haunted by the voices and fates of hundreds of women from every era. During a very long consultation, voiced one after another through this primordial woman, who is in a kind of trance, we hear a female sinner from the Bible, a nun locked away in a convent, an old lady condemned to be burned as a witch, a young peasant raped while gathering wood, an aristocrat obliged to sit still and suffocated by her heavy clothes, a wife forcibly consigned to an asylum by her husband and a prostitute killed by the after-effects of a clandestine abortion.

Dreuf does—more or less—hear Eva out, running the gamut of unsympathetic reactions, from boredom through distraction, mockery, impatience, worry and irritation. He wonders what he ought to do with this hysteric: send her to the asylum or merely knock her out with drugs? "Yes, of course, of course," he mumbles while she raves on. Memories of women who have frightened or humiliated him as a child parade through the mind of this gnome-like man, who clings to his science and mathematical formulae in order to ward off the terror inspired by the female of the species: "Paradise by the nun potency the fruit times the butcher and the root of the little girl soiled less the field of mud and the prostitute, that adds up to . . ." When the patient's tirade arrives at a witch-hunter, suddenly attentive, he remembers his master, Popokoff, "himself descended from a long line of eminent witch-hunters." He asks the young woman to describe this man to him. "He's a very nasty character," Eva replies. "He is wearing great leather boots, he holds a long hard cane and is wrapped in a vast cloak that's black as night. He is your age, Doctor, and . . . yes . . . Yes, I must tell you, there is something about him that reminds me of you, Doctor Dreuf!" The doctor beams, flattered, before clouding over again, for he feels he may have spotted "a faintly mocking modulation" in the voice of his analyzand.[35]

If Kandre had her sights set principally on Freud and psychoanalysis with this novel, behind these figures stand those of the doctor and the scientist more generally, as the targets of this delicious satire. Healthcare does indeed seem to provide the main stage on which modern science's war against women has been waged. Healthcare as we know it was built upon women's physical elimination: the witch-hunts first focused on female healers, as we have seen. Relying on their personal experience, these healers were generally much more effective than the official doctors of the time, many of whom were pitiful quacks but who nonetheless benefited from the removal of this "disloyal" competition—even while they appropriated many of the healers' discoveries. From the thirteenth century onward, however—in fact, long before the witch-hunts began—with the advent of medical schools at European universities, the medical profession had been off-limits to women. In 1322, Jacqueline Felice de Almania, a Florentine noble who had moved to Paris, was brought before judges by the city authorities for the illegal practice of medicine. Six witnesses confirmed that she had cured them, and one of them stated that she "was more knowledgeable in the art of surgery and medicine than the greatest male doctors and surgeons in Paris," but this only damaged her case further, for, as a woman, she was quite simply banned from medical practice.[36] The fate of the reference work that collected details of gynecological illnesses and was known as *Trotula* in homage to Trota, the famous female healer from Salerno, well demonstrates the process of women's effacement not only from practice, but also from the reference material of medical literature. Compiled around the end of the twelfth century, *Trotula* went through various vicissitudes and finally drifted into the hands of a German publisher, who published it as part of a much larger collection, the *Gynaeciorum libri*. Querying Trota's identity, he attributed this work to a male doctor called Eros. "Thus, the list of Greek, Roman and Arab-world contributors displays a remarkable homogeneity: all are men discoursing learnedly on the female body and setting themselves up as the true masters of gynecological knowledge," Dominique Brancher concludes.[37] In the US, where the medical profession is even more male-dominated than in Europe, women's expulsion occurred later on, in the nineteenth century. This ousting by middle-class white men in white encountered dogged resistance, notably through the Popular Health Movement, but was ultimately triumphant.[38]

The anonymous French hospital doctor who, in 2017, on the French radio station Europe 1, proudly claimed to "pat the backsides" of his female colleagues "for a laugh" would probably find it less funny if, sharing his concern for "everyone to chill out," one of those colleagues happened to give his meat and two veg a friendly pat or administer a slap to *his* backside.[39] The notorious phenomenon of cabin fever and the need for decompression, perennially trotted out to justify the sexual harassment of female doctors by their colleagues and managers, in all likelihood conceals the hostility their presence provokes.[40] The light-hearted excuses hide the conviction that women ought not to be there, that they are intruders, perpetuating a resentment with very old roots indeed. When, in 2018, a dozen mostly female junior doctors campaigned for the removal of a pornographic mural on their refectory wall at the Purpan Hospital in Toulouse, some of their male colleagues resisted, judging this "medical students' art" "an integral part of the history of medicine": one could hardly frame the problem any better![41] Similarly, one female surgeon reported her first boss's parting words to her, early in her career: "You may have a future in this profession, my dear. You are the first filly I haven't managed to make cry over the ops table."[42]

Female patients likewise bear the brunt of this men's locker-room scenario. Witness, for example, comments overheard about women's bodies while they are under sedation on the operating table, or the following experience reported by a young woman after a consultation with her gynecologist: "The last time, while I was going to request a follow-up date from his secretary, he went into his colleague's office and began describing my breasts. I heard them laughing. The secretary was petrified and I realized it wasn't the first time she'd heard this. I never went back."[43] Like the army, the medical world is a professional realm where a deep-rooted hostility toward women and a cult of macho attitudes seem to dominate—there is a horror of all forms of "sissy" behavior. But what surprises no one in an institution devoted to the exercise of violence is all the more shocking from a discipline that purports to be all about caring.

To a surprising degree, healthcare today still focuses on aspects of the science that were adopted during the witch-hunts: the spirit of aggressive domination and the hatred of women; belief in the omnipotence of science and of those who exercise it, but also in the separation of body and mind, and in a cold rationalism, shorn of all emotion. To begin with, the medical realm tends to perpetuate the impulse to dominate and subjugate, the beginnings of which Carolyn Merchant plots out in her book. And sometimes this is taken to cartoonish lengths: in December 2017, a British surgeon was tried for lasering his initials onto the livers of two patients during organ-transplant operations.[44] And this attitude can be at its worst in practice on female patients. First, as Florence Montreynaud notes, "Women's organs are mapped out with men's names," like flags affixed to various parts of our anatomy. She explains:

> The canals connecting each ovary to the uterus were, until 1997, known as the Fallopian Tubes, after the Italian surgeon who first described them in detail in the sixteenth century—before they became

the uterine tubes. The little sacs inside the ovaries where, between puberty and the menopause, an ovocyte matures every month are the Graafian follicles, named after Regnier de Graaf, a Dutch doctor in the seventeenth century. The glands that secrete liquid moistening the vulva and vaginal opening are called Bartholin's glands, after the seventeenth-century Danish anatomist. Worse still, in the twentieth century a pleasure zone within the vagina was given the appellation the "G-spot," celebrating the initial of the German doctor Ernst Grägenberg.

Imagine the equivalent for men: Garrett Anderson's corpus cavernosum or J. C. Wright's canals . . .[45]

Men's stranglehold on the profession is far from a broadly abstract force, either. The world of healthcare—especially when it comes to gynecology and reproductive rights—seems keen to exercise ongoing control over women's bodies and to ensure its own unlimited access to them. As if in never-ending reiteration of the joint project of taming nature and women, it seems these bodies must always be reduced to passivity, to ensure their obedience. For example, Martin Winckler questions why, in France, the annual gynecological check-up is considered an "immutable ritual," a "sacred obligation," from puberty onward, even if we're in perfect health. According to Winckler, there is no justification for this practice.

The idea that we must undergo "from the onset of sexual activity, and then every year" a gynecological exam, a breast exam and a smear test "so as not to miss anything" (i.e., in order not to miss a cervical, ovarian or breast cancer) is medically unsubstantiated, especially for women younger than thirty, among whom cancers are very rare and, in any case and as a rule, tend not to be discovered in generalist check-ups. And then, a year later, if the patient is doing well, the doctor can renew her contraceptive prescription *without examining her*! Why? It's quite simple: if the woman is feeling well, the likelihood that the doctor will find "something" is almost nil. Then, frankly, why harass her about the check-up in the first place?[46]

Why indeed? This ritual turns out to have some grim stories associated with it. Winckler recounts the case of two adolescents whose doctor (also the mayor of their local authority) insisted on a gynecological and breast exam every three months.[47] But the point of the institution, whether annual or more frequent, appears to be ideological more than anything else: it's about maintaining surveillance of women's bodies. Blogger and journalist Marie-Hélène Lahaye notes the eloquent title of a French obstetricians and gynecologists newsletter which, in June 2016, opposed widening the remit of independent midwives: the doctors denounced measures that would damage women's "medical surveillance . . ." For Mary Daly, this ritual perpetuates a state of anxiety in women from all walks of society—a situation comparable to that born of the pressures of beauty conventions—and constitutes a substantial drain on their resources.[48]

Many doctors are so sure of their rights that they can

cross the line into illegality without even noticing. In 2015, an internal note sent out by the South Lyon medical faculty inviting its gynecology students to practice vaginal examinations on patients sedated for operations was picked up online. On social media, as Marie-Hélène Lahaye reports, numerous doctors and students were offended by reminders that every medical action requires the patient's consent and that the introduction of fingers into the vagina meets the legal definition of rape. Some of them protested that there was "nothing sexual" in the practice and that they took "no pleasure at all" in it, thereby offering a brand-new and daring revision to the definition of rape. Others jumped from frying pan to fire by arguing that, if they were to respect procedure and request the patients' authorization, the latter might well refuse it. After reading and hearing from these quarters that vaginal and rectal exams were neutral acts without any sexual aspect, Lahaye suggested on Twitter that, in this case, the medical students could train in this work by practicing on each other: "I admit this was not received with wild enthusiasm."[49]

Another problematic ritual: the parade of medical personnel who show up when a woman is in the midst of giving birth and each in turn insert two fingers into her vagina to assess her cervical dilation, without requesting consent nor even informing her beforehand, and sometimes without being overly gentle either. Lahaye invites us to imagine the equivalent for other body parts: you are at the dentist and, at regular intervals, unfamiliar people come into the room and insert their fingers into your mouth; or you are seeing a specialist for a rectal exam and a dozen people take turns putting their finger into your anus . . . "Such a practice," Lahaye concludes,

"is inconceivable in any of the medical disciplines except obstetrics, the one that's all about access to women's genitals."[50]
We see here, in an extreme form, the assumption that wom-
en's bodies belong to everyone but themselves, which is found
to differing degrees throughout society and explains why we
are not expected to kick up a fuss over the odd pat on the
bottom.

A Bunch of Fantasists

Before we go on, I should be clear that I would never deny
the deep and genuine devotion shown by the great majority
of health professionals, operating in working conditions that
can be extremely testing. Like most patients and those close
to patients, I am indebted to these people and I would hate
to appear ungrateful or as though trying to denigrate them.
But budget cuts and the demands of profitability may not be
the only obstacles they face in defending their professional
image: consciously or not, they must also confront a structural
dynamic, a legacy of the way their profession has developed
historically—and this dynamic is plainly still espoused by
those of their colleagues who are demonstrably disdainful,
brutal and misogynistic. Mary Daly goes as far as proposing
that gynecology is a continuation of demonology by another
name. Just like the witch-hunter, the doctor can argue that
all he's doing is saving the woman from an evil to which her
fragile nature makes her peculiarly vulnerable; this evil used
to be called the Devil, but these days goes by "disease": "gynecology is of course streamlined Demonology, and the Devil
is Disease, to which women are especially susceptible."[51] Indeed, there's no denying the long history of violence inflicted

on women by medical authorities, which I won't go through in detail here. I will just pick out the removal of healthy ovaries, widely practiced in the 1870s and thought to remedy excessive sexual appetites or to correct "undisciplined behavior" (mostly within married couples); and removal of the clitoris—in the US, the last registered clitorectomy was carried out in 1948 on a girl of five, to "cure" her of masturbation;[52] and also lobotomies, which made it possible for "the patient to return to their family in an unchallenging condition, truly now a housecat"—that patient being, in the vast majority of cases, female.[53]

Nowadays, such cases of abuse and violence take their place alongside negligence and casual attitudes which, allied with the drive for profit and the cynicism of pharmaceutical companies, can lead to criminal consequences.[54] In the last few years, an impressive number of health scandals have turned patients' lives into a calvary, when they have not killed them: the French PIP breast implants, sold around the world in the tens of millions, from which silicone escaped into women's bodies; the Essure sterilization implants (made by Bayer), the metal of which wreaks havoc in some women's bodies; the third and fourth generation contraceptive pills, which significantly increase the risk of thrombosis, pulmonary embolism and stroke;[55] and the Prolift vaginal prostheses (by Johnson & Johnson) intended to help treat prolapsed organs, but which became instruments of torture for many, such that one victim reported, "I've never had the courage to commit suicide, but I was really hoping very hard not to wake up the next day."[56] To this we could add Servier's product, marketed as Mediator, an antidiabetic treatment which killed between 1,500 and 2,000 people and was mainly prescribed as a weight-loss aid, so principally to women.[57] Similarly, Levothyrox, the thyroid supplement drug taken by 3 million people in France, 80 percent of them women, for which, in 2017, the manufacturer Merck changed the formula; the new formula caused extremely damaging, even disabling side effects among thousands of its regular consumers.

After the Second World War, there was also the Distilbène or "DES" scandal: this medication was intended to prevent miscarriage, but also caused the daughters of women who took it fertility problems, unstable pregnancies, miscarriages, deformities and cancers. Prescription stopped in 1971 in the US and in 1977 in France, where, distributed by UCB Pharma, it had been given to 2,000 women. The effects have been felt through three generations—including among men. In 2011, a severely handicapped young man received compensation through the justice system: the Distilbène taken by his grandmother in 1958 had caused a uterine deformity in her daughter, who in 1989 had delivered her own baby severely prematurely.[58] And, in the same vein, Thalidomide, distributed between 1956 and 1961, and intended to relieve nausea in pregnant women, caused deformities in some 10,000 babies around the world. In 2012, the Diageo group paid out millions of dollars in compensation to an Australian woman born without arms or legs.[59]

We are also now beginning to see the degree to which prejudice about women undermines their medical care. "Despite showing the same symptoms, a female patient who complains of pressure in her chest will find herself prescribed anti-anxiety drugs, whereas a man will be sent to a cardiologist," neurobiologist Catherine Vidal explains, by way of example.[60] Similarly, many women suffer excessively painful menstruation in silence for years before anyone starts to suspect endometriosis. This disease affects one in ten women of childbearing age and is only now becoming better understood. In France, it was the subject of a national awareness-raising campaign in 2016.[61] Often, the system's misfires have to do with the notorious "it's all in your mind"—as in Dr. Dreuf's muttering, "Yes, of course, of course." The impossibility of making oneself heard or being taken seriously came to the fore again in the Levothyrox case. A female patient is seen as more likely to be making things up, exaggerating, or to be ignorant, emotional and irrational. (Need I add that I rarely say more idiotic things than precisely when faced with an unsympathetic doctor?) "Some studies point to the unconscious sexism of doctors, to their tendency to interrupt and cut women short more often than men," adds Martin Winckler.[62] Having so long considered women to be naturally weak, sick and impaired—in the nineteenth century, some upper-middle-class women were regularly known as chronic invalids and, as such, were enjoined to remain in bed, until they went crazy with boredom—the healthcare system now seems to have changed its mind. These days, it suspects all women's ailments of being "psychosomatic." In short, women have gone from being "physically sick" to being "mentally ill."[63] An American journalist, Annaliese Griffin, feels that the recent success among wealthy women of the wellness industry—with all its much-derided yoga, detoxing, smoothies, acupuncture, etc.—can be explained by the disenfranchisement and dehumanization women are experiencing within the dominant medical system. The wellness industry, she explains, "specializes in creating safe, welcoming, amber-lit spaces that make people feel cared-for and relaxed, and which treat the female body as its default."[64] And she quotes a fellow journalist: "Whatever you think of detox and the people who sell it, they are mostly people who care very much for you and who know how fragile happiness and health are and who want you to have a good life."[65]

In early 2018, the American medical drama series *Gray's Anatomy* gave a perfect illustration of the poor treatment afforded women in the conventional system. Convinced she is in the middle of a heart attack, Miranda Bailey, one of the series' female stars, heads to the nearest emergency center.[66] The doctor who receives her is skeptical and refuses to run the more specific tests she asks for. Then we watch a confrontation between a black woman doctor and her white colleague, a Yale graduate, who is condescending and arrogant to boot. Bailey's chances of being believed further diminish when she admits to suffering from obsessive compulsive disorder—she is sent to see a psychiatrist. In the end, it turns out that she was right, and viewers—female and male—can savor the hotshot male doctor's discomfiture. The episode was inspired by the experience of one of the series' writers, who was called a "neurotic Jewish woman" by her doctor.[67] But, when it aired, it also chimed with the story only recently revealed by tennis player Serena Williams: she had experienced great difficulty making herself heard when, in September 2017, shortly after giving birth, she reported the early symptoms of a pulmonary embolism—and was nearly fatally ignored. Her story shone a light on the fact that the US has the highest maternal mortality rate in the developed world and that the rate is even higher for black women: "Complications in pregnancy are killing three to four times more black mothers than white, non-Hispanic mothers, and the babies born to black women are twice as likely to die."[68] This goes back to their having among the worst living conditions, which is associated with worse medical care in general, and to the accumulated stress they live with, but also to racist prejudice which means they are often (still) not taken seriously—even when the patient is rich and famous and, in this case of a top-flight sportswoman, also has an excellent understanding of her own body. Two tragic cases have shown the deadly effects of this kind of contempt in France: in December 2017, the death of Naomi Musenga, a young Frenchwoman of Congolese origin, who was mocked by staff at the emergency-services reception when she tried to get help; and also, in 2007, that of Noélanie, a girl of Haitian origin, whose classmates called her "darkie" and tried to strangle her—but whom doctors refused to accept, having decided that she was "acting."[69]

The Birth of a Subliminal Solidarity

I hate doctors. The doctors are on their feet, the sick people are in bed. [. . .] And the doctors on foot march around the beds of the poor critters on their backs and about to die and, without really seeing the poor sods on their backs, the doctors toss Graeco-Latin words at them which they've no hope of understanding, and the poor people in bed don't dare ask so as not to bother the upstanding doctor who stinks of science and is hiding his own fear of death by disbursing definitive judgments and approximate antibiotics without batting an eyelid like the Pope at his balcony distributing words and the cough mixture of God over the crowd at his feet.[70]

Shortly before French humorist and broadcaster Pierre Desproges's death from cancer in 1988, I had felt a flash of recognition upon reading this indictment, declaimed by him on the *Tribunal des flagrants délires* ("Court of flagrant raving") satirical radio program. I was fifteen in 1988—my unhappy encounters with doctors came early in my life. Due to a health problem detected when I was twelve, I had been passed from specialist to specialist for years. A woman, young, timid and ignorant, facing mature men haloed with all the prestige of science, I had a fair insight into the asymmetrical power relations so well described by Mare Kandre. I think back to my younger self, standing half naked in the middle of a clinic, being examined from every angle by practitioners who talked about me as if I wasn't there and manipulated me roughly, without a care for my teenage modesty. I remember cold, fleshy hands, the smell of breath and aftershave, and the feel of white lab-coats brushing against my bare skin. Later, as an adult, I underwent a gynecological operation which ought not to have required an anesthetic, but went badly wrong. Considered prissy, I was shouted at. When the speculum hurt me, the doctor—a woman—saw red: I was treated to a poisonous and gratuitous, inappropriate comment which characterized me as incapable of tolerating anything in my vagina (speculums being, as everyone knows, perfectly pleasant). Although I am by nature a fairly docile patient, I rebelled: I fought when a mask was put on my face, meant to send me to sleep so they could finish the job. I demanded a minute to breathe before I put it on. Only one nurse seemed to sympathize; the other medics were furious about the time I was wasting for them.

In France, over the last few years, blogs and social media have highlighted issues around medical abuse, for example on the Tumblr *Je n'ai pas consenti* ("I did not consent").[71] Such online activism has percolated through to the mainstream, and other media outlets have picked up on it, with a particular focus on obstetrical malpractice, leading the secretary of state responsible for sexual equality to order an inquiry into the issue, in the summer of 2017.[72] This initial watershed of discussion around the question shared many similarities with the #MeToo movement, which was to kick off only a few weeks later, in the wake of the Harvey Weinstein affair, in effect catalyzing the reporting of sexual harassment and assault. In both fields, a massive collective movement was attempting to overturn the balance of power, to ensure the recognition of women's views and lived experience, and ultimately to subvert the hundreds of rhetorical tricks by which the aggressions aimed at women are downplayed. Other women's stories and their determination not to be steamrollered are persuading all women of their right to refuse certain behaviors. They are enabling us to acknowledge our own disgust, at last silencing the little voice that always used to say, "No, it's you who's being oversensitive, too prudish, too shy, too soft . . ." There is something elating, something galvanizing, in thus toppling the barriers between our separate experiences, or indeed in seeing a Miranda Bailey on our screens fighting to be heard, refusing to be intimidated, when you have yourself felt the crushing pressure of the medical establishment. I realize that new hopes of making a positive difference mean I am now actively interested in this area, whereas before I wanted only to forget my miserable experiences.

Boosted by this new, subliminal sense of solidarity, I am now not quite so petrified when I encounter unpleasant doctors (and of course I also come across entirely lovely ones). And I realize they don't like this. They may take a simple question about what they are doing, asked with genuine amicability, as an unacceptable affront, a crime against their exalted profession. A good patient, it seems, is one who keeps quiet. And they will rapidly move to clinch the argument: this procedure that you are daring to question could very well save your life. One of my friends gave birth in a "historic" Parisian maternity unit, a pioneering place where women's well-being is the top priority, yet she was shocked by the way things turned out, by the way she was frightened and roughly handled. Some time after her son's birth, she went back for a consultation and tried to raise the issue. The consultants interrupted her list of grievances, brusquely retorting, "You are healthy and your child is too; what more do you want?" It's a strange response. My friend was in good health and she had had a normal pregnancy: it was not surprising that she and her son were doing well; you might even say this was the minimum she could expect. But, as Marie-Hélène Lahaye writes, brandishing the specter of death is "the best weapon for dissuading women from aspiring to respect for their bodies and for perpetuating their submission to the medical powers that be."[73] And, if we are to believe Martin Winckler, it is also the best means of dissuading medical students from asking too many questions about the practices they are taught, terrorizing them with the likes of, "If you don't learn the right moves, and if you don't do them the way we say, your patients will die."[74] Often the risk is greatly exaggerated—especially when it comes to pregnant women, who are not ill. Be that as it may, sometimes the risk is real. Faced with a doctor, we are always in a position of weakness: because we are suffering with a more or less serious condition, which *may* kill us; because the doctor has knowledge we do not have and, if anyone has the power to save us, it is the doctor;[75] and because we are in bed and the doctor is up on his feet, as Desproges pointed out. But this position of vulnerability ought to mean that the doctor shows some basic courtesy, not that the sick person has to suck it up. And the contrasting postures tend to exaggerate all emotions: they make poor treatment all the more hurtful, and they prompt eternal gratitude to every doctor who acts with delicacy and empathy.

Treating Patients as People

We may think regretfully of what Western medicine could have been today had that power grab—from the female healers, from women in general, and in opposition to all the values associated with them—not happened. Driven out of the medical profession, as we have seen, women were first allowed to return as nurses. As Barbara Ehrenreich and Deirdre English observe, the nurse is an idealized woman—gentle, maternal, devoted—just as the doctor is an idealized man, haloed with the prestige of science; romance novelists are never wrong about these things. In his skilled hands lie the diagnostic decisions and prescriptions of treatment; in her gentle ones, all the follow-up and daily care. The great man will never "waste his talents or his expensive academic training on the tedious details of bedside care."[76] Winckler describes as follows the perpetuation of this labor division through the training given to French doctors: they are primarily taught to adopt "postures endorsing doctors" authority over that of all other citizens', and not to adopt "actions intended to relieve people who are suffering. Caring is the realm of the nursing profession, of the midwives, the physiotherapists and the counselors. Doctors' business is knowledge and the power that flows from it."[77]

Whereas, as Ehrenreich and English note, "Healing, in its fullest sense, consists of both curing and caring, doctoring *and* nursing. The old lay healers of an earlier time had combined both functions, and were valued for both."[78] When she returns to Barbados after the dark years in Salem, Maryse Condé's version of the witch Tituba once again establishes herself as a healer. One day, she is brought a young rebel slave, at death's door after the 250 strokes of the whip his master has inflicted: "I laid Iphigene (for that was his name) on a straw mattress in a corner of my bedroom so that I could hear his every murmur," she says.[79] Knowledge of the patient and the constant attention she gives him are an integral part of his treatment. They also require that she see him as a person rather than as a passive body, inert and interchangeable. By perpetuating the separation of body and spirit, the latter approach allows for abuse because it dehumanizes the sick person. It is this, in tandem with the controlling mindset described above, which explains how the patient may be manipulated quite casually by a doctor—like a mere mechanical system—and spoken of as if he or she is not there.

Putting yourself on an equal footing with your patient and addressing her or him as a whole person imply not only that you are *not* viewing their body as separate from their mind, but also that you are considering their body with more benevolence than a great scholar absorbed in rational purity tends to do. In the light of the new paradigm whose arrival we have traced, the body acts as a troubling, humiliating reminder of every human's fundamentally animal nature. For Silvia Federici, the obsession with excrement during the era of the witch-hunts, in particular, can be explained by "the bourgeois need to regulate and cleanse the body-machine from any element that could interrupt its activity" and by excrement's symbolism as "ill humors" thought to dwell in the body: for the Puritans, these humors "became the visible sign of the corruption of human nature, a sort of original sin that had to be combated, subjugated, exorcized. Hence the use of purges, emetics and enemas that were administered to children or the 'possessed' to make them expel their devilries."[80] Jules Michelet concurs that, in contrast, witches favored

> what may be called the reënfeoffment (rehabilitation) of the stomach and the digestive organs. They had the boldness to say, "There is nothing foul or unclean." [. . .] There is nothing foul but moral evil. In the natural world all things are pure; nothing may be withheld from our studious regard, nothing be forbidden by an idle spiritualism, still less by a silly disgust.[81]

According to Michelet, this attitude already ran counter to the standard medieval mindset, which, adhering to a hierarchy of "high" versus "low," considered the mind noble and the body non-noble, the sky noble and the abyss non-noble. Michelet argues as follows:

> Why? "Because heaven is high up." But in truth is it neither high nor low, being above and beneath alike. And what is hell? Nothing at all. Equally foolish are they about the world at large and the smaller world of men.
>
> This world is all one piece: each thing in it is attached to all the rest. If the stomach is servant of the brain and feeds it, the brain also works none the less for the stomach, perpetually helping to prepare for it the digestive *sugar*.[82]

Agreeing to look on patients as people, as equals, requires exposing yourself to feeling empathy for them; in other words, to feeling—horror of horrors—emotion. Now, in line with the myth of the cold, detached man of science, we also teach aspiring doctors to reject their emotions. "It all goes on as if, during their last hospital placements, we expect them not to get involved but rather to remain as emotionally distant from their patients as possible. Which, of course, is impossible," Martin Winckler observes. Often, medical students become desensitized during their studies, in an impulse of self-protective withdrawal, because they are stressed, overwhelmed and helpless before the suffering they are seeing, and because the stance of superiority they are taught to adopt implies appearing strong and therefore remaining unmoved. Some patients have even learned to feel reassured by this approach, or, at least, to assume that it does not preclude effective medical treatment. One idea Winckler takes care to knock on the head is that "There is no such thing as a 'cold, distant but competent' doctor."[83]

The idea that doctors could show their emotions seems to terrify both them and some of their patients, as if revealing their humanity and vulnerability would be to risk the loss of their skills, to reduce them to powerlessness—which says much about how we conceive the foundations of these skills. It's as if we fear a flood sweeping everything away in its path, transforming doctors into haggard wrecks and preventing them from doing their work. Yet I remember the oncologist who looked after a close relative. During the last few consultations, when it became clear that he could not keep his patient alive much longer, he sometimes had tears in his eyes. I was very moved when I learned this, later on; I felt sustained in my own grief. Those tears confirmed that the doctor knew he had a man sitting there, not a case. What could be more natural, having cared for this patient for some years? Recognition of their common humanity in no way made him less good as a doctor—quite the contrary. On the other hand, what message do we send when we appear impassive in the face of suffering? Is the psychopath implicitly our model for the good doctor? And does repressing your emotions really allow you to protect yourself?

When the Irrational is Not on the Side You Thought

Of all medicine's many branches, it's obstetrics that most plainly perpetuates both the war against women and the bias in modern science. "The witch and her counterpart, the midwife, were at the symbolic center of a struggle for control over matter and nature essential to new social relations in the spheres of production and reproduction," as Carolyn Merchant writes.[84] Two new tools enabled midwives to be sidelined and underpinned the market for "regular"—i.e. male—doctors: the speculum and the forceps. The speculum was invented in the 1840s by James Marion Sims, a doctor from Alabama who carried out numerous experiments on slaves; he forced one of them, called Anarcha, to go through thirty-odd operations without anaesthesia. "Racism and sexism is [sic] baked into the innocuous speculum itself—think of that next time you're in the stirrups," suggests Sarah Barmak, the Canadian author of *Closer*, about the ways women are now reclaiming sex for themselves.[85] As for the forceps, they were invented much earlier, in the sixteenth century, by Peter Chamberlen, a Huguenot migrant living in England. A century later, in 1670, his nephew Hugh attempted to demonstrate their use for the leading obstetrician, François Mauriceau, at the Hôtel-Dieu in Paris, but the operation was a disaster: it ended with the death of both mother and child. In England, the item was categorized as a surgical instrument, and the practice of surgery was forbidden to women . . . The midwives who accused doctors of using it to dangerous effect found they were protesting in vain.[86] Their petition against Peter Chamberlen III, in 1634, brought about no change. An aggressive smear campaign counter-accused the midwives of incompetence and obscurantism. By the late seventeenth century, birth was almost entirely in the hands of male practitioners.[87] In France, in 1760, Elizabeth Nihell, an English midwife working at the Hôtel-Dieu, confirmed she had never seen a birth requiring the assistance of any instrument. In her *Treatise on the Art of Midwifery*, she accused surgeons of using the forceps for their personal convenience, in order to foreshorten women's labor.[88]

In a grimly ironic twist, the doctors and surgeons managed to rid themselves of midwives by accusing them, in particular, of uncleanliness. Whereas, from the seventeenth to the nineteenth centuries, in the first maternity wards, where at the time only working-class women would give birth, puerperal fever was rife among the patients. In February 1866, for example, a quarter of the women who gave birth at the Paris maternity hospital died. American doctor Oliver Wendell Holmes describes how, in Vienna, circa 1840, the women were buried two to a coffin, in order to disguise the actual death rate.[89] In 1797, puerperal fever killed the English feminist intellectual Mary Wollstonecraft after the birth of her second daughter (Mary Shelley, future author of *Frankenstein*). In the mid-nineteenth century, Ignaz Philipp Semmelweis, then working at the hospital in Vienna, discovered the origin of this "epidemic": after dissecting bodies, the doctors would go off to assist at births—without having washed their hands . . . When he forced all his colleagues to wash their hands before entering the operating room, the mortality rate dropped dramatically. He was tormented by guilt: "God only knows the number of women whom I have consigned prematurely to the grave." But his discovery prompted outrage among his colleagues, who were offended by the notion that their own hands could be vectors of death. During the years that followed, Semmelweis had many doors closed in his face. Clinically depressed, he died in 1865 in a Vienna psychiatric asylum. Back in 1795, Alexander Gordon, a Scottish doctor, had proposed a similar hypothesis, but his theory met a wall of silence; and, having reached the same conclusions, Holmes was subject to similar attacks: he was labeled an irresponsible, attention-seeking social climber . . . Systematic handwashing was only instigated twenty years after Semmelweis's death.[90]

In her book *Accouchement: les femmes méritent mieux* ("Birth: women deserve better"), Marie-Hélène Lahaye goes beyond a mere exposé of obstetrical abuses: independently of the behavior, more or less well intended, of individual doctors, midwives and nurses, she sets out in detail all the absurdities and dubious practices involved in the way most of us came into the world and/or gave birth. Lahaye invites us to revise entirely how we conceptualize and organize birth—something that we are so used to doing the same old way, we can't imagine any other approach. Yet there is much in need of change, starting with the standard birth position: lying on your back is in fact the least convenient position for both woman and infant, for it deprives them of gravity's help. Uruguayan doctor Roberto Caldeyro-Barcia calls it the worst conceivable position "except for being hanged by the feet."[91] Certainly it suits only one of those present: the practitioner, who can sit or stand between the laboring woman's legs, from whom he steals the show. It is, in fact, equivalent to the missionary position in sexual intercourse, each being considered the only "appropriate" position, setting up "an active and hardworking man over a passive woman, preferably spread flat like a starfish."[92] It is revealing that, in 1663, when his mistress Louise de la Vallière was preparing to give birth, King Louis XIV is said to have asked the doctor to lay her on her back "so he could watch the birth while remaining hidden behind a canopy."[93] As ever, the obsession with surveillance . . . Five years later, the King's doctor, Mauriceau—the same man to whom Hugh Chamberlen had given his failed demonstration of the forceps—recommended this position in his influential treatise on giving birth.

Sketch for a Better World

In one corner, the labor ward as we know it: noisy, glaringly lit, with medical staff rushing in every direction and the laboring women duly neutralized, locked down by their monitors, on whom identical positions and procedures are imposed—an organizing model that is indeed "Fordist, in its production-line approach and its standardization," as Lahaye observes.[94] (Adrienne Rich, who made comparable observations in *Of Woman Born*, comments that we may indeed require assistance and support during a birth, but that "there is a difference between crying out for help and asking to be 'put under.'"[95]) In the other corner, the "natural birth rooms" in a clinic, where Lahaye gave birth herself, in the presence of her partner and her midwife. "In dim light and with relaxing music playing," she writes, "I freely took on the positions my body demanded, rearing like a panther between the room's fitted bars, swinging from the equipment like a monkey, as I wished. I did not feel pain, rather an incredible sense of power. I gave shouts of strength, yells of energy, moans of immensity."[96] Reading these two descriptions, I feel as though, in the first, I'm finding every element of the all-for-show culture that, as I've explained, makes me deeply uncomfortable, and that, in the second, I'm seeing the outline of how a different world could be, one that sustains a more peaceful relationship with nature—and with women. Two very different worlds into which to welcome a brand-new human being, and two very different ways of setting the tone for that being's life to come.

Lahaye's approach also interests me because she does not lay claim to an irrational position in opposition to a rational medical establishment; on the contrary, she challenges the establishment's very claim to rationality. Her book is stuffed with footnotes and scientific references. Although she calls for women to take back control in giving birth, she isn't doing so in the name of any imagined "instinct" that would give them some innate understanding of the process: birth, she says, is "a series of reflexes," something the body knows how to do already, like vomiting, "but with a much happier outcome," and for which the principal requirement is to be left to get on with it. Lahaye shows how the stress induced by hospital protocols causes the problems hospitals then pride themselves on solving:

> The noise of monitoring, and the shrill alarm that goes off if a sensor pulls away, can provoke a spike in adrenaline in the woman. Adrenaline production works to counter oxytocin production—the latter hormone being the one that leads, among other things, to the uterus contracting, and is essential for giving birth. The contractions then become less effective. To compensate, the medical team may inject a dose of oxytocin, which modifies the contractions and increases the woman's pain, due to her not releasing endorphins, another hormone. The mother may

then feel she needs an epidural to combat the pain, whose effect is then to stop her moving, which then leads to a further slowing of labor.[97]

This logic leads Lahaye to conclude that, of those women who say, "I would be dead if I'd not given birth in hospital," a good number might equally say, "They almost killed me at the hospital."[98] What's more, contrary to widespread belief, it wasn't the move to give birth in hospitals which led to the overall drop in maternal mortality: "The decline in mortality at birth between 1945 and 1950 is due far more to the effects of improved living conditions and hygiene, and to advances in general medicine, than to the practice of obstetric intervention at the moment of birth."[99]

Despite their parallel activity as sorceresses, about which we may be skeptical, and much more than the era's official doctors, the female healers targeted by the witch-hunts were already working within the parameters of the rational; indeed, they are characterized by Ehrenreich and English as "safer and more effective" than the "regular" doctors.[100] These doctors had studied Plato, Aristotle and theology; prominent among their repertoire were bloodletting and the application of leeches. However futile their claim to cure, doctors nonetheless encountered resistance from the religious authorities, for whom their efforts appeared to interfere with God's intentions. In the fourteenth century, doctors had the right to practice, but had to show "that their attentions to the body did not jeopardize the soul." ("In fact," Ehrenreich and English add, "accounts of their medical training make it seem more likely that they jeopardized the *body*."[101]) While medicine practiced officially

by and for the wealthier classes was tolerated, the women healers did not receive the same indulgence. They actively rejected
the fatalism when faced by illness that the clergy wished to
inculcate in their communities and which Michelet sums up
as follows: "Resign yourselves to suffer and to die. The Church
has prayers for the dead."[102] Similarly, women were obliged to
suffer when they brought children into the world in order to
expiate original sin. The healers eased their pain with ergot
of rye, from which even today certain derivatives form the
basis for medications used during and after childbirth. In fact,
many of the plants they used still contribute to our modern
pharmacopoeia. "It was witches who developed an extensive
understanding of bones and muscles, herbs and drugs, while
physicians were still deriving their prognoses from astrol-
ogy."[103] In other words, the daring and foresight, the refusal
to rely on old methods and the rejection of old superstitions
didn't necessarily come from the quarter we tend to expect.
As early as 1893, Matilda Joslyn Gage was explaining, "we
have abundant proof that the so-called 'witch' was among the
most profoundly scientific persons of the age."[104] Associating
witches with the Devil indicated that they had reached beyond
the realm to which men had tried to confine them, and were
now impinging on male privileges. Gage went on to remark
that "Death by torture was the method of the Church for the
repression of woman's intellect, knowledge being held as evil
and dangerous in her hands."[105]

The Revolt of the "Good Little Hysterics"

These days, the conflict over the symbolic order established
during the Renaissance is not, of course, confined to the realm

of healthcare. Let's go back to the repression of emotions and to the derogatory attribution of emotions to women alone—a dynamic that's especially marked among medics, but present throughout society. In 1985, African-American activist Cora Tucker was leading the protests against the installation of a radioactive waste storage site in the poor, majority black county of Halifax, in Virginia, where she lived. She described how hurt she had been at first when the (male, white) representatives of the authorities had called her a "hysterical housewife." Then, she had reconsidered, and, at the next encounter, when they reiterated their insult, she had replied, "You're exactly right. We're hysterical and when it comes to matters of life and death, especially mine, I get hysterical. [. . .] If men don't get hysterical, there's something wrong with them."[106] In short, our emotions don't always lead us astray; sometimes, on the contrary, when we listen to them, they can save us. This can work not only when people are trying to make us live on the edge of radioactive landfill sites, but also in situations of harassment and abuse, like those outlined above. By giving some credit to their feelings—whether disgust, anger, rejection or resistance—by listening to the alarms going off in their bodies and minds, victims may find the strength to defend themselves, especially when the voice of reason is just a front for the debilitating, intimidating voice of authority.

Of course, emotions can also blinker us and lay us open to manipulation. But we will not protect ourselves from this risk by attempting to block them out, for, in any case, the emotions will always be there. In Susan Griffin's opening acknowledgments in *Woman and Nature*, she thanks all those who have contributed to her "thinking." Griffin goes on to explain that she is using the word "think" "as it is constructed in Chinese calligraphy: 'brain' and 'heart' together."[107] Philosopher Michel Hulin reminds us that it is delusional to lay claim to a pure rationalism, free of all affect. He stresses that, at the root of all intellectual discipline, even the most rigorous and solidly grounded, there is an emotional preference— even if only that which makes us prefer "the organized to the chaotic, the clear to the muddled, the complete over the incomplete, the coherent over what is contradictory." He writes, "More fundamentally, our emotional life, along with its inevitable dimension of bias, sits at the very center of the act of understanding, in the sense that a consciousness that is perfectly neutral and impervious to all consideration of value would merely be content to leave things in the state in which they are presented to it." And he concludes that, "It is upon the shifting sands of emotional preference that the whole edifice of our theoretical constructions stands, in every realm of our knowledge."[108]

If we examine this question more closely, there is something childish about the highly implausible claim to a rationality that is immaterial, pure, transparent and objective—childish and deeply fearful. Faced with a character who appears impervious to doubt and sure of himself, his knowledge and his superiority—whether he's a doctor, a scholar, an intellectual or a barfly—it can be hard to remember that this stance may cloak a fundamental insecurity. And yet, this hypothesis is worth considering, as Mare Kandre implies in *The Woman and Dr. Dreuf,* in which she flushes out the terrified little boy hiding behind the great man of science. First of all, we should remember that the Cartesian world view was intended to avert a vast destabilization. By showing that the Earth spins around the Sun, Copernicus had turned the cosmogony of his times upside down, an act of iconoclasm that was further reinforced by the work of sixteenth-century Dominican friar Giordano Bruno, who posited that the universe could be infinite, thus polishing off the "snug, finite universe of the mediaeval imagination," as Susan Bordo described it.[109] At the same time, the first telescopes were catapulting observers into the celestial void. From now on, "infinity had opened its jaws," in Arthur Koestler's words.[110] Descartes' task was to respond to the anxiety born of this bonfire of the certainties, to lead "the journey from doubt and despair to certainty and hope."[111] As if in a fit of pique or self-defense, in his approach to this universe now viewed as vast and empty, indifferent and cold, Descartes cultivated an attitude of maximum detachment. His masterstroke was the transformation of an experience of "estrangement and loss" into an engine promoting understanding and human progress.[112] With this transition, to all intents and purposes, complete, "the nightmare landscape of the infinite universe has become the well-lighted laboratory of modern science and philosophy."[113]

Those who nowadays see inconveniences to living in this laboratory often come up against the incomprehension and disapproval of their peers. They are accused of opposing the technological society on which they are nonetheless dependent and the comforts of which they enjoy—even if this argument is losing credence as the effects of the ecological crisis become ever more direct and flagrant. This logic follows the same pattern as attempts to silence patients criticizing the medical system on the pretext that their health and sometimes their lives depend on it. We are thus to be neutralized by guilt and condemned to submission and resignation. Can we be held responsible for the society into which we were born and in relation to which our room for maneuver is inevitably limited? To use this as grounds to ban all critique of our society amounts to tying our hands in the face of disaster, hamstringing thought and, more broadly, stifling imagination, desire and the capacity to recall that things are not doomed to be as they currently are.

Besides, it is quite strange that many people seem not even to dream that history could have been different, that progress could have taken different paths and we could have had—could still have—the benefits without the problems. It's an attitude brutally summed up by the binary adage, or rather, blackmail, that offers only "the nuclear age or the stone age" (with the result that we'll likely be stuck with both at once). Hence, at the end of his thoroughly researched history of the witch-hunts in Europe, which veils none of the horror, reconstructs the story as it unfolded and presents a rich and complex discussion of their cultural significance, Guy Bechtel comes to the surprising conclusion that, in essence, you can't make an omelette without breaking a few eggs. Indeed, he feels that this episode should be seen as a "revolution," and revolutions, Bechtel argues, "can only be achieved by the annihilation of opposing positions and of those who uphold them (or claim to uphold them)."[114] He says, "The movement that tried to kill the witches is also, unwittingly of course, that which paved the way, later on, for the lives and thought of Montesquieu, Voltaire and Kant." In conclusion, he gives his blessing to a logic that he sums up with the maxim: "Killing the women of the past to create the men of the future."[115] And, in doing so, Bechtel shows, once again, that historians of the witch-hunts are themselves products of the world that hunted the witches, and that they remain locked inside the frame of reference that the witch-hunts created. Bechtel's point of view is a stark contrast to the very different views of Barbara Ehrenreich and Deirdre English, who describe not only individual tragedies—the quashed aspirations and broken spirits of the hunts' victims—but also all that society denied itself by outlawing them, all that these women were prevented from developing and passing to future generations. Ehrenreich and English speak of "the sheer waste of talent and knowledge" represented by the witch-hunts, and urge us to undertake the "important task [. . .] of recovering, or at least pointing out, what was lost."[116]

Bechtel's determination to forcibly insert the horrendous history he has just pieced together into the virtuous account of the dawn of progress prompts him to come up with theories that are far-fetched to say the least: "It is likely that we are, at least partially, indebted to the unjustifiable massacre of the witches for a change in mindset toward greater rationalism, greater justice, stronger support for the right to legal defense and general awareness of human rights," as he puts it.[117] An attempt to justify what you have, in the same sentence, just called unjustifiable? Matilda Joslyn Gage's analysis (as early as 1893) seems altogether more plausible:

> During the witchcraft period the minds of people were trained in a single direction. The chief lesson

of the church that betrayal of friends was necessary to one's own salvation created an intense selfishness. All humanitarian feeling was lost in the effort to secure heaven at the expense of others, even those most closely bound by ties of nature and affection. Mercy, tenderness, compassion were all obliterated. Truthfulness escaped from the Christian world; fear, sorrow and cruelty reigned pre-eminent. [. . .] Contempt and hatred of women was inculcated with greater intensity; love of power and treachery were parts of the selfish lessons of the church. All reverence for length of years was lost. The sorrows and sufferings of a long life appealed to no sympathetic cord in the heart.[118]

A much more appropriate tableau to offer overexcited and gushy humanists requiring a cold shower.

Thinking Two Liberations in One

Even if the symbolic order that fetishizes detachment and objectivity was largely created in opposition to women and all that is associated with them, these days, as we would expect—and all the more effectively, now, five centuries from its origins—the order has fought free of this dynamic. In our daily interactions as in our intellectual lives, it has been subject to challenges from all quarters, both incidental and deliberate, and many of these challenges are framed independently of any reference to gender. Even while some men and women (such as myself) exemplify the opposing positions to the point of caricature—that is, we embody respectively a masculine rationality or a feminine emotionality—this system is criticized by many men and espoused by many women. But we can also choose to oppose it from a feminist point of view. Many of the witches in these pages express a lucid and determined disagreement with the world view of those who would crush them beneath their heels. "She taught me that everything lives, has a soul and breathes. That everything must be respected. That man is not the master riding through his kingdom on horseback," says Maryse Condé's Tituba about the old slave whose legacy of knowledge she received.[119]

Some women thinkers lead this critique by reclaiming the association between women and nature previously made by the philosophers, and by giving new credence to the idea that women may be "closer to nature" than men, that they have particular affinities with the natural world. The best-known supporter of this theory, although she never mentions the origins of modern science and does not belong to the ecofeminist movement, is without question Clarissa Pinkola Estés, author of the bestseller *Women Who Run With the Wolves*.[120] This work exemplifies the essentialism which has provoked impassioned debate within—and, perhaps most importantly, around—the ecofeminist movement, some elements of which have been accused of promoting a similar vision. This movement began in the 1980s when, in the English-speaking world, activists made the link between the exploitation of natural resources and the male domination they were personally struggling with. But can we be satisfied with a wholesale rejection of such essentialism, along the lines of Janet Biehl's work, which was strongly influenced by the eco-socialist theorist Murray Bookchin?[121] According to philosopher Catherine Larrère, "in order to free women from the domination that keeps them down, it isn't enough to deconstruct their naturalization for the sake of repatriating them on the same side as men—on the side of 'culture.' This would be to do only half the job and to leave nature high and dry. Nature's cause would lose out—but so would women's."[122] Ecofeminists, as Émilie Hache explains, want to be able to reclaim, to regain control of and celebrate the body, which has been demonized (literally), degraded and vilified for centuries. They also want to challenge the warring, antagonistic approach to nature that we have developed in parallel. As they see it, the problem can be framed like this: "How to (re)build a connection with a nature from which we have been excluded or from which we have excluded ourselves due to being forcibly and negatively identified with it?"[123]

At the same time, ecofeminists refuse to let "nature" become a pretext for imposing on them a normative outcome or behavior such as motherhood or heterosexuality. The little-known experience of the "back-to-nature" separatist lesbian communities in 1970s Oregon offers solid proof of this view's tenacity (as well as offering all we need to finish off those who, in France at least, go ballistic at the mere idea that women—or victims of racism—might organize a couple of hours' encounter without any men involved).[124] "Why should we hand heterosexuals the monopoly on having 'natural' sex lives and imagine that queer movements could only emerge in cities, far from and in opposition to nature?" Larrère asks. She sees "no reason to build feminism upon a denial of nature."[125] Similarly, why should the rediscovery of our connection with nature require imposing motherhood on women who don't want it and thereby violating their sovereignty over their own bodies? Historically, as we have seen, the war on nature has gone hand in hand with the war waged against women wanting to take control of their fertility. This demonstrates the ineptness of today's Christian reactionaries, who base their anti-abortion crusade on a would-be "ecological fundamentalism" and are hoping, according to the appalling slogan of their figurehead in France, Eugénie Bastié, "to save both the penguins and the embryos."[126] Environmentalism has proved a convenient new way to oppress women.

Émilie Hache notes with alarm that certain ecofeminist writers have only to celebrate women's bodies or mention "the goddess" for "scandalized yelps" and accusations of essentialism to ensue. "What has happened to make all reference to the body, i.e. to the [cis] female body, impossible?" she asks.[127] A demonstration of the thousand and one tricks of misogyny, in all its depth and tenacity, perhaps? Hache calls for a much more open-minded attitude: "Instead of seeing this as an assertion of biological essence and a reiteration of patriarchal discourse, we should read these texts as acts of healing and empowerment, as pragmatic attempts at cultural repair after centuries of women's denigration, and as a move to reconnect with the Earth and nature."[128] Hache regrets that disproportionate anxiety over the bogeyman of essentialism ends up inhibiting both thought and action. But, more than anything, she sees what emerges here, in the vehemence of the opposition, as principally a means of punishing the ecofeminist movement for its audacity. For it is audacious, there's no question. And audacity is what we need if we're to challenge not only our own destinies, but also the global order in which they participate. To me, this audacity is on a continuum with the spike in resistance we have seen these last few years over sexual harassment and medical malpractice. It is simply an extension of this work: as ever, the point is to compel the world to hear our stories and our views, to expose what is going on behind the scenes and to bring it into the light of day.

Your World Does Not Work for Me

In the winter of 2018, an episode in the Harvey Weinstein affair jumped out at me as a textbook study for this point. The long-awaited testimony of the actor Uma Thurman completely destroyed the monument to pop culture that was *Kill Bill*, volumes 1 and 2 (2003 and 2004), a pair of films directed by Quentin Tarantino and produced by Weinstein's company, Miramax.[129] Until this moment, the films had been billed as feminist, presenting an invincible and resourceful heroine, both strong and sexy, played by an actor at the top of her Hollywood game and allied to her director by a rock-solid understanding. At the end of Thurman's testimony, we are faced with the horrifying tale of an actor who, already raped at the age of sixteen, was then subjected to further sexual harassment, like dozens of her peers, by her film's producer. As for Tarantino, after repeatedly behaving in a sick and sadistic way toward Thurman throughout the film shoot, he almost managed to kill her by forcing her to do her own stunt, in which she had to drive an unsafe car that went out of control and crashed into a tree—Thurman eventually posted footage of the accident on Instagram, as a bitter counterpoint to the film, after waiting years for it to be released to her. Far from becoming one with the glorious warrior she played on screen, or with the ethereal and sultry star, perfected by Pilates and beauty treatments and sold to us by the magazines, Thurman came out of this as the survivor of an ordeal, still suffering the episode's consequences in her injured neck and knees. Even the photo illustrating her interview in the *New York Times*, showing a forty-something woman who is visibly well off and privileged, though still human and unextraordinary, with a rather tired expression, marked a break from the smooth and unrealistic imagery of Thurman's usual Photoshop creations. Suddenly, with testimony from Thurman and hundreds of others, we could really see how drastically the world through women's eyes differs from the world we are sold every day. What we meant by that standard term "speaking out" effectively cast a kind of spell, it became a magic mantra, unleashing storms and lightning strikes, sowing chaos amid our settled world. The great legends of our culture have been toppling like dominoes, and those who, on social media, have credited us with censorious intentions as we relayed these dramatic changes of perspective surely exposed their own alarm at finding the ground crumbling beneath their feet. Having myself grown up with these legends, and having been fully signed up to them—I still occasionally get a reflex impulse to quote Woody Allen witticisms—I was no less thunderstruck than anyone else. But, unlike its critics, I welcome this crisis as a liberation, a decisive breakthrough, a reconfiguration of our social universe. It feels like a brand-new world view is struggling to take over and replace the old.

Your world does not work for me: the cult of the goddess, practiced by Starhawk and other witches, may represent the most radical way of asserting this and of seeking to remedy it, even if their choice does at first look like a New Age fad. Although we live in largely secular societies, and although many women and men no longer believe in God, as ecofeminist writer Carol P. Christ explains, the patriarchal religions fashioned our culture, values and ideas, and the male authority model that resulted directly from their influence is still ingrained in us. "The reason for the continuing effect of religious symbols is that the mind abhors a vacuum. Symbol systems cannot simply be rejected, they must be replaced."[130] It follows, then, that a woman who practices the cult of the goddess and nourishes herself with these images is deliberately displacing one representation with another. This is about re-centering, allowing yourself to be the source of your own salvation and finding your resources within you, instead of always relying on standard male authority figures. A friend who had never heard of the neo-pagan cult of the goddess told me that, when she needs to be in touch with her own strength, she pictures herself in the form of the sea goddess from *Ponyo,* Hayao Miyazaki's 2008 animation feature: that is, as a mother figure who is both gentle and powerful, which makes perfect sense for my friend, for whom motherhood is an important dimension of her life.

In 2017, black artist Harmonia Rosales reinterpreted Michelangelo's fresco for the Sistine Chapel, *The Creation of Adam.* She replaced Adam and God, both white men in Michelangelo's depiction, with two black women, and she called her piece *The Creation of God:* a way of proclaiming that the emperor has no clothes. Her painting knocks the viewer off balance. It forces us to realize how arbitrary, relative and provisional the old, familiar representations are. Susan Griffin's book *Woman and Nature* creates the same effect: by drawing up a catalog of the great truths about men, women, nature and knowledge, the world, etc., which have become embedded over the centuries, and by offering them up for critical analysis, Griffin invites us to see them with fresh eyes and so to identify the prejudices that linger in our minds.[131] And this is a supremely exciting invitation to embrace freedom and creativity—exciting, but also crucial, for the system we have inherited looks about to breathe its last.

In her conclusion to *The Death of Nature,* Carolyn Merchant made the following diagnosis: "The world must once again be turned upside down."[132] She was writing the day after the 1979 Three Mile Island nuclear explosion, the worst nuclear power accident in the US to date. If we want to decide today what might justify such a conclusion, we are spoiled for choice. Turning the world upside down is no small undertaking. But there can be great joy—the joy of audacity, of insolence, of a vital affirmation, of defying faceless authority—in allowing our ideas and imaginations to follow the paths down which these witches' whisperings entice us. Joy in bringing into focus an image of this world that would ensure humanity's well-being through an even-handed pact with nature, not by a Pyrrhic victory over it—this world, where the untrammeled enjoyment of our bodies and our minds would never again be associated with a hellish sabbath.

Acknowledgments

Thank you, Guillaume Barou, Akram Belkaïd, Otto Bruun, Irina Cotseli, Thomas Deltombe, Eleonora Faletti, Sébastien Fontenelle, Alain Gresh, Madmeg, Emmanuelle Maupetit, Daria Michel Scotti, Joyce A. Nashawati, Geneviève Sellier, Maïté Simoncini, Sylvie Tissot and Laélia Véron for all of your reading recommendations, your links and clippings, your discussions and encouragement. Of course, the finished product is mine and nothing in it should be laid at any door other than mine.

Thank you, Serge Halimi, for the sabbatical I took to work on this book.

And my deepest gratitude goes to Katia Berger, Dominique Brancher and Frédéric Le Van for your invaluable readings and your judicious comments.

I must also thank my editor, Grégoire Chamayou.

And special thanks, once more, to Thomas Lemahieu.

Notes

Epigraph

1. *See:* https://www.versobooks.com/blogs/4588-witchy-bitchy.

Foreword

1. And, if she's Baba Yaga, her house is a hut and her hut has chicken legs.

    2. I would be remiss, here, if I didn't quote Lindy West's searing op-ed responding directly to this comment: "The witches are coming, but not for your life. We're coming for your legacy . . . We don't have the justice system on our side; we don't have institutional power; we don't have millions of dollars or the presidency; but we have our stories, and we're going to keep telling them. Happy Halloween." (Lindy West, "Yes, This Is a Witch Hunt. I'm a Witch and I'm Hunting You." *New York Times,* October 17, 2017.)

Introduction

1. Maria Gripe, trans. Sheila La Farge, with drawings by Harald Gripe, *The Glassblower's Children* (London: Abelard-Schuman, 1973), p. 11.

    2. Mona Chollet, *Beauté fatale. Les nouveaux visages d'une aliénation féminine* (Paris: La Découverte Poche, 2012).

3. Gripe, op. cit., p. 12.

4. In this series of books for young readers by Georges Chaulet, Fantômette is a clever and resourceful schoolgirl who wears a cape and a mask at night and beats up bad guys.

5. Guy Bechtel, *La Sorcière et l'Occident: La destruction de la sorcellerie en Europe, des origines aux grands bûchers* (Paris: Plon, 1997), p. 641.

6. Bechtel, op. cit., p. 8.

7. Bechtel, op. cit., p. 106.

8. Françoise d'Eaubonne, *Le Sexocide des sorcières* (Paris: L'Esprit frappeur, 1999).

9. Bechtel, op. cit., p. 224.

10. In other cases, we may note a symmetry between anti-Semitism and plain misogyny: in Germany, rumors claimed that Jewish men, having been circumcised, bled every month (Barstow, *Witchcraze: A New History of the European Witch Hunts* [New York, NY: HarperCollins, 1994]).

11. Bechtel, op. cit., p. 157.

12. Bechtel, op. cit., p. 199.

13. Bechtel, op. cit., p. 431.

14. Johann Sprenger, quoted in Barrière-Flavy, *La Chronique Criminelle d'une Grande Province sous Louis XIV* (Paris: Occitania, 1926), available at https://archive.org/stream/LaChroniq ueCriminelleDuneGrandeProvinceSousLouisXiv/Barriere_Flavy _Chronique_Criminelle_djvu.txt.

15. Christopher S. Mackay, *The Hammer of Witches: A Complete Translation of the Malleus Maleficarum* (Cambridge: Cambridge University Press, 2006), vol. II, pp. 120–1.

16. Anne L. Barstow, *Witchcraze* (San Francisco, CA / London: Pandora, 1995), p. 142.

17. Barstow, op. cit., p. 41.

18. Bechtel, op. cit., p. 461.

19. Silvia Federici, *Caliban and the Witch* (Brooklyn, NY: Autonomedia, 2004), p. 189.

20. Bechtel, op. cit., p. 463.

21. Bechtel, op. cit., p. 465.

22. William Shakespeare, *La Tempête*, trans. François Guizot (Paris, 1864), Act V, Scene I, note 24 (my translation). *See:* https://www.gutenberg.org/files/15071/15071-h/15071-h.html.

23. Barstow, op. cit., p. 130.

24. Barstow, op. cit., p. 11.

25. Bechtel, op. cit., p. 535.

26. Carol F. Karlsen, *The Devil in the Shape of a Woman* (New York, NY / London: Norton, 1998), p. 262.

27. Barstow, op. cit., p. 142.

28. Barstow, op. cit., p. 5.

29. Bechtel, op. cit., p. 241.

30. Jean Delumeau, *La Peur en Occident* (Paris: Librairie Arthème Fayard, 1978), ch. 10: "Les agents de Satan III: la femme," heading 2: "La diabolisation de la femme," ebook location 61% / empl. 8829.

31. Guy Bechtel, *Les Quatre Femmes de Dieu: La putain, la sorcière, la sainte et Bécassine* (Paris: Plon, 2000), p. 72.

32. Delumeau, op. cit., ch. 10: "Les agents de Satan III: la femme," heading 4, "Une production littéraire souvent hostile à la femme," ebook location 65% / empl. 9346.

33. *The Works of Voltaire: A Contemporary Version.* A Critique and Biography by John Morley, notes by Tobias Smollett, trans. William F. Fleming (New York: E. R. DuMont, 1901). In 21 vols. Vol. V. *See:* https://oll.libertyfund.org/titles/voltaire-the-works-of-voltaire-vol-v-philosophical-dictionary-part-3.

34. Colette Arnould, *Histoire de la sorcellerie* (Paris: Tallandier, 1992, 2009).

35. Quoted in Barstow, op. cit., p. 3 (emphasis added by Barstow).

36. Karlsen, op. cit., p. 263.

37. Barbara Ehrenreich and Deirdre English, *Witches, Midwives and Nurses: A History of Women Healers* (New York, NY: Feminist Press, 1973, 2010), second edition, p. 14.

38. Robert Muchembled, *Les Derniers Bûchers: Un village de France et ses sorcières sous Louis XIV* (Paris: Ramsay, 1981).

39. Agathe Duparc, "Anna Göldi, sorcière enfin bien-aimée," in *Le Monde*, September 4, 2008.

40. Barstow, op. cit., p. 167.

41. Duparc, op. cit.

42. Matilda Joslyn Gage, *Woman, Church, & State* (New York: The Truth Seeker Company, 1893), p. 291. *See:* https://sacred-texts .com/wmn/wcs/wcs07.htm.

43. Kristen J. Sollée, *Witches, Sluts, Feminists: Conjuring the Sex Positive* (Berkeley, CA: ThreeL Media, 2017), p. 48.

44. Robin Morgan, *Going Too Far: The Personal Chronicle of a Feminist* (New York, NY: Random House, 1977), p. 76.

45. Morgan, op cit, p. 72.

46. For a detailed (and illustrated) survey of the evolution of the witch and her cultural transformations through the ages, see Julie Proust Tanguy, *Sorcières! Le somber grimoire du féminin* (Bordeaux: Les Moutons Électriques, 2015).

47. I recommend Québécoise singer Pauline Julien's version, which can be found on YouTube.

48. Sollée, op. cit., p. 61.

49. Starhawk, *Dreaming the Dark* (Boston, MA: Beacon Press, 1982).

50. Mæl, "Tremate tremate, le streghe son tornate! Tremblez tremblez, les sorcières sont de retour!—Introduction à la sorcellerie," Simonae.fr, September 11, 2017.

51. Starhawk, *The Spiral Dance: A Rebirth of the Ancient Religion of the Goddess* (20th Anniversary Edition) (New York, NY: HarperCollins, 1999), pp. 4–5.

52. Mona Chollet, *La Tyrannie de la réalité* (Paris: Calmann-Lévy, 2004); *Chez soi: Une odyssée de l'espace domestique* (Paris: Éditions La Découverte, 2016).

53. Starhawk, *Dreaming the Dark* (Boston, MA: Beacon Press, 1982), p. 10.

54. Starhawk, *A Pagan Response to Katrina*, September 14, 2005. *See:* https://starhawk.org/Activism/activism%20writings/2005

-August-Hurricane-Katrina/2005–09–14-A-Pagan-Response-to
-Katrina.pdf.

55. E. Orrell, "'I just like thinking about the moon and light-ing candles': 21st-century Witches on Instagram" in *Ethnographic Encounters,* vol. 10, no. 1, 2019. *See:* https://ojs.st-andrews.ac.uk /index.php/SAEE/article/view/1963.

56. https://medium.com/defiant/use-this-spell-to-bind-trump -and-his-cronies-a5b6298f5c69.

57. Alex Mar, *Witches of America* (New York, NY: Sarah Crichton Books, 2015).

58. Corin Faife, "How Witchcraft Became a Brand," Buzz-Feed.com, 26 July 2017. *See:* https://www.buzzfeed.com/corinfaife /how-witchcraft-became-a-brand.

59. Jean Baudrillard, *The Consumer Society: Myths and Structure* (London: Sage, 1998), p. 31.

60. K-Hole, *A Report on Doubt,* August 2015, p. 10. *See:* http://khole.net/issues/05/.

61. https://www.susannekaufmann.com/pages/origin.

62. Mary Daly, *Gyn/Ecology: The Metaethics of Radical Feminism* (Boston, MA: Beacon Press, 1990 [first published 1978]), ch. 1.

63. D'Eaubonne, op. cit. (my translation).

64. Bechtel, *La Sorcière et l'Occident,* op. cit.

65. Barstow, op. cit., p. 105.

66. Armelle Le Bras-Chopard, *Les Putains du Diable: Le procès en sorcellerie des femmes* (Paris: Plon, 2006), p. 196.

67. Garthine Walker, "The Strangeness of the Familiar: Witchcraft and the Law in Early Modern England," in Angela McShane and Garthine Walker (eds.), *The Extraordinary and the Everyday in Early Modern England* (Basingstoke: Palgrave Mac-millan, 2010), pp. 105–24.

68. Barstow, op. cit., p. 135.

69. Federici, op. cit., p. 12.

70. Bechtel, *La Sorcière et l'Occident,* op. cit.

71. Gage, op. cit., p. 275.

72. Federici, op. cit., p. 25 etc. (Chapter: "The Struggle on the Commons.")

73. Federici, op. cit., e.g. pp. 12–13.

74. Chollet, *Chez soi*, op. cit.

75. Diane Wulwek, "Les cheveux gris ne se cachent plus," *Le Monde 2*, February 24, 2007.

76. Sophie Fontanel, *Une apparition* (Paris: Robert Laffont, 2017). Cf. Mona Chollet, "La revanche d'une blande," La Méridienne (blog), June 24, 2017. *See:* http://www.la-meridienne.info/La -revanche-d-une-blande.

77. Katie Couric, quoted in Rebecca Traister, *All the Single Ladies: Unmarried Women and the Rise of an Independent Nation* (New York, NY: Simon & Schuster, 2016), p. 119.

78. Pam Houston, "The trouble with having it all," in Meghan Daum (ed.), *Selfish, Shallow, and Self-Absorbed: Sixteen Writers on the Decision Not to Have Kids* (New York, NY: Picador, 2015).

79. Fontanel, op. cit., p. 26 (my translation).

80. *The Mindscape of Alan Moore* (documentary), written and directed by Dez Vylenz and Moritz Winkler, 2005.

Chapter 1: A Life of One's Own

1. *Gloria: In Her Own Words* (documentary), directed by Peter Kunhardt, HBO, 2011.

2. Rebecca Traister, *All the Single Ladies* (New York, NY: Simon & Schuster, 2016), pp. 264–5.

3. Traister, op. cit., p. 266.

4. Betty Friedan, "Up from the kitchen floor," in *New York Times*, March 4, 1973. *See:* https://www.nytimes.com/1973/03/04 /archives/up-from-the-kitchen-floor-kitchen-floor.html.

5. Traister, op. cit., p. 24.

6. This does not mean—of course—that marriage had never been attacked before. See, for example, Voltairine de Cleyre, *Le mariage est une mauvaise action* [1907] (Paris: Éditions du Sextant, 2009).

7. Quoted in Traister, op. cit., p. 27.

8. Stephanie Cootz, *A Strange Stirring: The Feminine Mystique and American Women at the Dawn of the 1960s* (New York, NY: Basic Books, 2011), p. 123.

9. Cf. Kaitlyn Greenidge, "Secrets of the South," Lenny Letter (website), October 6, 2017. *See:* https://www.lennyletter.com/story/secrets-of-the-south.

10. Traister, op. cit., p. 23.

11. "'Welfare Queen' Becomes Issue in Reagan Campaign," in *New York Times*, February 15, 1976. *See:* https://www.nytimes.com/1976/02/15/archives/welfare-queen-becomes-issue-in-reagan-campaign-hitting-a-nerve-now.html.

12. Eric Bradner, "Jeb Bush to women on welfare in 1994: 'Get a husband,'" CNN Politics (website), June 12, 2015. *See:* https://edition.cnn.com/2015/06/11/politics/jeb-bush-to-women-on-welfare-in-1994-get-a-husband/index.html.

13. Ariel Gore, *We Were Witches* (New York, NY: Feminist Press, 2017), ebook location 51% / empl. 1911.

14. Mike Martindale, "Michigan rapist gets joint custody," in *Detroit News*, October 6, 2017. *See:* https://eu.detroitnews.com/story/news/local/michigan/2017/10/06/rape-victim-attacker-joint-child-custody/106374256/.

15. Robert Rector, "Marriage: America's Greatest Weapon Against Child Poverty," the Heritage Foundation (report), September 5, 2012. *See:* https://www.heritage.org/poverty-and-inequality/report/marriage-americas-greatest-weapon-against-child-poverty.

16. Traister, op. cit., p. 195.

17. Traister, op. cit., p. 298.

18. "Nixon Says Woman Could Be President," in *New York Times*, January 3, 1972. See: https://www.nytimes.com/1972/01/03/archives/nixon-says-woman-could-be-president.html.

19. Eve Kay, "Call me Ms," in *Guardian*, June 29, 2007. *See:* https://www.theguardian.com/world/2007/jun/29/gender.uk.

20. Alix Girod de l'Ain, "Après vous Mademoiselle?," in *Elle*, October 19, 2011. *See:* https://www.elle.fr/Societe/Edito/Apres-vous-Mademoiselle-1769892.

21. Claire Schneider, "N'appelez plus les féministes 'Mademoiselle!',", in *Marie Claire*, September 27, 2011. *See:* https://www.marieclaire.fr/,mademoiselle-osez-le-feminisme-chiennes-de-garde,20123,431653.asp.

22. Heather Havrilesky, "Ask Polly: 'Tell me not to get married!,'" in *The Cut*, September 27, 2017. *See:* https://www.thecut.com/2017/09/ask-polly-tell-me-not-to-get-married.html.

23. Charlotte Debest, *Le choix d'une vie sans enfant* (Rennes: Presses Universitaires de Rennes, 2014), p. 128.

24. Gloria Steinem, *Revolution from Within: A Book of Self-Esteem* (New York, NY: Little, Brown, 1992), pp. 255–6.

25. Érika Flahault, *Une vie à soi. Nouvelles formes de solitude au féminin* (Rennes: Presses Universitaires de Rennes, 2009), pp. 59–60.

26. Maurice de Waleffe, "Les Femmes Isolée: L'art de vivre en société," in *Paris-Midi*, April 29, 1927, cited in Flahault, op. cit., p. 62.

27. André Soubiran, *Lettre ouverte à une femme d'aujourd'hui* (Paris: Rombaldi, 1973 [first published 1967]), cited in Flahault, op. cit., p. 53.

28. An adaptation of the first novel by Miles Franklin, a pioneer of Australian feminism.

29. Cf. Laurie Lisle, *Without Child: Challenging the Stigma of Childlessness* (New York, NY: Ballantine Books, 1996), p. 147.

30. Erica Jong, *Fear of Flying* (London: Panther, 1974), p. 18 and p. 123.

31. Jong, op. cit., p. 194.

32. Jong, op. cit., p. 78.

33. Jong, op. cit., p. 79.

34. Gloria Steinem, *My Life on the Road* (New York, NY: Penguin Random House, 2016), p. xxiv.

35. Steinem, *My Life . . .* op. cit., p. 4.

36. Steinem, *My Life . . .* op. cit., p. 23.

37. Steinem, *My Life . . .* op. cit.

38. Steinem, *My Life . . .* op. cit., p. 250.

39. Leah Fessler, "Gloria Steinem says Black women have always been more feminist than White women," in *Quartz*, December 8, 2017. *See:* https://qz.com/1150028/gloria-steinem-on-metoo-black-women-have-always-been-more-feminist-than-white-women/.

40. Flahault, op. cit., p. 147.

41. Nadia Daam, "À quel moment les femmes célibataires sont devenues des 'femmes à chat'?," in *Slate*, January 16, 2017. *See:* https://www.slate.fr/story/134552/femmes-celibataires-chat.

42. Nadia Daam, *Comment ne pas devenir une fille à chat. L'art d'être célibataire sans sentir la croquette* (Paris: Mazarine, 2018).

43. Judika Illes, *The Weiser Field Guide to Witches: From Hexes to Hermione Granger, From Salem to the Land of Oz* (San Francisco, CA: Red Wheel/Weiser, 2010), p. 220.

44. Matilda Joslyn Gage, *Woman, Church, & State* (New York: The Truth Seeker Company, 1893), p. 218. *See:* https://sacred-texts.com/wmn/wcs/wcs07.htm.

45. Susan Faludi, *Backlash: The Undeclared War Against American Women* (New York, NY: Crown Press, 1991), p. 52.

46. Faludi, op. cit., p. 79.

47. Quoted in Faludi, op. cit., p. 96.

48. Megan Marshall, *The Cost of Loving: Women and the New Fear of Intimacy* (New York, NY: Putnam, 1984), quoted in Faludi, op. cit., p. 5.

49. Faludi, op. cit., p. 100.

50. Faludi, op. cit., p. 88.

51. Faludi, op. cit., p. 106.

52. Cited by Érika Flahault, "La triste image de la femme seule," in Christine Bard (ed.), *Un siècle d'antiféminisme* (Paris: Fayard, 1999), pp. 393–4.

53. Flahault, *Une vie à soi*, op. cit., p. 82.

54. Faludi, op. cit., p. 338.

55. Flahault, *Une vie à soi*, op. cit., p. 89 (citing *Antoinette*, February 1985).

56. Quoted by Flahault, *Une vie à soi*, op. cit., p 89.

57. Furrows running from the nose to the corners of the mouth: a favorite target for cosmetic surgery.

58. Tracy McMillan, "Why You're Not Married," in *HuffPost*, February 13, 2011. *See:* https://www.huffpost.com/entry/why -youre-not-married_b_822088?guccounter=1&guce_referrer=aH R0cHM6Ly91ay5zZWFyY2gueWFob28uY29tLw&guce_referrer _sig=AQAAAJWwz79Dv59kPiyJCL1RbMq1LyJGqIYOxWh DHwmOKgWF7NocWShYck4sVBCK1sjJH_exEfkVN8hJ4 -ZsWl5AzGfrPVouzt7nmxfjjHnn-mUrK5up2igspMQ0rR1IIsQ xBeTdhIEBK4Bzty5Cjs2VTt2t8pU0EfT-ljPUdB_-GbNw.

59. Cf. Mona Chollet, "L'hypnose du bonheur familial" (ch. 6), in Chollet, *Chez soi: Une odyssée de l'espace domestique* (Paris: Éditions La Découverte, 2016).

60. Bruce Fretts, "*Fatal Attraction* oral history: rejected stars and a foul rabbit," in *New York Times,* September 14, 2017. *See:* https://www.nytimes.com/2017/09/14/movies/fatal-attraction-oral -history.html.

61. Faludi, op. cit., p. 112.

62. Fretts, op. cit.

63. Faludi, op. cit., p. 120.

64. Faludi, op. cit., p. 448.

65. Faludi, op. cit., p. 449.

66. *Les Sorcières* (discussion program), Hors-Serie, February 20, 2015. *See:* https://www.hors-serie.net/En-acces-libre /2015–02–20/Les-Sorcieres-id64.

67. "Au Ghana, des camps pour 'sorcières,'" TV5 Monde, August 11, 2014. *See:* https://information.tv5monde.com/terriennes /au-ghana-des-camps-pour-sorcieres-3331.

68. Cited by Guy Bechtel, in *Les Quatre Femmes de Dieu: La putain, la sorcière, la sainte et Bécassine* (Paris: Plon, 2000).

69. Aline Kiner, *La Nuit des béguines* (Paris: Liana Levi, 2017).

70. Cf. Titiou Lecoq, "'Elle s'appelait Aurélie, elle avait 34 ans, il lui a tire dessus au fusil de chasse:' une année de meurtres conjugaux," in *Libération*, June 30, 2017. *See:* https://www.liberation.fr

/france/2017/06/30/elle-s-appelait-aurelie-elle-avait-34-ans-il-lui
-a-tire-dessus-au-fusil-de-chasse-une-annee-de-meurt_1580445.

71. *See:* "Les mots tuent," on Tumblr: https://lesmotstuent
.tumblr.com.

72. At first glance, *Bewitched* appears to present a similar scenario. However, the series does at least offer a counterpoint to it, through the character of Endora, Samantha's mother, who is dismayed by her daughter's submissiveness and by her dim-witted son-in-law.

73. Armelle Le Bras-Chopard, *Les Putains du Diable: Le procès en sorcellerie des femmes* (Paris: Plon, 2006), p. 147.

74. Pam Grossman, "Foreword," in Taisia Kitaiskaia and Katy Horan, *Literary Witches: A Celebration of Magical Women Writers* (New York, NY: Seal Press, 2017), p. 5.

75. As with the action at the Stock Exchange, with hindsight, Morgan is strongly critical of this demonstration, particularly because the release of the mice "frightened and humiliated the visitors and their mothers, not to mention the way it frightened and humiliated the mice themselves." Robin Morgan, *Going Too Far: The Personal Chronicle of a Feminist* (New York, NY: Random House, 1977), p. 80.

76. Colette Cosnier, "Maréchal, nous voilà! ou Brigitte de Berthe Bernage," in Bard, op. cit., p. 242.

77. Quoted by Cosnier, in Bard, op. cit., p. 244.

78. Orna Donath, *Regretting Motherhood: A Study* (Berkeley, CA: North Atlantic Books, 2017), p. 76.

79. Titiou Lecoq, *Libérées: Le combat féministe se gagne devant le panier de linge sale* (Paris: Fayard, 2017), p. 14.

80. Adrienne Rich, *Of Woman Born: Motherhood as Experience and Institution* (London: Bantam, 1977), pp. 6–7.

81. Rich, op. cit., p. 156.

82. Éliette Abécassis, *Un heureux événement* (Paris: Albin Michel, 2005).

83. Barbara Ehrenreich and Deirdre English, *Complaints and Disorders: The Sexual Politics of Sickness* (New York, NY: Feminist Press, 1993 [first published 1973]), p. 27.

84. Ehrenreich and English, *Complaints and Disorders* . . . op. cit., p. 28.

85. McMillan, op. cit.

86. Rich, op. cit., pp. 28–9.

87. Rich, op. cit., p. 37.

88. Corinne Maier, *No Kid: Quarante raisons de ne pas avoir d'enfant* (Paris: Michalon, 2007), p. 138.

89. Lecoq, op. cit.

90. Barbara Ehrenreich and Deirdre English, *Witches, Midwives and Nurses: A History of Women Healers* (New York, NY: Feminist Press, 1973, 2010), second edition, pp. 4 and 36–7.

91. Julia Blancheton, "Un tiers des femmes travaillent à temps partiel," in *Le Figaro,* July 8, 2016.

92. "Répartition femmes/hommes par métiers: l'étude de la Dares," from the French ministry responsible for sexual equality, December 13, 2013. *See:* https://dares.travail-emploi.gouv.fr/publications/la-repartition-des-hommes-et-des-femmes-par-metiers.

93. Silvia Federici, *Caliban and the Witch* (Brooklyn, NY: Autonomedia, 2004), p. 31.

94. Rachida El Azzouzi, "Marie Pezé: 'Les violences sexuelles et sexistes sont dans le socle de notre société,'" in *Mediapart,* May 12, 2016. *See:* https://www.mediapart.fr/journal/france/120516/marie-peze-les-violences-sexuelles-et-sexistes-sont-dans-le-socle-de-notre-societe.

95. Jackson R. Bryer and Cathy W. Barks (eds.), *Dear Scott, Dearest Zelda: The Love Letters of F. Scott and Zelda Fitzgerald* (New York, NY: Scribner, 2002), p. 207.

96. Jong, op. cit., p. 43, but also pp. 140–1.

97. Jong, op. cit., p. 110.

98. Jong, op. cit., p. 113.

99. Jong, op. cit., p. 47.

100. Quoted by Pam Houston, "The trouble with having it all," in Meghan Daum (ed.), *Selfish, Shallow, and Self-Absorbed: Sixteen Writers on the Decision Not to Have Kids* (New York, NY: Picador, 2015), p. 166.

101. Cf. Nathalie Bajos and Michèle Ferrand, "La contraception, levier réel ou symbolique de la domination masculine," in *Sciences sociales et santé*, vol. 22, no. 3, September 2004.

102. Of course, the principle of contradictory imperatives applies here, too. In 2010, in southern France, Odile Trivis had her three-year-old son, whom she was raising alone, taken away from her because she was too "smothering" toward him. That she had good reason to have become so—during her pregnancy she'd had to cope with both separation from the boy's father and a cancer—apparently made no difference. Ought we to conclude that over-investment in the maternal role becomes problematic whenever it brings no benefit to a partner? Antoine Perrin, "Une mère séparée de son fils car elle l'aime trop," BFMTV, December 28, 2010. *See:* https://www.bfmtv.com/police-justice/une-mere-separee-de-son-fils-car-elle-l-aime-trop_AN-201012280012.html.

103. Rich, op. cit., p. 24.

104. Sylvie Chaperon, "Haro sur Le Deuxième Sexe," in Bard, op. cit., p. 277.

105. Quoted by Flahault, *Une vie à soi,* op. cit., p. 52.

106. Jancee Dunn, "Women are supposed to give until they die," Lenny Letter (website), November 29, 2017. *See:* https://lennyletter.com/story/women-are-supposed-to-give-until-they-die.

107. Les Chimères, *Maternité esclave* (Paris: 10/18, 1975), p. 81.

108. Cited by Mardy S. Ireland, *Reconceiving Women: Separating Motherhood from Female Identity* (New York, NY: Guilford Press, 1993), p. 27.

109. Les Chimères, op. cit., p. 310.

110. Traister, op. cit., p. 134.

111. Cited by Lucie Joubert, *L'Envers du landau: Regard extérieur sur la maternité et ses débordements* (Montréal: Triptyque, 2010), p. 9.

112. Nathalie Loiseau, *Choisissez tout* (Paris: Jean-Claude Lattès, 2014); Amy Richards, *Opting In: Having a Child Without Losing Yourself* (New York, NY: Farrar, Straus and Giroux, 2008).

113. To date, there is no study done on the division of labor within same-sex couples' households.

114. Nathacha Appanah, "La petite vie secrète des femmes," in *La Croix*, May 18, 2017. *See:* https://www.la-croix.com/Debats /Chroniques/petite-vie-secrete-femmes-Nathacha-Appanah -2017–05–18–1200848116.

115. Erica Jong, *Fear of Fifty: A Midlife Memoir* (New York, NY: Harper Paperbacks, 1995), p. 198.

116. Jeanette Winterson, interviewed for "The Art of Fiction" in the *Paris Review*, no. 145, Winter 1997, pp. 107–8.

Chapter 2: Wanting Sterility

1. Les Chimères, *Maternité esclave* (Paris: 10/18, 1975), p. 16.

2. Adrienne Rich, *Of Woman Born: Motherhood as Experience and Institution* (London: Bantam, 1977), p. xv.

3. Rich, op. cit., p. 155.

4. Corinne Maier, *No Kid: Quarante raisons de ne pas avoir d'enfant* (Paris: Michalon, 2007), p. 144.

5. Cited by Rebecca Traister, *All the Single Ladies* (New York, NY: Simon & Schuster, 2016), p. 224.

6. In the US, contraception and abortion were made illegal at the end of the nineteenth century. Contraception remained illegal up until 1965 and abortion until 1973.

7. Maryse Condé, *Moi, Tituba, sorcière noire de Salem* (Paris: Gallimard, "Folio" collection, 1998 [first published 1986]); also, *I, Tituba, Black Witch of Salem*, trans. Richard Philcox (Charlottesville, VA: University of Virginia Press, 2009).

8. Condé, *I, Tituba*, op. cit., p. 50, etc.

9. Condé, *I, Tituba*, op. cit., p. 92.

10. Condé, *I, Tituba*, op. cit., p. 122.

11. Condé, *I, Tituba*, op. cit., p. 120.

12. "Mère infanticide en Gironde: l'accusée évoque un 'enfermement' et un 'déni total,'" in *Paris-Match*, March 21, 2018. *See:* https://www.parismatch.com/Actu/Faits-divers/Mere-infanticide

-en-Gironde-l-accusee-evoque-un-enfermement-et-un-deni-total-1483160.

13. Rich, op. cit., p. 261.

14. Rich, op. cit., p. 267.

15. Collectif, *Réflexions autour d'un tabou: l'infanticide* (Paris: Cambourakis, 2015), p. 14. Even if we don't agree with all its conclusions, this book is valuable in stimulating discussion of a subject which is almost universally avoided.

16. Collectif, op. cit., p. 15.

17. Collectif, op. cit., p. 19.

18. Jules Michelet, *The Witch*, trans. Lionel James Trotter (Simpkin, Marshall & Co, 1863 [originally published 1862]), p. 71.

19. Michelet, op. cit., p. 161.

20. Michelet, op. cit., p. 220.

21. Michelet, *La Sorcière* (Paris: Calmann Lévy, 1878), p. 164 (quote translated for this book by Sophie R. Lewis).

22. Alexandros Papadiamantis, *The Murderess,* trans. George X. Xanthopoulides (London: Doric Publications, 1977), p. 46.

23. Papadiamantis, op. cit., p. 71.

24. Papadiamantis, op. cit., p. 17.

25. Papadiamantis, op. cit.

26. Guy Bechtel, *La Sorcière et l'Occident: La destruction de la sorcellerie en Europe, des origines aux grands bûchers* (Paris: Plon, 1997), p. 318.

27. Collectif, op. cit., p. 47.

28. Anne L. Barstow, *Witchcraze* (San Francisco, CA / London: Pandora, 1995).

29. Carol Costello, "Can you be pro-life and pro-death penalty?" CNN (website), May 28, 2014. *See:* https://edition.cnn.com/2014/05/14/opinion/costello-pro-life-pro-death-penalty/index.html.

30. Source: Gun Violence Archive. *See:* www.gunviolencearchive.org.

31. "En 2015, un décès sur six dans le monde était lié à la pollution," in *HuffPost,* October 20, 2017. *See:* https://www.huffingtonpost

.fr/2017/10/20/en-2015-un-deces-sur-six-dans-le-monde-etait-lie-a
-la-pollution_a_23249807/.

32. Françoise Vergès, *Le Ventre des femmes: Capitalisme, racial-
isation, féminisme* (Paris: Albin Michel, 2017).

33. Carolyn M. Morell, *Unwomanly Conduct: The Challenges of
Intentional Childlessness* (New York: Routledge, 1994), p. 38.

34. Morell, op. cit., p. 39.

35. Laurie Lisle, *Without Child: Challenging the Stigma of
Childlessness* (New York, NY: Ballantine Books, 1996), p. 222.

36. Morell, op. cit., p. 19.

37. Maier, op. cit., pp. 111–2.

38. *Sorcières, mes soeurs,* directed by Camille Ducellier, Larsens
Production, 2010. *See:* www.camilleducellier.com.

39. Chloé Delaume, *Une femme avec personne dedans* (Paris:
Seuil, 2012), pp. 124 and 121 (my translations); also her novel, *Les
Sorcières de la République* (Paris: Seuil, 2016).

40. Charlotte Debest, Magali Mazuy and the team from the
"Fecond" survey, "Rester sans enfant: un choix de vie à contre-
courant," in *Population & Sociétés,* no. 508, February 2014.

41. Charlotte Debest, *Le choix d'une vie sans enfant* (Rennes:
Presses Universitaires de Rennes, 2014), p. 43.

42. Gaëlle Dupont, "Natalité: vers la fin de l'exception française,"
in *Le Monde,* January 16, 2018. *See:* https://www.lemonde.fr
/societe/article/2018/01/16/natalite-la-fin-de-l-exception-francaise
_5242408_3224.html.

43. Lauren Sandler, "Having It All Without Having Children," in *Time* magazine ("The Childfree Life" issue), August
12, 2013. *See:* http://content.time.com/time/magazine/article
/0,9171,2148636,00.html.

44. Laura Kipnis, "Maternal instincts," in Meghan Daum
(ed.), *Selfish, Shallow, and Self-Absorbed: Sixteen Writers on the Decision Not to Have Kids* (New York, NY: Picador, 2015), p. 45.

45. "Soaring childlessness among southern European
women—report," BBC News (website), January 11, 2017. *See:*

https://www.bbc.co.uk/news/world-europe-38582100#:~:text
=%22While%20childlessness%20has%20broadly%20stabilized,
in%20central%20and%20eastern%20Europe.%22.

46. Éva Beaujouan et al., "La proportion de femmes sans enfant a-t-elle atteint un pic en Europe?" in *Population & Sociétés*, no. 540, January 2017.

47. Debest, *Le choix d'une vie sans enfant*, op. cit., p. 82.

48. Lisle, op. cit., p. 33.

49. Jeanne Safer, "Beyond *Beyond Motherhood*," in Daum, op. cit., p. 190.

50. Pam Houston, "The trouble with having it all," in Daum, op. cit., p. 169.

51. Anne Gotman, *Pas d'enfant: La volonté de ne pas engendrer* (Paris: Éditions de la MSH, 2017), p. 30.

52. Gotman, op. cit., p. 45.

53. Gotman, op. cit., p. 41.

54. Betsy Salkind, "Why I didn't have any children this summer," in Henriette Mantel (ed.), *No Kidding: Women Writers on Bypassing Parenthood* (Berkeley, CA: Seal Press, 2013), p. 127.

55. Rebecca Solnit, "The Mother of All Questions," in *Harper's Magazine*, October 2015. *See:* https://harpers.org/archive/2015/10/the-mother-of-all-questions/.

56. Michèle Fitoussi, "Le pire de Maier," in *Elle*, June 25, 2007.

57. Laura Carroll, *Families of Two: Interviews with Happily Married Couples Without Children by Choice* (Bloomington, IN: Xlibris, 2000), pp. 145–6.

58. Carroll, op. cit., p. 45.

59. As attributed here: https://dicocitations.lemonde.fr/citations/citation-63284.php (quote translated for this book by Sophie R. Lewis).

60. Cited by Muriel Salle and Catherine Vidal, *Femmes et santé, encore une affaire d'hommes?* (Paris: Belin, 2017).

61. Salle and Vidal, op. cit.

62. Salle and Vidal, op. cit.

63. Moira Weigel, "The foul reign of the biological clock," in *Guardian*, May 10, 2016. *See:* https://www.theguardian.com/society/2016/may/10/foul-reign-of-the-biological-clock.

64. Richard Cohen, "The Clock is Ticking for the Career Woman," in *The Washington Post*, March 16, 1978. *See:* https://www.washingtonpost.com/archive/local/1978/03/16/the-clock-is-ticking-for-the-career-woman/bd566aa8-fd7d-43da-9be9-ad025759d0a4/.

65. Lisle, op. cit., p. 199.

66. David Le Breton, "Le genre de la laideur" ("The gender of ugliness"), preface to Claudine Sagaert, *Histoire de la laideur féminine* (Paris: Imago, 2015).

67. Martin Winckler, *Les Brutes en blanc: La maltraitance médicale en France* (Paris: Flammarion, 2016), p. 103.

68. Mare Kandre, *La Femme et le Docteur Dreuf,* translated from Swedish by Marc de Gouvenain and Lena Grumbach (Arles: Actes Sud, 1996 [originally published in Sweden, 1994]), pp. 149–50 and 152 (quotes translated from the French for this book by Sophie R. Lewis).

69. Erica Jong, *Fear of Fifty: A Midlife Memoir* (New York, NY: Harper Paperbacks, 1995), p. 277.

70. Geneviève Serre, "Les femmes sans ombre ou la dette impossible: Le choix de ne pas être mère," in *L'Autre*, vol. 3, no. 2, 2002.

71. Debest, *Le choix d'une vie sans enfant*, op. cit., p. 96.

72. Serre, op. cit.

73. Lucie Joubert, *L'Envers du landau: Regard extérieur sur la maternité et ses débordements* (Montréal: Triptyque, 2010), p. 23.

74. Véronique Cazot and Madeleine Martin, *Et toi, quand est-ce que tu t'y mets? Celle qui ne voulait pas d'enfant* (vol. 1) (Paris: Fluide. G, 2011).

75. Lisa Capretto, "What Elizabeth Gilbert Wants People To Know About Her Choice Not To Have Children," in *HuffPost*, 10 October 2014. *See:* https://www.huffpost.com/entry/elizabeth-gilbert-children-choice_n_5953950?guccounter=1&guce_.

76. Martine Tartour with Gaëlle Guitard and Melval, "Le people qui a changé ma vie," *Cosmopolitan* (French edition), September 2006.

77. Cited by Mantel, op. cit., p. xii.

78. Chantal Thomas, *Coping with Freedom: Reflections on Ephemeral Happiness,* trans. Andrea L. Secara (New York, NY: Algora, 2001), p. 83.

79. Simone de Beauvoir, *The Prime of Life*, trans. Peter Green (New York, NY: Paragon House, 1992), pp. 15–16.

80. Beauvoir, op. cit., pp. 66–7.

81. Gloria Steinem, *My Life on the Road* (New York, NY: Penguin Random House, 2016), p. vii.

82. Steinem, op. cit., p. 12.

83. Steinem, op. cit., p. 250. See also, "Ruth's song (because she could not sing it)," in Gloria Steinem, *Outrageous Acts and Everyday Rebellions* (New York, NY: Holt, Rinehart and Winston, 1983).

84. Joubert, op. cit., pp. 31 and 53.

85. Lisle, op. cit.

86. Debest, *Le choix d'une vie sans enfant,* op. cit., p. 65.

87. Solnit, op. cit.

88. "Épisode 4: Un lieu pour les femmes (Virginia Woolf)," *La Compagnie des auteurs,* on France Culture, January 28, 2016. *See:* https://www.franceculture.fr/emissions/la-compagnie-des-auteurs /virginia-woolf-4-un-lieu-pour-les-femmes.

89. Pam Grossman, "Foreword," in Taisia Kitaiskaia and Katy Horan, *Literary Witches: A Celebration of Magical Women Writers* (New York, NY: Seal Press, 2017).

90. Susan Faludi, *Backlash: The Undeclared War Against American Women* (New York, NY: Crown Press, 1991), p. 99.

91. Ann Snitow, "Motherhood: reclaiming the demon texts," in Irene Reti (ed.), *Childless by Choice: A Feminist Anthology* (Santa Cruz, CA: HerBooks, 1992).

92. Lisle, op. cit., pp. 36–7.

93. Christine Delphy, "La maternité occidentale contemporaine: le cadre du désir d'enfant," in Francine Descarries and Christine Corbeil, *Espaces et temps de la maternité* (Montréal: Éditions du Remue-Ménage, 2002), quoted in Joubert, op. cit., p. 51.

94. Debest, *Le choix d'une vie sans enfant,* op. cit., p. 182.

95. Jeanne Safer, "Beyond *Beyond Motherhood,*" in Daum, op. cit., p. 190.

96. Debest, *Le choix d'une vie sans enfant,* op. cit., p. 91.

97. Thomas, op. cit., p. 81.

98. Not to mention the accusations of rape that have been made against him, as in Alain Brassart, "Les femmes vues par Woody Allen," in *Le Monde diplomatique,* May 2000 (*see:* https://www.monde-diplomatique.fr/2000/05/BRASSART/2292); and Maureen Orth, "10 Undeniable Facts About the Woody Allen Sexual-Abuse Allegation," in *Vanity Fair,* February 7, 2014 (*see:* https://www.vanityfair.com/news/2014/02/woody-allen-sex-abuse-10-facts).

99. Serre, op. cit.

100. Voluntary sterilization was legalized in France in 2001.

101. *J'ai décidé d'être sterile* (web documentary), created by Hélène Rocco, Sidonie Hadoux, Alice Deroide and Fanny Marlier, 2015. *See:* https://www.lesinrocks.com/actu/jai-decide-detre-sterile-le-webdocumentaire-sur-la-sterilization-volontaire-des-femmes-qui-ne-veulent-pas-etre-meres-340532–26–09–2015/.

102. Joubert, op. cit., p. 21.

103. Debest, *Le choix d'une vie sans enfant,* op. cit., p. 149.

104. Maier, op. cit. pp. 12 and 141.

105. Fitoussi, op. cit.

106. Nolwenn Le Blevennec, "tre mère et le regretter: 'Je me suis fait un enfant dans le dos,'" Rue89 (website), June 28, 2016. *See:* https://www.nouvelobs.com/rue89/20190430.OBS12321/anemone-je-me-suis-fait-un-enfant-dans-le-dos.html.

107. Le Blevennec, op. cit.

108. Orna Donath, *Regretting Motherhood: A Study* (Berkeley, CA: North Atlantic Books, 2017), p. xvi. Also the source for the following quotations, except where otherwise indicated.

109. "Regretter d'être mère? 'L'amour n'est jamais à débattre,'" Rue89 (website), July 1, 2016. *See:* https://www.nouvelobs.com /rue89/rue89-nos-vies-connectees/20160701.RUE3304/regretter -d-etre-mere-l-amour-n-est-jamais-a-debattre.html.

110. Donath, op. cit.

111. Danielle Henderson, "Save yourself," in Daum, op. cit., p. 155.

112. Michelle Huneven, "Amateurs," in Daum, op. cit., pp. 136 and 142.

113. Donath, op cit, p. 58.

114. Rich, op. cit., p. 254.

115. Le Blevennec, op. cit.

116. Debest, *Le choix d'une vie sans enfant,* op. cit., p. 91.

117. Henderson, "Save yourself," in Daum, op. cit., p. 157.

118. Rich, op. cit., pp. 252–3.

Chapter 3: The Dizzy Heights

1. Cynthia Rich, "Ageism and the politics of beauty," in Barbara Macdonald (with Cynthia Rich), *Look Me in the Eye: Old Women, Aging and Ageism* (San Francisco, CA: Spinsters Ink., 1983), p. 142.

2. "The Crone issue," *Sabat,* Spring–Summer 2017. *See:* www.sabatmagazine.com.

3. Barbara Macdonald, "Barbara's introduction," in Macdonald (with Rich), op. cit., p. 5.

4. Barbara Macdonald, "Do you remember me?," in Macdonald (with Rich), op. cit., p. 16.

5. Macdonald, "Do you remember . . ." op. cit., p. 30.

6. Macdonald, "Do you remember . . ." op. cit., pp. 40–1.

7. Cynthia Rich, "Cynthia's afterword," in Macdonald (with Rich), op. cit., pp. 102 and 104.

8. Sophie Rosemont, "Pourquoi, 40 ans plus tard, Gloria Steinem règne toujours sur le féminisme," in *Vanity Fair* online, February 3, 2017. *See:* https://www.vanityfair.fr/culture/people /diaporama/gloria-steinem-icone-feministe-de-la-pop-culture /40535.

9. Rich, "Cynthia's afterword," in Macdonald (with Rich), op. cit., p. 105.

10. Susan Sontag, "The double standard of aging," in *Saturday Review*, September 23, 1972. *See:* https://www.unz.com/print/SaturdayRev-1972sep23–00029.

11. For example, Juliette Rennes, "Vieillir au féminin," in *Le Monde diplomatique*, December 2016. *See:* https://www.monde-diplomatique.fr/2016/12/RENNES/56899.

12. Gwyneth Paltrow, "Penelope Cruz," in *Interview* magazine, October 4, 2017. *See:* https://www.interviewmagazine.com/film/penelope-cruz-gwyneth-paltrow.

13. Jean Swallow, "Both feet in life: interviews with Barbara Macdonald and Cynthia Rich," in Collectif, *Women and Aging: An Anthology by Women* (Corvallis, OR: Calyx Books, 1986), p. 195.

14. Martin Winckler, *Les Brutes en blanc: La maltraitance médicale en France* (Paris: Flammarion, 2016), ebook location 47% / empl. 2268.

15. Daphnée Leportois, "L'anormal silence autour de l'âge des pères," in *Slate*, March 2, 2017. *See:* http://www.slate.fr/story/138194/silence-sexiste-age-pere.

16. "À 73 ans, Mick Jagger est papa pour la huitième fois mais séparé de la maman," in *Gala*, December 8, 2016. *See:* https://www.gala.fr/l_actu/news_de_stars/a_73_ans_mick_jagger_est_papa_pour_la_huitieme_fois_mais_separe_de_la_maman_380790. Also, Sam Tonkin, "'Jumpin' Jack Dash! Mick Jagger, 73, catches last-minute 3,500-mile private jet flight to be at the bedside of his ballerina girlfriend, 29, as he becomes a father for the EIGHTH time,' in *Daily Mail*, December 8, 2016. *See:* https://www.dailymail.co.uk/news/article-4014018/Rolling-Stones-frontman-Sir-Mick-Jagger-father-age-73.html.

17. Irene E. De Pater, Timothy A. Judge and Brent A. Scott, "Age, gender, and compensation: a study of Hollywood movie stars," in *Journal of Management Inquiry*, October 1, 2014.

18. Suzi Parker, "Rush Limbaugh's obsession with Hillary Clinton," in *Washington Post*, December 17, 2012. *See:* https://www

.washingtonpost.com/blogs/she-the-people/wp/2012/12/17/rush
-limbaughs-obsession-with-hillary-clinton/.

19. Yanan Wang, "Carrie Fisher strikes back at haters: youth
and beauty are not accomplishments," in *The Washington Post*,
December 30, 2015. *See:* https://www.washingtonpost.com/news
/morning-mix/wp/2015/12/30/carrie-fisher-strikes-back-at-haters
-youthbeautyrnot-accomplishments/.

20. Lauren Said-Moorhouse, "Carrie Fisher shuts down
body-shamers over *Star Wars: The Force Awakens* appearance,"
CNN (website), December 30, 2015. *See:* https://edition.cnn.com
/2015/12/30/entertainment/carrie-fisher-star-wars-aging-response
-twitter/index.html.

21. For this film, Fisher was asked to lose fifteen kilos, which
may be one of the factors behind her premature death from car-
diac arrest on 27 December 2016, at the age of sixty. See Joanne
Eglash, "Carrie Fisher autopsy: did *Star Wars* weight loss, drugs,
bipolar disorder contribute to death at 60?," *Inquisitr* (website),
January 2, 2017. *See:* https://www.inquisitr.com/3846223/carrie
-fisher-autopsy-did-star-wars-weight-loss-drugs-bipolar-disorder
-contribute-to-death-at-60/.

22. Guillemette Faure, "Teinture pour hommes, l'impossible
camouflage?," in *M le Mag*, December 29, 2017.

23. Sontag, op. cit.

24. Fabienne Daguet, "De plus en plus de couples dans
lesquels l'homme est plus jeune que la femme," in *Insee Première*,
no. 1613, September 1, 2016.

25. Vincent Cocquebert, "L'irrésistible attrait pour la jeunesse,"
in *Marie Claire*, September 2016. *See:* https://www.marieclaire.fr/,
l-irresistible-attrait-pour-la-jeunesse,827963.asp.

26. Cocquebert, op. cit.

27. Cocquebert, op. cit.

28. "Breaking news: les femmes de 42 ans sont belles,"
Meufs (website), July 11, 2014. *See:* https://m-e-u-f-s.tumblr.com
/post/91449345947/breaking-news-les-femmes-de-42-ans-sont
-belles.

29. Katy Waldman, "In Praise of 56-Year-Old Men," in *Slate*, July 10, 2014. *See:* https://slate.com/human-interest/2014/07/in -praise-of-56-year-old-men-a-response-to-esquire-s-ode-to-42 -year-old-women.html.

30. Sharon Waxman, "Maggie Gyllenhaal on Hollywood Ageism: I was told 37 is 'too old' for a 55-year-old love interest," *The Wrap* (website), May 21, 2015. *See:* https://www.thewrap.com /maggie-gyllenhaal-on-hollywood-ageism-i-was-told-37-is-too -old-for-a-55-year-old-love-interest/.

31. Cf. Kyle Buchanan, "Leading men age, but their love interests don't," *Vulture* (website), April 18, 2013 (*see:* https://www .vulture.com/2013/04/leading-men-age-but-their-love-interests -dont.html); Christopher Ingraham, "The most unrealistic thing about Hollywood romance, visualized," in *The Washington Post*, August 18, 2015 (*see:* https://www.washingtonpost.com/news/wonk /wp/2015/08/18/the-most-unrealistic-thing-about-hollywood -romance-visualized/).

32. "Et dans le cinéma français, les hommes tombent-ils amoureux de femmes de leur âge?," in *HuffPost*, May 22, 2015. *See:* https://www.huffingtonpost.fr/2015/05/22/cinema-francais -hommes-amoureux-femmes-age_n_7421374.html.

33. Nardine Saad, "George Clooney puts Tina Fey on notice after Golden Globes joke," in *Los Angeles Times*, January 20, 2014. *See:* https://www.latimes.com/entertainment/envelope/la-xpm -2014-jan-20-la-et-mg-george-clooney-tina-fey-golden-globes -joke-20140120-story.html.

34. "Brigitte Macron enceinte: la Une de 'Charilie Hebdo' provoque une tollé sur Internet," Europe 1 (website). *See:* https://www .europe1.fr/medias-tele/brigitte-macron-enceinte-la-couverture -de-charlie-hebdo-provoque-un-tolle-sur-internet-3325979. Also covered in the English-language press: Chloe Farand, "Charlie Hebdo publishes cartoon of Emmanuel Macron's wife pregnant with caption 'he will do miracles,'" in *Independent*, May 10, 2017. *See:* https://www.independent.co.uk/news/world/europe/charlie

-hebdo-emmanuel-macron-wife-cartoon-pregnant-brigitte-he
-will-do-miracles-satire-magazine-a7728496.html.

35. Clément Boutin, "Les hommes sont-ils eux aussi victimes 'd'age-shaming'?," Les Inrockuptibles (website), June 17, 2017. *See:* https://www.lesinrocks.com/actu/les-hommes-sont-ils-eux-aussi -victimes-dage-shaming-50010–17–06–2017/.

36. Camille Laurens, *Celle que vous croyez* (Paris: Gallimard, 2016).

37. Sylvie Brunel, *Manuel de guérilla à l'usage des femmes* (Paris: Grasset, 2009).

38. Sylvie Brunel, op. cit., p. 215.

39. "Famille monoparentale rime souvent avec pauvreté," Observatoire des Inégalités, November 30, 2017. *See:* https://www .inegalites.fr/Famille-monoparentale-rime-souvent-avec-pauvrete ?id_theme=15.

40. Cf. Irène Jonas, *Moi Tarzan, toi Jane: Critique de la réhabilitation scientifique de la différence hommes/femmes* (Paris: Syllepse, 2011).

41. Michel Bozon and Juliette Rennes, "Histoire des normes sexuelles: l'emprise de l'âge et du genre," in *Clio,* no. 42, the "Âge et sexualité" issue, 2015.

42. Quoted by Boutin, op. cit.

43. Marie Bergström, "L'âge et ses usages sexués sur les sites de rencontres en France (années 2000)," in *Clio,* no. 42, the "Âge et sexualité" issue, 2015.

44. David Le Breton, "Le genre de la laideur" ("The gender of ugliness"), preface to Claudine Sagaert, *Histoire de la laideur féminine* (Paris: Imago, 2015), p. viii.

45. Mary Daly, *Gyn/ecology: The Metaethics of Radical Feminism* (Boston, MA: Beacon Press, 1990 [first published 1978]), p. 15.

46. Cynthia Rich, "The women in the tower," in Macdonald (with Rich), op. cit., p. 80.

47. Walter Isaacson, interview with Woody Allen, "The Heart Wants What It Wants," in *Time* magazine, June 24,

2001. *See:* http://content.time.com/time/magazine/article/0,9171,160439,00.html.

48. *Broad City,* "Witches," episode 6, season 4, Comedy Central, October 25, 2017.

49. Sophie Fontanel, "Les super-models défilent pour Versace: l'image la plus virale de la mode," in *L'Obs,* September 25, 2017. *See:* https://o.nouvelobs.com/mode/mode-pour-tous/20170925.OBS5112/les-super-models-defilent-pour-versace-l-image-la-plus-virale-de-la-mode.html.

50. Isabel Flower, "Looking at Nicholas Nixon's forty-third portrait of the Brown sisters," in the *New Yorker,* December 12, 2017. *See:* https://www.newyorker.com/culture/photo-booth/looking-at-nicholas-nixons-forty-third-portrait-of-the-brown-sisters.

51. Michelle Lee, "*Allure* magazine will no longer use the term 'anti-aging,'" in *Allure,* August 14, 2017. *See:* https://www.allure.com/story/allure-magazine-phasing-out-the-word-anti-aging.

52. Christine Talos, "Elle ne supportait pas de vieillir, Exit l'a aidée à partir," in *La Tribune de Genève,* October 6, 2016. *See:* https://www.tdg.ch/suisse/supportait-vieillir-exit-aide/story/24585273.

53. Sophie Fontanel, *Une apparition* (Paris: Robert Laffont, 2017), pp. 120–1.

54. Cited by Rennes, "Vieillir au féminin," op. cit.

55. Fontanel, *Une apparition,* op. cit. p. 153.

56. Sarah Harris, "I've had gray hair since I was 16," in *Telegraph,* September 16, 2016. *See:* https://www.telegraph.co.uk/women/life/ive-had-gray-hair-since-i-was-16/.

57. Anne Kreamer, *Going Gray: What I Learned about Beauty, Sex, Work, Motherhood, Authenticity, and Everything Else that Really Matters* (New York, NY: Little, Brown, 2007), pp. 4–5.

58. Fontanel, *Une apparition,* op. cit., p. 179.

59. *Dans le genre,* ". . . de Sophie Fontanel," interview with Géraldine Serratia, *Radio Nova* (podcast), May 14, 2017.

60. Sontag, op. cit.

61. In conversation with Sophie R. Lewis, November 17, 2020.

62. Isaacson, interview with Woody Allen, op. cit.

63. On this point, see Liv Strömquist's graphic book *Prins Charles Känsla* (Stockholm: Ordfront/Galago, 2010); French edition published as *Les Sentiments du prince Charles*, trans. Kirsi Kinnunen and Stéphanie Dubois (Paris: Rackham, 2016). (No English translation.)

64. Apparently quoted by Irène Jonas in *Moi Tarzan, toi Jane*, p. 79—but I can't find the quote in the book she's quoting from! Bradley Gerstman et al., *What Men Want: Three Professional Single Men Reveal What it Takes to Make a Man Yours* (New York: Cliff Street Books, 1998).

65. Valerie Solanas, *SCUM Manifesto* (London: Olympia Press, 1971), pp. 25–6.

66. Michael Gross, *Model: The Ugly Business of Beautiful Women* (New York, NY: It Books, 2011 [first published 1995]), pp. 449–50.

67. Mona Chollet, *Beauté fatale. Les nouveaux visages d'une aliénation féminine* (Paris: La Découverte Poche, 2012), p. 280.

68. *Cloclo, 40 ans après, ultimes révélations* (documentary), TMC, January 31, 2018.

69. Anne L. Barstow, *Witchcraze* (San Francisco, CA / London: Pandora, 1995), p. 27.

70. Barstow, *Witchcraze*, op. cit.

71. Guy Bechtel, *La Sorciere et l'Occident: La destruction de la sorcellerie en Europe, des origines aux grands bûchers* (Paris: Plon, 1997), p. 746.

72. Kristen J. Sollée, *Witches, Sluts, Feminists: Conjuring the Sex Positive* (Berkeley, CA: ThreeL Media, 2017), p. 112.

73. Bruno Jeudy, "Quand Laurent Wauquiez recevait *Paris Match* sur ses terres," in *Paris Match*, October 11, 2017. *See:* https://www.parismatch.com/Actu/Politique/Laurent-Wauquiez -nous-a-recus-sur-ses-terres-1368563.

74. Starhawk, *The Spiral Dance: A Rebirth of the Ancient Religion of the Great Goddess* (20th Anniversary Edition) (New York, NY: HarperCollins, 1999), p. 153.

75. Lynn Botelho, "Les Trois Âges et la Mort du peintre Hans Baldung (xvie siècle)," in *Clio,* no. 42, the "Âge et sexualité" issue, 2015. *See:* https://www.cairn-int.info/journal-clio-women-gender-history-2015–2-page-191.htm.

76. Audre Lorde, *The Cancer Journals* (San Francisco, CA: Aunt Lute Books, 1997), pp. 64–5.

77. Gloria Steinem, *Revolution from Within: A Book of Self-Esteem* (New York, NY: Little, Brown, 1992), pp. 322–3.

78. Brunel, op. cit., pp. 238 and 241.

79. Olivia de Lamberterie, "Immortel Frédéric Beigbeder," in *Elle,* December 29, 2017.

80. Virginie Despentes, *King Kong Theory,* trans. Frank Wynne (London: Fitzcarraldo Editions, 2020), p. 111.

81. Jean Delumeau, *La Peur en Occident* (Paris: Librairie Arthème Fayard, 1978) ebook location 59% / empl. 8582 ("Les agents de Satan: la femme").

82. Cited in Guy Bechtel, *Les Quatre Femmes de Dieu: La putain, la sorcière, la sainte et Bécassine* (Paris: Editions Plon, 2000), p 55.

83. Le Breton, "Le genre de la laideur," in Sagaert, op. cit., p. x.

84. Daniel White, "Donald Trump Calls Clinton's Bathroom Break 'Disgusting,'" in *Time* magazine, December 21, 2016. *See:* https://time.com/4158303/donald-trump-hillary-clinton-disgusting-schlonged/.

85. Delumeau, op. cit. ebook location 58% / empl. 8453 ("Les agents de Satan: la femme").

86. Delumeau, op. cit., ebook location 66% / empl. 9510 ("Une iconographie souvent malveillante").

87. Cited by Sagaert, op. cit., p. 58.

88. Pierre de Ronsard, trans. Anthony Hecht, "Invective Against Denise, a Witch," in *American Scholar,* vol. 48, no. 4, Autumn 1979. *See:* https://www.jstor.org/stable/41210559.

89. Sarah H. Matthews, *The Social World of Old Women* (Beverly Hills, CA: Sage Publications, 1979), cited by Cynthia Rich, "Aging, ageism and feminist avoidance," in Macdonald (with Rich), op. cit., p. 57.

90. Rich, "The women in the tower," in Macdonald (with Rich), op. cit., p. 77.

91. "Sophie Fontanel, une beauté jaillissante," Mai HUA (website), December 2015. *See:* https://www.maihua.fr/2015/12 /sophie-fontanel-une-beaute-jaillissante/.

92. Fontanel, *Une apparition,* op. cit., pp. 85–6.

93. Fontanel, *Une apparition,* op. cit., p. 133.

94. Delumeau, op. cit., ebook location 58% / empl. 8453.

95. Geoffrey Wagner (trans.), *Selected Poems of Charles Baudelaire* (New York, NY: Grove Press, 1974).

96. Bechtel, *La Sorcière et l'Occident,* op. cit., p. 233.

97. Botelho, op. cit.

98. Barstow, op. cit., p. 137.

99. Erasmus, *In Praise of Folly,* trans. John Wilson (1668) (Oxford: Clarendon Press, 1913), p. 61. *See:* https://warburg.sas.ac .uk/pdf/nah7375b2325486.pdf.

100. Fontanel, *Une apparition,* op. cit., p. 133.

101. Gabrielle Lafarge, "Alors, heureuse?" in *Grazia,* November 17, 2017.

102. Valentine Pétry, "La couleur de l'argent . . . ," in *L'Express Styles,* March 19, 2014.

103. Judika Illes, *The Weiser Field Guide to Witches: From Hexes to Hermione Granger, From Salem to the Land of Oz* (San Francisco, CA: Red Wheel/Weiser, 2010), p. 263.

104. Sheila, "Patti Smith Forced to Explain Her Hair to *NYT,*" *Gawker* (website), July 11, 2008. *See:* https://gawker.com /5024385/patti-smith-forced-to-explain-her-hair-to-nyt.

105. Erasmus, *In Praise of Folly* (1876), (Gutenberg edition, 2009). *See:* https://www.gutenberg.org/files/30201/30201-h/30201 -h.htm.

106. Dany Jucaud, "Monica Bellucci: 'Quelque chose d'érotique chez les hommes d'expérience,'" in *Paris Match,* September 7, 2016. *See:* https://www.parismatch.com/People/Monica-Bellucci -Quelque-chose-d-erotique-chez-les-hommes-d-experience -1063858.

107. Sontag, op. cit.

108. Sylvie Braibant, "Quand la justice européenne doit réaffirmer le droit des femmes de plus de 50 ans à une sexualité épanouie," TV5 Monde (website), August 10, 2017. *See:* http://information .tv5monde.com/terriennes/quand-la-justice-europeenne-doit -reaffirmer-le-droit-des-femmes-de-plus-de-50-ans-une.

109. Catherine Achin and Juliette Rennes, "La vieillesse: une identité politique subversive. Entretien avec Thérèse Clerc," in *Mouvements,* no. 59, "La tyrannie de l'âge" issue, 2009.

110. Feminist by some lights, the film is still quite conventional in its recourse to the cliché of female rivalry.

111. Colette, *Chéri* and *The Last of Chéri,* trans. Roger Senhouse (London: Secker & Warburg, 1951), pp. 214, 215, 221 and 264.

112. Claude Benoit, "L'art de 'bien vieillir' chez deux grandes femmes de lettres: George Sand et Colette," in *Gérontologie et société,* vol. 28, no. 114, 2005.

113. "Les inégalités face aux retraites," Observatoire des Inégalités, September 5, 2013. *See:* https://www.inegalites.fr/Les -inegalites-face-aux-retraites.

Chapter 4: Turning the World Upside Down

1. Cynthia Rich, "Cynthia's introduction," in Barbara Macdonald (with Cynthia Rich), *Look Me in the Eye: Old Women, Aging and Ageism* (San Francisco, CA: Spinsters Ink., 1983), p. 11.

2. Susan Griffin, *Woman and Nature: The Roaring Inside Her* (London: The Women's Press, 1984 [first published 1978]), p. 14.

3. Molière, *The Learned Women,* trans. Charles Heron Wall, Act II, Scene vii. *See:* http://www.fullbooks.com/The-Learned -Women.html.

4. Marine Le Breton, "Une pub de Cdiscount pour les soldes accusée de véhiculer un cliché sur les femmes et les sciences," in *HuffPost,* January 10, 2018. *See:* https://www.huffingtonpost .fr/2018/01/10/une-pub-de-cdiscount-pour-les-soldes-accusee -de-vehiculer-un-cliche-sur-les-femmes-et-les-sciences_a_233 29690/.

5. Rebecca Solnit, *Men Explain Things to Me* (Chicago: Haymarket Books, 2014), pp. 4–5.

6. Solnit, *Men Explain Things to Me,* op. cit., p. 11.

7. Rebecca Solnit, "Men Explain Things to Me," in *Guernica,* August 20, 2012. *See:* https://www.guernicamag.com/rebecca-solnit-men-explain-things-to-me/.

8. "Les hommes et les femmes sont-ils égaux face aux mathématiques?," *Franceinfo* (website), November 29, 2013. *See:* https://www.francetvinfo.fr/replay-radio/info-sciences/les-hommes-et-les-femmes-sont-ils-egaux-face-aux-mathematiques_1758325.html.

9. Mary Daly, *Gyn/Ecology: The Metaethics of Radical Feminism* (Boston, MA: Beacon Press, 1990 [first published 1978]), pp. 184–5, etc.

10. Gloria Steinem, *Revolution from Within: A Book of Self-Esteem* (New York, NY: Little, Brown, 1992), p. 129.

11. Cf. Mona Chollet, "À l'assaut du réel," in *La Tyrannie de la réalité* (Paris: Calmann-Lévy, 2004).

12. René Descartes, *Discourse on Method* (1637), Part IV. *See:* https://www.bartleby.com/34/1/6.html.

13. Cf. Augustin Berque, *Écoumène: Introduction à l'étude des milieux humains* (Paris: Belin "Alpha," 2016 [first published 2000]).

14. Jean-François Billeter, *Chine trois fois muette* (Paris: Allia, 2000).

15. Michael Löwy & Robert Sayre, *Romanticism Against the Tide of Modernity,* trans. Catherine Porter (Durham, NC: Duke University Press, 2002), p. 40.

16. On this point, I refer readers to Jun'ichiro Tanizaki, *In Praise of Shadows,* trans. Gregory Starr (Sora Books, 2017 [first published 1933]).

17. Carolyn Merchant, *The Death of Nature: Women, Ecology, and the Scientific Revolution* (San Francisco, CA: HarperOne, 1990 [first published 1980]).

18. Merchant, op. cit., p. 478.

19. Merchant, op. cit., pp. 68, 102 and 233.

20. Susan Bordo, *The Flight to Objectivity: Essays on Cartesianism and Culture* (Albany, NY: State University of New York Press, 1987), pp. 59, 78 and 97.

21. Bordo, op. cit., p. 9.

22. Guy Bechtel, *La Sorcière et l'Occident: La destruction de la sorcellerie en Europe, des origines aux grands bûchers* (Paris: Plon, 1997), p. 859.

23. Sandra Harding, quoted in Bordo, op. cit., pp. 8 and 104.

24. Bordo, op. cit., p. 105.

25. Francis Bacon, quoted in Bordo, op. cit., p. 8.

26. René Descartes, *Discourse on Method* (1637). *See:* https://archive.org/stream/renedescartesmeditations/RENE%20DES CARTES%20Meditations_djvu.txt.

27. Susan Bordo has also published a key work of reference on the relationship between the body and the obsession with thinness in contemporary Western culture, which I refer to often in *Beauté fatale*. Susan Bordo, *Unbearable Weight: Feminism, Western Culture and the Body* (Berkeley, CA: University of California Press, 1993).

28. Descartes, *Discourse on Method* (1637), op. cit.

29. Merchant, op. cit., p. 127.

30. Merchant, op. cit., p. xxi.

31. Merchant, op. cit., p. 169.

32. Merchant, op. cit., p. 171.

33. Aldo Leopold, *A Sand County Almanac* (Oxford: Oxford University Press, 1989), p. 68.

34. Mare Kandre, *La Femme et le Docteur Dreuf,* translated from Swedish by Marc de Gouvenain and Lena Grumbach (Arles: Actes Sud, 1996 [originally published in Sweden, 1994]), p. 12 (quotes translated from the French for this book by Sophie R. Lewis).

35. Kandre, op. cit., p. 64.

36. Barbara Ehrenreich and Deirdre English, *Witches, Midwives and Nurses: A History of Women Healers* (New York, NY: Feminist Press, 1973, 2010), second edition, p. 18.

37. Dominique Brancher, *Équivoques de la pudeur: Fabrique d'une passion à la Renaissance* (Genève: Droz, 2015).

38. Ehrenreich and English, *Witches, Midwives and Nurses,* op. cit., pp. 24–5.

39. "Harcèlement sexuel à l'hôpital: 'Franchement, il y a des fois où on met des mains au cul,'" Europe 1 (website), October 25, 2017. *See:* https://www.europe1.fr/societe/harcelement-sexuel -a-lhopital-franchement-il-y-a-des-fois-ou-on-met-des-mains-au -cul-3473753.

40. Aude Lorriaux, "Comment le sexisme s'est solidement ancré dans la médecine française," in *Slate,* February 5, 2015. *See:* http://www.slate.fr/story/97555/comment-pourquoi -sexisme-medecine-francaise. Cf. Paye Ta Blouse (website), www .payetablouse.fr.

41. Soazig Le Nevé, "Des internes du CHU de Toulouse obtiennent le retrait d'une fresque jugée sexiste," in *Le Monde,* March 19, 2018.

42. Martin Winckler, *Les Brutes en blanc: La maltraitance médicale en France* (Paris: Flammarion, 2016), p. 196.

43. Winckler, op. cit., p. 99.

44. "Un chirurgien jugé pour avoir gravé ses initiales . . . sur le foie de ses patients," in *L'Express,* December 14, 2017. *See:* https:// www.lexpress.fr/actualite/monde/europe/un-chirurgien-juge-pour -avoir-grave-ses-initiales-sur-le-foie-de-ses-patients_1968930 .html. "'Liver branding' surgeon Simon Bramhall fined £10,000," BBC News (website), January 12, 2018. *See:* https://www.bbc.co.uk /news/uk-england-birmingham-42663518.

45. Florence Montreynaud, *Appeler une chatte . . . Mots et plaisirs du sexe* (Paris: Calmann-Lévy, 2004), pp. 45–6.

46. Winckler, op. cit., part II: "De la maltraitance médicale en France," ebook location 31% / empl. 1518.

47. Winckler, op. cit., p. 128.

48. Daly, op. cit.

49. Marie-Hélène Lahaye, *Accouchement: les femmes méritent mieux* (Paris: Michalon, 2018), pp. 101–2, 104.

50. Lahaye, op. cit., p. 109.

51. Daly, op. cit., p. 264.

52. Barbara Ehrenreich and Deirdre English, *Complaints and Disorders: The Sexual Politics of Sickness* (New York, NY: Feminist Press, 1993 [first published 1973]), p. 34.

53. Lynda Zerouk, "Durant 50 ans, 84% des lobotomies furent réalisées sur des femmes, en France, Belgique et Suisse," TV5 Monde (website), December 5, 2017. *See:* https://information .tv5monde.com/terriennes/durant-50-ans-84-des-lobotomies -furent-realizees-sur-des-femmes-en-france-belgique-et?fbclid=I wAR2YOxavE18wSh66I77hfFSpIOd2aTqVrbM0x4OSmeejVw2 1W5QSJCu2tMw.

54. See, for example, Mélanie Déchalotte, *Le Livre noir de la gynécologie* (Paris: Éditions First, 2017). Also, *Un podcast à soi*, "Le gynécologue et la sorcière" (episode 6), March 7, 2018. *See:* https://www .arteradio.com/son/61659783/le_gynecologue_et_la_sorciere_6.

55. "Pilules contraceptives: 'accident médical' reconnu pour la bordelaise Marion Larat après un AVC," France Info (website), February 13, 2018. *See:* https://france3-regions.francetvinfo.fr /nouvelle-aquitaine/gironde/bordeaux/pilules-contraceptives -accident-medical-reconnu-bordelaise-marion-larat-apres-avc -1423275.html.

56. Nolwenn Le Blevennec, "Prothèse vaginale: Cathy, 59 ans, transformée par la douleur," Rue89 (website), October 28, 2017. *See:* https://www.nouvelobs.com/rue89/nos-vies-intimes /20171011.OBS5857/prothese-vaginale-cathy-59-ans-transformee -par-la-douleur.html.

57. Eric Favereau, "Procès Mediator: 'Ce drame est une histoire de femmes,'" Libération (website), June 24, 2020. *See:* https:// www.liberation.fr/france/2020/06/24/ce-drame-est-une-histoire -de-femmes_1792321/.

58. "Handicapé, un petit-fils 'Distilbène' obtient réparation," in *Elle*, June 9, 2011. *See:* https://www.elle.fr/Societe/News/Handicape -un-petit-fils-Distilbene-obtient-reparation-1612064.

59. "Née sans bras ni jambes, elle obtient des millions de dollars," in *Elle*, July 18, 2012. *See:* https://www.elle.fr/Societe/News /Nee-sans-bras-ni-jambes-elle-obtient-des-millions-de-dollars

-2119410. Also, "Australian woman reaches settlement with UK-based Thalidomide distributor," in *Guardian*, July 18, 2012. *See:* https://www.theguardian.com/business/2012/jul/18/australian -woman-settlement-thalidomide-distributor.

60. Marie Campistron, "Les stéréotypes de genre jouent sur l'attitude des médecins comme des patients," in *L'Obs*, January 13, 2018. *See:* https://www.nouvelobs.com/sante/20180111.OBS0488 /les-stereotypes-de-genre-jouent-sur-l-attitude-des-medecins -comme-des-patients.html.

61. Chrysoula Zacharopoulou, "Endométriose: enfin, cette maladie gynécologique sort de l'ombre," in *Le Plus*, March 22, 2016. *See:* https://leplus.nouvelobs.com/contribution/1497920 -endometriose-enfin-cette-maladie-gynecologique-sort-de-l-ombre .html. Also, Sarah Boseley, Jessica Glenza and Helen David-son, "Endometriosis: the hidden suffering of millions of women revealed," in *Guardian*, September 27, 2015. *See:* https://www .theguardian.com/society/2015/sep/28/endometriosis-hidden -suffering-millions-women.

62. Winckler, op. cit., part II, chapter 1: "La maltraitance médicale ordinaire," ebook location 19% / empl. 900.

63. Ehrenreich and English, *Complaints and Disorders*, op. cit., p. 79.

64. Annaliese Griffin, "Women are flocking to wellness be-cause modern medicine still doesn't take them seriously," in *Quartz*, June 15, 2017. *See:* https://qz.com/1006387/women-are-flocking -to-wellness-because-traditional-medicine-still-doesnt-take-them -seriously/.

65. Taffy Brodesser-Akner, "We have found the cure! (Sort of . . .)," in *Outside*, April 11, 2017. *See:* https://www.outsideonline .com/2170436/we-have-found-cure-sort.

66. *Grey's Anatomy*, "(Don't fear) the reaper," episode 11, sea-son 14, ABC, February 1, 2018.

67. Taylor Maple, "Miranda Bailey's heart attack on *Grey's Anatomy* was inspired by a writer's own story," in *Bustle*, February 1, 2018. *See:* https://www.bustle.com/p/miranda-baileys-heart-attack

-storyline-on-grays-anatomy-was-inspired-by-a-show-writers
-own-experience-8052783.

68. Frantz Vaillant, "États-Unis: pourquoi cette mortalité record pour les femmes noires dans les maternités?," TV5 Monde
(website), February 7, 2018. *See:* https://information.tv5monde
.com/terriennes/etats-unis-pourquoi-cette-mortalite-record-pour
-les-femmes-noires-dans-les-maternites.

69. "Le calvaire de la petite Noélanie mal prise en charge par le
samu," in *Marie Claire,* May 9, 2018. *See:* https://www.marieclaire
.fr/samu-mort-sante,1264055.asp.

70. Pierre Desproges, *Vivons heureux en attendant la mort*
(Paris: Points Seuil, 1997 [first published 1983]).

71. Je n'ai pas consenti (blog), http://jenaipasconsenti.tumblr
.com.

72. Marie-Hélène Lahaye, "L'été historique où les violences
obstétricales se sont imposées dans les médias," Marie accouche
là (website), August 8, 2017. *See:* http://marieaccouchela.net/index
.php/2017/08/18/lete-historique-ou-les-violences-obstetricales-ont
-fait-le-buzz/.

73. Lahaye, *Accouchement: les femmes méritent mieux,* op. cit.,
p. 33.

74. Winckler, op. cit., part III, chapter 2: "Les chapelles
médicales françaises," ebook location 63% / empl. 3056.

75. The feminist movement has consistently campaigned to
reduce this dependency as far as possible. See, in particular, Rina
Nissim, *Une sorcière des temps modernes: Le self-help et le mouve-
ment femmes et santé* (Genève : Éditions Mamamélis, 2014), and the
Boston Women's Health Book Collective, *Our Bodies, Ourselves*
(New York, NY: Simon & Schuster, 2011).

76. Ehrenreich and English, *Witches, Midwives and Nurses,* op.
cit., p. 39.

77. Winckler, op. cit., part III: "La fabrique des brutes en
blanc," ebook location 59% / empl. 2860.

78. Ehrenreich and English, *Witches, Midwives and Nurses,* op.
cit., p. 40.

79. Maryse Condé, *I, Tituba, Black Witch of Salem*, trans. Richard Philcox (Charlottesville, VA: University of Virginia Press, 2009), p. 159.

80. Silvia Federici, *Caliban and the Witch* (Brooklyn, NY: Autonomedia, 2004), pp. 153–4.

81. Jules Michelet, *The Witch*, op. cit., pp. 127–8.

82. Michelet, op. cit., p. 128.

83. Winckler, op. cit., part II, chapter 1: "La maltraitance médicale ordinaire," ebook location 23% / empl. 1127.

84. Merchant, op. cit., p. 151.

85. Sarah Barmak, *Closer: Notes from the Orgasmic Frontier of Female Sexuality* (Toronto: Coach House Books, 2016), p. 57. Also, Thomas Belleaud, "Le spéculum, inventé par un misogyne et testé sur des esclaves," Terrafemina (website), July 30, 2015. *See:* https://www.terrafemina.com/article/le-speculum-invente-par-un-misogyne-et-teste-sur-des-esclaves_a281148/1.

86. Ehrenreich and English, *Witches, Midwives and Nurses*, op. cit.

87. Merchant, op. cit.

88. Adrienne Rich, *Of Woman Born: Motherhood as Experience and Institution* (London: Bantam, 1977), p. 138.

89. Rich, op. cit., p. 144.

90. Rich, op. cit., pp. 144–8.

91. Quoted in Rich, op. cit., p. 174.

92. Lahaye, *Accouchement: les femmes méritent mieux*, op. cit., p. 119.

93. Lahaye, *Accouchement: les femmes méritent mieux*, op. cit.

94. Marie-Hélène Lahaye, "On impose aux femmes un accouchement 'fordiste,' au détriment de l'accompagnement," in *L'Humanité*, February 13, 2018. *See:* https://www.humanite.fr/marie-helene-lahaye-impose-aux-femmes-un-accouchement-fordiste-au-detriment-de-laccompagnement.

95. Rich, op. cit., p. 181.

96. Marie-Hélèn Lahaye, "La promesse," Alors Voilà (website), January 16, 2018. *See:* https://www.alorsvoila.com/2018/01/16/3656/.

97. Lahaye, *Accouchement: les femmes méritent mieux,* op. cit., p. 37.

98. Lahaye, *Accouchement: les femmes méritent mieux,* op. cit., p. 79.

99. Lahaye, *Accouchement: les femmes méritent mieux,* op. cit., p. 75.

100. Ehrenreich and English, *Witches, Midwives and Nurses,* op. cit., p. 24.

101. Ehrenreich and English, *Witches, Midwives and Nurses,* op. cit., p. 16.

102. Michelet, op. cit., p. 117.

103. Ehrenreich and English, *Witches, Midwives and Nurses,* op. cit., p. 17.

104. Matilda Joslyn Gage, *Woman, Church, & State* (New York: The Truth Seeker Company, 1893), p. 233. *See:* https://sacred-texts.com/wmn/wcs/wcs07.htm.

105. Gage, op. cit., pp. 242–3.

106. Cora Tucker, "Women Make it Happen," in *Empowering Ourselves: Women and Toxics Organizing* (Falls Church, VA: Center for Health, Environment & Justice, 1989, 2012), p. 5. *See:* http://chej.org/wp-content/uploads/Empowering%20Ourselves%20-%20PUB%20092.pdf.

107. S. Griffin, *Woman and Nature,* op. cit., p. xi.

108. Michel Hulin, *La mystique sauvage* (Paris: PUF, 1993), pp. 196–7.

109. Bordo, *The Flight to Objectivity,* op. cit., p. 13.

110. Quoted in Bordo, op. cit.

111. Bordo, op. cit., p. 15.

112. Bordo, op. cit., p. 100.

113. Bordo, op. cit., p. 99.

114. Bechtel, *La Sorcière et l'Occident,* op. cit., p. 900.

115. Bechtel, *La Sorcière et l'Occident,* op. cit., p. 859.

116. Ehrenreich and English, *Witches, Midwives and Nurses,* Introduction to the second edition, pp. 21 and 22.

117. Bechtel, *La Sorcière et l'Occident,* op. cit., p. 900.

118. Gage, op. cit., pp. 274–5.

119. Condé, *I, Tituba, Black Witch of Salem*, op. cit., p. 9.

120. Clarissa Pinkola Estés, *Women Who Run With the Wolves: Myths and stories of the wild woman archetype* (New York, NY: Ballantine, 1992).

121. Janet Biehl, "Féminisme et écologie, un lien 'naturel'?," in *Le Monde diplomatique*, May 2011. *See:* https://www.monde-diplomatique.fr/2011/05/BIEHL/20467.

122. Catherine Larrère, "L'écoféminisme ou comment faire de la politique autrement," in Hache (ed.), *Reclaim*, op. cit., p. 373.

123. Émilie Hache, "Reclaim ecofeminism!," in Hache (ed.), *Reclaim*, op. cit., p 51.

124. Catriona Sandilands, "Womyn's Land: communautés séparatistes lesbiennes rurales en Oregon," in Hache (ed.), *Reclaim*, op. cit.

125. Larrère, "L'écoféminisme . . . ," in Hache (ed.), *Reclaim*, op. cit., pp. 373–4.

126. *Avortement, les croisés contreattaquent* (documentary), directed by Alexandra Jousset and Andrea Rawlins-Gaston, Arte, March 6, 2018.

127. Hache, "Reclaim ecofeminism!," in Hache (ed.), *Reclaim*, op. cit., p. 30.

128. Hache, 'Reclaim ecofeminism!', op. cit., p. 31.

129. Maureen Dowd, "This is why Uma Thurman is angry," in *New York Times*, February 3, 2018. *See:* https://www.nytimes.com/2018/02/03/opinion/sunday/this-is-why-uma-thurman-is-angry.html.

130. Carol P. Christ, "Why Women Need the Goddess," in Carol P. Christ and Judith Plaskow (eds.), *Womanspirit Rising: A Feminist Reader in Religion* (San Francisco, CA: Harper One, 1992), p. 275.

131. S. Griffin, *Woman and Nature,* op. cit.

132. Merchant, op. cit., p. 295.

Index

About the Author

Mathieu Zazzo

MONA CHOLLET is a Franco-Swiss writer and
journalist. *In Defense of Witches* is her first book
to be translated into English. She lives in Paris,
France.